About *Essential Truths: The Bay Area in Color*

Essential Truths assembles in one anthology a diverse array of Bay Area poets, writers, artists and activists, speaking their truths in a racially divisive time when the voices of Asian Pacific Islanders, Black, Indigenous, People of Color, LGBTQ+ and allies need to be heard.
—Poet/storyteller Andre LeMonte Wilson

The poems, essays and artwork from the 130 creators in *Essential Truths* are, at their core, about ordinary people of color overcoming major obstacles in order to live their best lives in extraordinary times.
—Joshua Rotter, *San Francisco Examiner*

What are the essential truths that you hold on to in hard times? This is the guiding question of Write Now! SF Bay's fourth anthology, *Essential Truths: The Bay Area in Color*. It's filled with compelling stories of loss and love told through poetry, prose and visual art in a variety of styles from talented writers of color from the Bay Area.
—Daniella Lake, *The Daily Californian*

Editor Shizue Seigel is a literary troublemaker, a canary in the coal mine of white supremacy, as it still dominates literature, as major white publishers continue to turn their backs on the fact that San Francisco and California are respectively white-minority city and state.
—Dennis J. Bernstein, Executive Producer, *Flashpoints,* Pacifica Radio (KPFA)

Other books from Write Now! SF Bay:

Standing Strong! Fillmore and Japantown
Voices from Write Now! Fillmore and Write Now! Japantown

Endangered, Species, Enduring Values
An Anthology of San Francisco Area Writers and Artists of Color

Civil Liberties United
Diverse Voices from the San Francisco Bay Area

WRITE NOW! SF BAY

ESSENTIAL TRUTHS
THE BAY AREA IN COLOR

Edited by Shizue Seigel

Pease Press • San Francisco

ESSENTIAL TRUTHS
The Bay Area in Color

Shizue Seigel • Write Now! SF Bay
www.WriteNowSF.com

Pease Press
1717 Cabrillo Street, San Francisco, CA 94121
www.peasepress.com
First edition July 2021. Second printing October 2021.
Printed in the United States of America.
Orders: www.peasepress.com/EssentialTruths

Book design by Shizue Seigel. www.shizueseigel.com

Front cover: Designed by Eiselle Ty and Shizue Seigel. Clarion Alley mural by WHOLE9 (@hitch_w9 and @simo_w9). Photo by Edsel River, inspiration from Kelechi Ubozoh.
Back cover: "The Eyes of Bai Bibyaon Ligkayan Bigkay" by Cece Carpio.
Uncredited photos throughout book by Shizue Seigel

Library of Congress Cataloging-in-Publication Data

Essential Truths: The Bay Area in Color
Edited by Shizue Seigel
Library of Congress Control Number: 2019941693

ISBN: 978-0-9904173-9-2

About this Book

In the San Francisco Bay Area, we are guests on the unceded ancestral homelands of the Ohlone, Miwok, and other original stewards of this land. In gratitude and solidarity, we seek to restore balance and harmony within ourselves, with each other, and in community.

The vitality of the San Francisco Bay Area arises from its diversity. Fully 60% of its residents are people of color. We have long been overlooked, but we have always made essential contributions to Bay Area life and culture. Long familiar with turbulence, uncertainty and loss, we have learned draw strength from flexibility and openness. We seek to blend the best of American ideals with precolonial legacies and present-day activism around the globe. We are constantly learning, adapting and including. We are bi- or multicultural because we have to be. We are expanded by the rich exchange of culture, history and spirituality that makes the Bay Area so vibrant.

This book includes poetry, prose and visual art from 130 contributors—Black, Brown, Indigenous, People of Color and a few White allies. We range from poets laureates and PhDs to high-school students and closet writers; from fire commissioners to the formerly unhoused. Our work is not always polished, but it arises from the lived experience of grappling with real issues of the day.

Our sense of community (or the ache of its erosion) and our roots in Native America, Africa, Asia, Latin America, the Middle East, and Europe give us strength to face uncomfortable realities without blinking.

We may write in the vernacular, or English may be our second or third language. If our rhythms are unfamiliar, ask yourself why—is our work inflected by other tongues and vernaculars, rusty from disuse, scattered by stress or trauma, struggling out of silence, or hastily scribbled on borrowed time?

Old ways are dissolving, and change is in the air. BIPOC arts and activism have been here all along. Now we are stepping into the light.

—Shizue Seigel, Editor and
Director of Write Now! SF Bay
www.WriteNowSF.com

About the Editor and Write Now! Sf Bay

Essential Truths: The Bay Area in Color was edited, designed and produced by Shizue Seigel, a third-generation Japanese American writer, visual artist, and community activist who explores complex intersections of history, culture, and spirituality through prose, poetry, and visual art.

A college dropout who learns by doing, her creative vision is informed by her family's WWII incarceration; her childhood experiences in segregated Baltimore, Occupied Japan, California farm labor camps, skid-row Stockton; and her 55 years as a San Francisco resident. She's witnessed many of the city's changes, from Western Addition redevelopment and Haight-Ashbury counterculture in the 1960s to feminist and alternative school movements of the 1970s, Financial District corporate life in the greed-is-good 1980s, HIV prevention efforts in public housing and needle exchanges in the 1990s, and the demographic and political shifts of a post-9/11 21st century.

In addition to the Write Now! anthologies, her books include *Distillations: Meditations on the Japanese American Experience* (Pease Press 2010), *In Good Conscience: Supporting Japanese Americans During the Internment* (AACP, Inc. 2006) and *My First Hundred Years* (Pease Press 2019, first printed as *A Century of Change* in 2002). Her prose and poetry have appeared in the anthologies *(Her)oics: Women's Lived Experience during the Pandemic, All the Women in My Family Sing, Your Golden Sun Still Shines, InvAsian, Cheers to Muses, Empty Shoes,* and *My Words Are Gonna Linger* and in *Away Journal, Soundings East, sPARKLE + bLINK, Eleven Eleven, Persimmon Tree, Whirlwind Magazine,* and elsewhere. She is working on a two-volume memoir.

She is a four-time VONA/Voices fellow who has been awarded grants and residencies from the San Francisco Arts Commission, California Humanities, Center for Cultural Innovation, Zellerbach Family Foundation, Asian Pacific Islander Cultural Center, Jentel, Atlantic Center for the Arts, Newnan Art Rez, and Hypatia-in-the-Woods. Her papers are archived at UC Santa Barbara's California Ethnic and Multicultural Archives.

She facilitates Write Now! SF Bay's free monthly writing workshops at the San Francisco Main Library. For details, see www.WriteNowSF.com.

Acknowledgements:

Essential Truths: The Bay Area in Color is Write Now! SF Bay's fourth anthology of Bay Area writers and artist of color. The seeds for Write Now! were planted in 2015 when Shizue Seigel was awarded a San Francisco Arts Commission Individual Artist Commission to explore overlapping communities in the City's Western Addition. Subsequent anthologies were supported by SFAC, the Asian Pacific Islander Cultural Center, and the Zellerbach Family Foundation. Intersection for the Arts became our fiscal sponsor in December 2018.

Essential Truths was made possible with support from the San Francisco Arts Commission, California Humanities, and Center for Cultural Innovation. Special thanks to the Editorial Committee: Andre Wilson, Christl Perkins, Darzelle Oliveros, Kevin Madrigal Galindo, Tehmina Khan, and Yaminah Abdur-Rahim; proofreader Rosalie Cavallaro; and production artist Pat Koren. We're grateful to all the writers and artists for their richly varied submissions, and for help and advice from Poet Laureate Emerita Kim Shuck, Karen Seneferu of *The Black Woman Is God* project, Shawna Sherman and Anissa Malady of the San Francisco Public Library, Mihee Kim of the Kearny Street Workshop, Alison Snopek of Intersection for the Arts, designer Eiselle Ty, arts consultant Lenore Naxon, Jon Finck of Encore Communications 2.0, and participants of Write Now! SF Bay's on-going monthly creative workshops.

Write Now! SF Bay offers free or donation-based virtual writing workshops for writers of coor every 2nd Tuesday and every 3rd Saturday, Share your work and build community with BIPOC writers writing in any genre, at any level. Find out more about us here: www.WriteNowSF.com.

Fiscally sponsored by Intersection for the Arts, a historic 501(c)(3) non-profit artsorganization supporting people working in arts and culture. Supported by the San Francisco Arts Commission. This project was made possible with support from California Humanities, a non-profit partner of the National Endowment for the Humanities. Visit www.calhum.org.

Table of Contents

I
in place

Shizue Seigel, photograph, plaster Buddha,
Argonne Community Garden, San Francisco, 2020.

A Poem and Three Images by Adrian Arias

I walk on the stones that you left me on purpose
one over the other, in apparent total equilibrium
like your hair when you comb it in slow motion,
as the coordinated scream of those who protest and march without fear
like the silence of the astronaut who looks at planet earth while floating
and feel that this is all a dream.

I walk on the verb, without adjectives, I slip, I fall, I get up.

A will o´ the wisp arises at every corner.
The animals returned to the empty streets for a few days
checking over the territory that we took from them,
contemplating the strange allegories to progress we've built.
I bite my lips

while the consonants lost in the babble of what I couldn't tell you
indiscreetly touch each other
making that guttural and invisible noise that characterizes them.
I walk on the salt of dry and elusive tears.

The afternoon glow returns your silence to me.
You're gone and there's no reason to be sad while I bite my sandwich,
the universe becomes an empty glass, I'm thirsty.

In the distance a star collapses,
thousands of planets are born that we will never know but they are there
and they will have their own love stories
their own pandemics, their own revolutions.

On the rustic formation of clouds stopped in a paper sky I see you
and I approach you without fear, to say goodbye
six feet away.

And suddenly it's already tomorrow.

I just want to feel like I can still get home
where I will finally take the stones out of my pocket
I'll take off the mask that slows my breathing.

Adrian Arias, "Painting the Ritual Moon," live painting at Machina Loci
gallery in Berkeley. Photo by Carol Mancke and Richard Spencer.

I will wet the shore the brightness the oblivion,
and without haste I will write a poem for someone I do not know
a poem for you
where my hands warm your feet,
where my lips silently kiss your skin.

I'll sew all the silences that somebody left lying all over the place
and I'll have a blanket that keeps me warm without grudges.

I will fall asleep on the edge of the cosmos
I'll be the nothing that people don't like
I'll be my own eclipse
I'll be a forbidden word
and I will have the possibility to disappear
without fear of being forgotten.

Bio: Adrian Arias is an American poet, visual artist and performer born in Peru and a San Francisco Bay Area resident since 2000. Winner of important visual-arts and poetry prizes in Peru, Argentina, Japan, Macedonia and the US, Adrian reinvents animals, creates dream-based languages and codes, explores the absurd and the surreal visually and creates paintings in action and murals related to the pandemic and the social revolution that we are experiencing.

Photo by Stella Adelman.

Adrian Arias in front of "8:46" altar dedicated to George Floyd at 2020 *Dia de los Muertos/Day of the Dead* exhibition at SOMArts Cultural Center.

.............I CRY CREATIVITY
..(inspired by the Music of Erik Jekabson)
Avotcja

I was asleep
Secure & comfortably asleep
Dreaming of peace & love
Hypnotized
By a mirage of unity & togetherness
Dancing away demons of war & hate
In what I thought was a Land of plenty
In what I'd been taught was the land of the free
Then I opened my eyes
Was slapped in the face
By a wide awake nightmare
A senseless, suicidal madness
A world of selfishness
Insatiable gluttony & rampant homelessness
Created by / Shortsighted Masters of fantasy
So used to
Dealing from their deck of unfulfillable promises
That they can no longer feel anything real
I opened my eyes
And found myself sadly looking at
Those who are empty inside
And seem to think they can fill their emptiness
With all kinds of pretty things & tons of money
&
More & more money & the newest prettier things
And all I could do is cry
Cry for those blindly drunk on greed as I write
And smile as another Poem is born
A Poem
About all the beauty the greedy can no longer see
I believe
If we Artists could only bottle our tears
No one would ever die of thirst
Our tears would become unifying melodies
Creative love filled organic harmonious medicine
And we... an inspiring army of creativity
Just might be able to
Heal the World... one note at a time

Un Milagro En El Estado De Las Pulgas

Avotcja

¡Acá! ¡Aquí estoy!
¡Yo! Como una sombra en la oscuridad
Invisible
Sin importancia, ignorada, despreciable
Una vez más
Me encuentro al cruce de caminos
Como una Mariposa Nocturna
Volando a solas
Una aparecida inapreciable que no vale ná
Nadie me vé
Una indeseada más
Yo no soy nadie
Entre miles y miles de indeseadas ignoradas
Peónes perdidos en el sendero de los olvidados
   Invisibles
Somos vagabundas embriagadas
Emborrachadas
De tragar demasiado del gran sueño imposible
Enjambres desmoralizados de necios embrujados
Confundidos
Por tragar de una botella llena de fantasías ajenas
Espejismos alucinantes nacidos de promesas fracasadas
Y
Un bello montón de engaños resbaladizos
Tesoros prometidos y un saco de deseo superficial
Siempre fuera del alcance
   ¡Aca! ¡Aquí estoy!
¡Yo! Una plaga insignificante
Atrapada una vez más
Como una polilla perdida en una mentira luminosa
Bailando como una equilibristita sin equilibrio
Como una marioneta en la penumbra
Buscando y buscando y buscando milagros
Entre la basura de los ricos
Escarbando como un minero obsesionado
Por los basureros de una civilización falsificada
En el cementerio de un mundo incivilizado
Yo soy nada más que
Una polilla fanática en busca de una luz sagrada
Buscando la sabiduría en un callejón interminable

¡Ay, que cosa increible!
Somos las hijas cómicas de la naturaleza
Como la Mariposa Nocturna
Un bellísimo enigma
Bien cansada, pero laboriosa todavía
Buscando incesantemente
Pá reclamar el derecho de vivir con dignidad
Pá mantener una vida sin miedo
Una vida libre, libre como el viento
Libre en un mundo lleno de integridad mundial
     ¿Cansada? ¡Absolutamente!
     ¿Rendida? ¡Nunca!
Somos
Como bellas Mariposas Nocturnas
En el estado de las Pulgas vampiricas
Juguetes transitorios pá los ricos en un parque de sanguijuelas
     ¡Acá! ¡Aquí estoy!
Y por las buenas o por las malas
¡Yo! Inolvidable
Como una fenómena majestuosa
Somos una fuerza incesante
Gimnastas chiquititos con cabezas y ganas de acero
¡Irrefrenable!
Siempre buscando
Eternamente buscando esa Luz

See next page for English t4anlation.

Avotcja is an award winning poet, multi-instrumentalist and popular Bay Area DJ and radio personality on KPFA and KPOO. She has been widely published in English & Spanish in the USA, Mexico and Europe. She has shared stages with Sonia Sanchez, Janice Mirikitani, Michael Franti, Rahsaan Roland Kirk, Bobi & Luis Cespedes, John Handy, Nikki Giovanni, and many others. Her group Avotcja & Modúpue has performed at the Asian-American Jazz Festival. Her poetry and music has been performed by dance groups in the Bay Area and New York City. She's been featured at AfroSolo, San Francisco's Carnival, New York's Henry Street Settlement Theater, and The Women On The Way Festival in San Francisco.

She continues to teach creative writing, storytelling & drama in public schools and was a California Arts Council Artist in Residence at the Milestones Project and the San Francisco Penal System. She is a member of Disability Advocates Of Minorities Organization, PEN Oakland, California Poets in the Schools, International Women's Writers Guild and ASCAP.

A Miracle In A World Of Fleas
Avotcja

Here   I am right here
Me! … Like a shadow in the darkness
Invisible
Scorned, unimportant, ignored
Once again
I find myself at the Crossroads
Like a Moth
Flying all alone
A worthless, unwanted apparition
No one would see me
Just one more of the undesirable
I am nobody
Inside the thousands & thousands of undesirables
Lost pawns on the path of the forgotten
Invisible
We are drunken wanderers
Sloppy drunk from swallowing too much of the impossible dream
Disheartened swarms of the bedazzled foolish
All mixed up
From drinking from a bottle full of other folks' fantasies
Hallucinatory mirages born of broken promises
And
A beautiful pile of slippery tricks
Promised treasures & a bag of empty wishes
Always just out of reach
Here   I am right here
Me! …An insignificant pest
Trapped again
Like a Moth lost in a shiny lie
Dancing like a clumsy Acrobat
Like a puppet in the twilight
Searching & searching & searching for miracles
In the garbage of the rich
Digging like an obsessed miner
Through the trashcans of a counterfeit civilization
In the cemetery of an uncivilized world
I'm nothing more than
A fanatical Moth in search of the light of illumination
Trying to find wisdom in an unending alley

Incredible!!!
We are Mother Nature's comical children
Like the Moth
A beautiful enigma
Tired as hell, but still going strong
Always searching
Trying to reclaim the right to a dignified life
To a sustainable life without fear
A life that's free as the wind is free
Free in a world that's full of international integrity
      Tired? …Definitely!
      Ready to give up? …Never!
We are
Like beautiful Moths in a world of blood sucking Fleas
Passing toys for the rich in a playground of leeches
      Here   I am right here
¡Me! Unforgettable
Like a majestic phenomenon
Through the best & worst of times
We are an unending force
Little tiny gymnasts with iron wills & hard heads
Unstoppable!
Searching
Eternally searching for that Light

Malik Seneferu, untitled—one of 500+ pieces in his series *From the Hill and Beyond*, 48 x 36 inches, 2016.

See bio on p. 13.

A Play in Two Parts
Tongo Eisen-Martin

English is a lukewarm relationship with your people
      With practice, I met every white person in the world

The state's pastel gibberish and
      White noise watchlists transmuted by agents who
                    point finger pistols
                  at Black children
                        …for funded nature

          And now it's winter…or adulthood in america

Retail awards and standard issue bullets left on a plate outside my door
Plate design inspired by the gold-trim razor wire around mother Afrika
                    —A congressional motif

Rope tickles neck

I am a human sacrifice/ my parallel employment—pocket full of fists—
defining efforts to be part of a famous family/ the hospital bed shakes
          Now I am a white man's son

              to quote the people who left me for dead

Nervous energy all over the constitution
              …I owe you a war

I had a firm grasp on my mortality
I had an idea for a sonnet and a prison wall all picked out

Besides the nightstick, I know no other colors today

My double grows in Mississippi
My shoulders turned towards where lesser gods landed
Where the light changes revolutions

Pure america now confronts the woman I love
Our forearms bathed in Louisiana tithes
Forearms under each other's palms
I close my eyes one floor beneath eyes already closed
One league beneath the sweetest laugh I've ever known
Psalm sketched
A sketch of gallows foreplay
        You've taken me back
                Your humble narrator

Gallows band stand
and every place she turned my life into decent artwork

Imagine us, the death of commerce
        velvet gloves passing around our FBI file

Police station muscling for robber baron free associations
The sum of all corporate defense mechanisms

                        Maybe a pale horse hoof

Policing that don't involve populations
Just population-symbols

Rope tickles a trumpet of God's

In the beginning was the word for a little bit
                        so I put sound first

She pushes my soul back into my tear ducts
Her classic bravery

She is loved back by her books
Black proletariat bathed in her late evening smoke

Rope tickles the water

Out-evolved by the police state, the suburbs retract
bullwhips dealt liberally in a prison society
vice president's initials on every nightstick
        saying, "the next person out the door better mean america no harm"

every place she turned my life into decent artwork

I've been blinded by this sun sitting on the wall

Our door hinges now in the water
Water and Richmond, California pollution

I wish my imagination was formal

Deathtrap narrator book-burning the hospital lobby

                    I am a revolutionary there too

lazy eyes giving me an ovation

a one
a four
escape art

jazz-ready
the drums you love while kneeling
                unintelligible chariot-talk

        the horn's breastplate pierced by a roman soldier

Psalm of the woman I love
Our house is ascending
this sketch spinning in unmarked air

                a one
                a sacrament
                a four

Tongo Eisen-Martin was recently named San Francisco's 8th Poet Laureate. He was born and raised in San Francisco and earned his MA at Columbia University. He is the founder of Black Freighter Press and the author of *someone's dead already* (Bootstrap Press, 2015). His poetry collection *Heaven Is All Goodbyes* (City Lights, 2017) received a California Book Award and an American Book Award in 2018 and was shortlisted for the Griffin Poetry Prize. As an educator and organizer, his work centers on issues of mass incarceration, extrajudicial killings of Black people, and human rights.

Only made of light now… like an autobiography ends

I close my eyes
   one floor beneath the Five-Spot

gallows king
instrument of a new people
     laughter briefly fitting a psalm
        commenting on the sea line
           putting boots to whirlwind

did you come all the way back from the Harlem Renaissance just to have a word with me?

I am for sure
   your poetry too

Malik Seneferu, "Little Bobby Hutton," 48 x 36 inches, 2014. In 1966, 16-year-old Bobby Hutton became the first member of the Black Panther Party, serving as party treasurer. Two years later, during the turmoil following the murder of Martin Luther King, Jr., he became the first Panther to be shot and killed by police, under disputed circumstances.

Malik Seneferu, an award-winning artist and teacher, grew up in San Francisco's Hunter's Point and now lives in Richmond with his artist wife Karen. He is prolific in many styles, working with the humble materials of his childhood, like paint, pencil, ballpoint pen, scrap wood, markers, and oil pastels. He is deeply committed to the social, political, environmental and spiritual challenges of people targeted for oppression. His work has been widely exhibited in the Bay Area, at the Schomburg Center in New York City, the Smithsonian in Washington DC, and in London, South Africa, Italy, Haiti and Kenya.

Which headstones are these?
Kim Shuck

Misplaced trust
We are,
She says,
A nation of laws
Laws that set limits at the extremes
That define the edges not the heart
And every new report makes clear what is protected
That the plea
Don't kill us
Is a bigger threat than a stew of
Guns and misogyny
That our prayers are met with violence
The way that racism can't see racism
The way that deadly cosplay
Stands in for heroism
Because some other guys did it before
Some other time
In defense of a thought
We can't even hire people to defend these days
Are presented with terrorism selfies
And a song we already know

Kim Shuck is the 7th poet laureate of San Francisco emerita. Shuck is a citizen of the Cherokee Nation of Oklahoma. Kim has read her work in different contexts and continents, in back rooms of bars and in the Library of Congress and many places in between. Her latest published work is *Whose Water,* from Mammoth Publishing.

Hillside
Tehmina Khan

Passover passes us by,
and neighbors turn on computers
and sing with faces on screens,
tell the story of suffering and resistance,
while savoring a seder feast they cannot share.

Holy Saturday in Jerusalem.
Five hundred faces gather onscreen
from the far corners of the world,
to pray
for science and solidarity to resurrect us
from this virus.
Candles,
alone together,
offer light to the occupied, to the imprisoned,
the sick, the caregivers.
Faces on screens speak The Lord's Prayer
in their own language,
overlapping into a global chorus.

I ride my bicycle across the deserted city,
and return to the hill as the sun sets
to seek out the sliver of Ramadan moon,
which beckons me
to begin
my daily journeys of hunger
as the moon grows big and then small again,
to hold space in my emptiness
for healing and wholeness.

Outside the shuttered door of St. Kevin's Church,
a woman in white veil
crosses herself and bows.

Evenings at eight,
neighbors clang pots and pans
echoing the bells of Tassajara Zen Monastery,
chiming gratitude and remembrance.

Rafael the poet holds a stick of palo santo,
swirling its sacred smoke
through my computer screen,
invoking the east, the west, the south, the north,
calling me deeper into the planet.

On a concrete ledge
where men used to gather to drink,
my neighbor Ofelia sits,
Estoy orando, she says, por todos los enfermos
because only Dios can heal us.
She recites in Spanish as my grandmother recited in Arabic:
La ilaha illallah, La ilhaha illallah
each incantation calling her deeper into the Divine
as the wind prays
as the water falling through my fingers prays.

What can I do but practice softness?

As we watch the grasses grow on the hillside.

Tehmina Khan is a daughter of Indian immigrant scientists who has spent her adult life writing, teaching, resisting, and mothering. She has taught science to preschoolers and citizenship to octogenarians; she now teaches English at City College of San Francisco, where she defends everyone's right to a quality education. Her work has been published in *PoetsEleven*, *Written Here*, *OccuPoetry*, *Civil Liberties United*, *The City is Already Speaking*, and *Muslim Writers at Home*.

City Snapshots. Spring
Shizue Seigel

Time remains elusive
        sense and schedule virus scattered
                but meaning's crystal clear
Earth and sky are calling us
        to remember who's in charge.
Skies unload after winter drought
        upon a super bloom of spring
a wealth of dudleya and acacia
native Californians and Australian imports flourish
        alongside a proliferation of tents mushrooming
                mushrooming as the world turns upside
                        down and backwards.
Celestial cycles grind on.
        Fallen caesars and pharaohs
                are they laughing now?
        Earth mounds and monoliths
                Pyramids and skyscrapers
Humanity's been here before
        too many times to know

How the mighty rise and fall
        but the poor will endure.
                Can we bridge the salt of the earth
                    To stars in our eyes
                everlasting gold in the heart?

In my neighborhood of stubborn weeds
        did COVID arrive just in time to save us
                from total eradication, preserving the last of the grit
from million-dollar scrubs of virgin
        olive oil, oatmeal and sage consumed by the pampered few who
                can afford to bathe their skins with what lesser folk could eat?
Will the virus slow them down
        like the bursting of dot.com 1 or the '89 earthquake?
Coastal fog used to be enough
        to keep away those who did not love this land:
                the fragile interface with sea and
                sky sometimes unseen all summer long.

Fog tendrils in microdroplets
  burst against our cheeks, reminding us
    like warning blasts and mourning bleats
    signaling ships at sea and landlubbers alike
that we are all adrift on life—reality rising and falling
  heaving and lulling, by turns.
There are no guarantees,
  only the invitation to risk.

We are a hardy people
  buckwheat and sorrel, dandelion and succulents.
Look down your nose at us,
  indulge yourself elsewhere
    with showy blooms and gourmet grazings.
We are a plain people whose meager dollars
  sent a generation to college so
  they could look down on us, too.
Now they are learning something priceless:
  there are no guarantees except
    death comes to all of us.
  Life reveals by
    how you
      rise to meet it.

In a rent-controlled apartment
  a women liberated from an office
    breathes herself into a new life,
propelled from an enclosing womb
  where she was bathed in the amniotic fluid of
    guilt, shame, fear, rage
bathed in others' thoughts
  and the impulse to make things right—for them.

Liberated into new life
  she lets the universe suffuse her
    like a tender newborn.
Perhaps she brings joy just by being—
  right here   in this moment
As dawn lightens the sky.
  In a now-hushed city,
    birds stir to a new day.

Strangers wave from across the street.
      Even cars stop
      to let her walk.

Across town, the Mission is deserted.
      Its streets and shops
            no longer a pulse of the city
a thready reed
      profound
            connection.
How deeply one
      could love
            a stranger
a wordless bow
      from the heart
sharing for a moment
      ancient stones calling
            the earth's core turning
                  the wheel of stars across the sky.
Who could not
      taste the love in a plato
            your 20% tip
                returned as
                    a double spoonful of beans.
Today, a young woman a shade lighter than café au lait
      bleached dreads tied in a topknot with a stylish scarf
            talks loudly—into a cell phone?
No, she argues with herself
      with sharp yips and sudden jumps
            as if to leap out of her body,
                escape her own skin.
I want to take her in my arms, calm her with my eyes
      she who fears touch yet longs for it.
            Before I can reach her, she turns the corner and disappears.

Another woman sits on the sidewalk
      legs crossed as if in meditation, hoodied head erect,
            searching for that peace she knows exists
                But not today, not in Mission Street grit
She's haloed by orange peels—discards or a gift?
A man towers over her, screeching like a banty rooster.
      Her neck shrinks down into her shoulders as

he spits invective en español. Does she understand?
I wait until he walks away
      Our eyes connect as I slip her a five, rolled tight
          so he won't notice she now has
               something more he can take.
Her face is grimy, brown as the street
a darker shade than when she left
      Sri Lanka? Kerala? I wish I could tell her
          It'll be all right. But all I have left is a silent prayer.

In the Tenderloin, a clot of homeless shelter in place
      on a Medusa raft of sidewalk
          side by side, huddling close
      heads declined to the same angle
          shielding each other from hate
               that kills as surely as virus.

Back in the western city, the produce man misses his wife;
      she's denied re-entry from a visit home to Greece.
      The Brits appropriated xenophobia along with Elgin marbles
          but Peter lives by philoxenia, love of strangers.
      Recalling what the Nazis did in the mountains of his boyhood,
          he hires refugees from Salvador and Albania
               who suffuse his vegetables with fortitude and love.
      Fierce-eyed Alma folds conservative prayers into paper angels
      while cousin Lefty shrugs. But her eyes twinkle
          over our shared mrmory of ripe figs.
In the secret green heart of my stucco-rimmed block
      willows sway in the salt air, and a riot of succulents
          shoot golden stars toward the sun
      weeks of rampant glory
          before heads drop on withered stems
      native California survivors and hardy migrants
      winter frost and summer drought.

Shizue Seigel is a Japanese American writer who has led community writing projects for 20+ years. She established Write Now! SF Bay to support Bay Area writers and artists of color through workshops, events and anthologies. She's written or edited seven books and her prose and poetry have appeared in *Soundings East, Away Journal, Eleven Eleven, sPARKLE + bLINK*, and the anthologies *We've Been Too Patient, All the Women in My Family Sing, Cheers to Muses, InvAsian*, and elsewhere.

Seigel, Casa Maria Market #2, Visitacion Valley, now closed.

I Am The Town
Tony Aldarondo

I am the Town …

I am the Athletic
the Raider
that Golden State
Warrior.

The Indian
the African
the Asian
the Latino
the colors
of the rainbow yo …

I am the Town.

I am that liquor store
on International Boulevard
between Fate
and Destiny

where lovers walk
yet crimes are committed …

where flowers
blossom and bloom

yet bullets
singing last lullabies
fly by …

and way too many
black and brown
young men
and women
in Oakland
have to die …

I am the Town …

But why oh why
must our young go so soon
to meet their doom …

Today I speak as their poet …

Yet I am the elephant
in the room.

I am the Town ...

I am that
Oakland teacher
who can barely live
on that ridiculous
teacher's wage ...

who's living paycheck
to paycheck—
which should be a
warning label
at the bottom of my doctor's
prescriptions page ...

I am the Town ...

I am that
East Bay resident
who sleeps under
an Oakland moon ...
where the police
are blindfolded
by dollar bills
and cheap thrills ...

where they avoid the
East Oakland
and
West Oakland
But not them
Oakland Hills.

I am the Town ...

I am that brave father

who deep in his heart
weeps in his heart ...
and wants so bad
to do so good.

But the way things are
on the streets today ...

is too afraid
of the folks
in his own
neighborhood.
I am the Town ...

I am joyed
and pained
at the same time ...
yet this poet
is willing to do
what he has to do
to help make
Oakland shine ...

Oak-
land
California ...

where we build
communities up

and not
tear them down ...

I shout out loud ...

I ... AM ... THE TOWN.

Tony Aldarondo is a San Francisco Bay Area poet and actor. He studied theater at the American Conservatory Theater, toured two seasons with the San Francisco Shakespeare Festival, taught Shakespeare summer camp, and is a member of the Screen Actors Guild. Tony has performed his music and poetry in venues from L.A. to the Bay.

Writing in the Time of Pandemic and Racist Attack 2020
Catalina Cariaga

The ***Extreme Headache Series*** is a collection of type, poetic gesture, text, digitized art on cheap Daiso cards and envelopes that I found hoarded in drawers. Instead of writing formal poems, I found myself using a typewriter to make small constricted bits of text on cards no bigger than two by three inches. Perhaps these are personal meditations on the bold murals by pinay artist Cece Carpio on Broadway in uptown Oakland painted during the BLM protests during the pandemic lock down. Anything I write is photographed on my Android smartphone. Then the image of the text is digitally enhanced. The end result is an extreme close up of typewritten text reflecting the pressurized personal view of a global pandemic and current events from the steps of my home in Oakland.

Catalina Cariaga has an MFA from San Francisco State University and a book of poetry, *Cultural Evidence*, Subpress Collective, 1999. She has been published in *Chain*, *ZYZYVA*, *Pinoy Poetics*, *Babaylan* (Aunt Lute Books) and forthcoming in *Tripwire*. She is a contributing editor to *Poetry Flash*. She will soon retire from UC Berkeley as a financial analyst and complete her next book, *Manifest*. She lives with her husband and college age son in the Maxwell Park neighborhood of Oakland.

The Neighbors Are At It Again
Faith Adiele
With thanks to Pamela Painter

The neighbors are at it again. Tossing their mattresses into the street (invariably when we have company, African families sprinting onto our porch in matching wax print outfits, unisex hipsters in knit caps). Rows of pickup trucks idle in broad daylight beside the narrow strip of park across the street, a repurposed former streetcar line with WELCOME mosaicked into a retaining wall above a dry creek bed choked with blackberry bushes. Colonies of feral cats crouch in the underbrush, watching intently as drivers lean out to dump old chairs, broken electronics, plastic tubs, busted strollers, bags bags bags of clothes and trash onto the pathways and scrub grass.

The neighbors are at it again. Actually, their mattresses are being tossed into the street (invariably when we have company, aging Berkeley liberals carrying good wines into our lanterned backyard, creatives from a sampling of Oakland's fifty neighborhoods and 125 languages). Waves of sheriffs or paid thugs, whoever it is who does the never-ending evicting, wash in. Kids from the nearby high school (67% Latinx, 20% Black, 10% API, 53% below the poverty line) slump on the retaining wall, watching disinterestedly the cyclical chaining of fences, the painful padlocking of doors, the cruel casting of baby clothes in wide, rainbow colored arcs into potholes as Oakland becomes richer, whiter.

The neighbors are at it again. Jumping fences, zigzagging across lawns, dropping handguns, dodging the cr-cr-crackle of cop radios as ch-ch-choppers chase and whirr overhead. I reach for Tylenol, crank up the Afropop. The doorbell rings, jangly blue uniforms on the doorstep asking Have you seen Have you seen Have you How can you afford this house? The phone vibrates and buzzes, everyone on NextDoor chirping What the what What's that Who's that Suspect is suspect is suspect suspect. I swipe and watch, awaiting the invariable responses: Don't say it Don't say it Don't say What has race got to do with it.

The neighbors are at it again. Inventing new culture right here in the street, revving modified engines on steamy summer nights, rims sparking, tires screeching, thick black lines scuffing the exit ramp. Sirens wail as blue scanners pick up news about the latest Sideshow. NextDoor chirps Hear that Where's that Where's that Here. Girls gleam in Puffs Weaves Braids Twists Locs Knots, cheering fresh-faced boys who stunt. They ghost, dancing alongside cars that glide without drivers. They race, spinning defiant doughnuts in perfect continuous geometry. Phones post clips, post coordinates, jangle warnings and fresh-faced boys disappear in clouds of acrid smoke. Keep disappearing, their cars felling stop signs and traffic lights, slamming into my sister-in-law's car with metallic indifference as she rushes in scrubs to pass these neighbors who are at it at it at it. Again.

The neighbors are at it again. Gleaming girls marching in masks, delivering meals and socks and sanitizer in broad daylight to colonies of the unhoused. Fresh-faced boys in bright Ts and gloves, stuffing trash from the street into bags. A van idles beside a sea of tattered tents and makeshift plywood huts. Beneath every overpass. Alongside train stations. Momentarily in the narrow strip of park across the street with WELCOME mosaicked into a retaining wall above a dry creek bed. I open my door to watch intently as this sampling of Oakland's neighborhoods and languages descends. Calling greetings, they pick their way through old chairs, broken electronics, plastic tubs, and busted strollers with steaming boxes of food. Laughing and chatting, they pick up the potholes clean of clothes and trash. These neighbors are at it again.

Faith Adiele (http://adiele.com) is author of memoirs *Meeting Faith* and *The Nigerian Nordic Girl's Guide to Lady Problems*; co-editor of *Coming of Age Around the World: A Multicultural Anthology;* and writer for *My Journey Home* (PBS), *Sleep Stories* (Calm App), and *A World of Calm* (HBO Max). She resides in Oakland and teaches at California College of the Arts, VONA/Voices, Left Margin LIT and the Writers Grotto.

Aquí Se Habla Español
Susana Praver-Pérez

Mimi told me
    her tongue was whipped
    by a wasp of a woman
        for speaking
            Spanish.

This was not rural Florida, a Burger King
        where days before,
    two white patrons pounced
    the Puerto Rican manager,
    told him to go back to his "Mexican country"
        for speaking
            Spanish.

This was liberal San Francisco, the Presidio
      former fortress by the sea
          seized by the U.S. from Mexico
              in a bloody land grab war.

I might've flicked the wasp away, snarled
    "Translate this!!"
        middle finger in the air.
But Mimi wears pearl earrings and said,
    "Excuse me?!"
        right eyebrow hiked to her hairline.

What's happening to the Bay?
Who's flipping barrios to bohemian chic?
Who's arrived?
What do they add and subtract?
And who does the math?

Money pours in through silicon
    while black and brown stream out.

Realtors are the new rock stars.
    Mortgage bankers rumble the bass.
        And they're all gettin' high
           on the boom.
We said goodbye to a neighbor
    off to convert
        gritty factories
           to glittery condos.

A pin-striped party guest asked, "Where?"
"Jingletown," she giggled.

I leaned in with Oakland history of that
    working-class Mexican neighborhood—
How back in the day, men coming home could be heard
    half a block away,
        day's pay
           jingling
             in their pockets.

My story was sliced midair by the pin-striped guest—"Is it safe??"
I'd said Mexican. He'd heard criminal.

I left the bash, shared my despair with a friend.

"He may not be the racist you say," he said,
        playing devil's advocate.

(Who the hell lawyers for Lucifer?!)

"People get a certain image
        when you say ghetto," he added.

I didn't say ghetto—
I said, working-class Mexican neighborhood.

    ¡Dios mío! ¡Ayúdanos Señor!

      ****

In the locker room at a public pool,
        two English-speakers ping-pong words.

Consonants bounce
        off concrete walls,
        sprout an ache
            in the nape of my neck.
        I hold my tongue—they have every right.
But when I think of Mimi,
        of who's allowed, who's disavowed,
            bile burns my mouth.

I summon antidotes, distill words,
        conjure
        what Mimi might've said:

    Esta linda tierra era mexicana.
    Todavía se oyen los dulces retumbos.
    Aquí, <u>sí</u>, se habla español.

Susana Praver-Pérez is an Oakland-based, Pushcart-nominated poet. By day she works at La Clínica de la Raza in Oakland. By night she reads at poetry events from San Francisco to San Juan. By nature, she's a storyteller. Susana's first full-length book of poetry, *Hurricanes, Love Affairs and Other Disasters*, will be released by Nomadic Press in 2021.

Walking Monks
Clara Hsu

Are we passing through time
or has time passed us?
Nine months of furling
bound and deprived.
New variants borne
by the invisible strain,
are they passing through
or are we done
squabbling, squandering
    time
with its sly fingers
wrinkles the surface of our skin.

They walk, silent.
Each measured breath—
the redemption of one soul

not seen   not heard   not felt

Clara Hsu is the director of Clarion Performing Arts Center in San Francisco Chinatown. She is a poet, translator, playwright and children's theater director. During COVID-19 Shelter-in-Place, Clara produced *The Piano, a play-movie* and other video skits on YouTube. She is hosting Book Talk @ Clarion, a forum for Asian American authors on Zoom. Please visit: clarahsu.com

II

alone together

Joan Osato, "Ashley Smiley, Playwright," from the photographic
portrait series *unseen labor*, 2020.

Joan Osato, "Bijou McDaniel, DJ/Production Manager," from the
photographic portait series *unseen labor,* 2020.

Joan Osato
Artist Statement

unseen labor was created while in production for numerous projects and plays
over the past year. My project *Industry* looks at the pandemic through the
lens of labor. It proposes as its end result to have a series of portraits, video
interviews, and community discussions centered around Bay Area industries,
and those who labor in them. I will focus on industries which formed the
backbone of creative resilient spaces, and hope to examine the critical role that
these industries and their unseen workforce play in the current ecology of the
Bay Area. I'm hoping the project will prompt discussion that elevates the labor
of the designer, the production manager, the artist, the playwright, and other
unseen members of the aggregate labor force that makes live theater possible.
Interviews, portrait sessions, discussion, and on-site or virtual exhibition will
heighten public appreciation of the specific obstacles that face them as they
make their unique contributions to Bay Area community life.

Joan Osato is a photographer from San Francisco. As an artist and producer she
is an awardee of prestigious grants from the MAP Fund, Wattis Foundation,
Surdna Foundation Artist for Social Change Award, Theater Bay Area Award
for Excellence in Video Design, Prix de Photographie and the Arte Laguna
Prize. Her next project *Last Days at Pu'unene Mill* documents communities in
Hawai'i and California through the plantation and sugar industry.

in limbo
norm mattox

like it or not

shelter in place
self quarantine
an opportunity
to go inside…

maybe...
build a rocket to
explore your 'innerverse'.

maybe...
invent the fuel for a rocket
you've already built…

maybe...
leave your skin
in a pile at the door
hand sanitizing raw knuckles

peeling outta gloves
like a snake
shedding lives
between a rock
and a hard head

say goodbye to
superficial thinking
poets are the scouts
exploring with 'innervision'
bring your telescope,
time to go deep!

---

norm mattox is a retired bilingual educator from new york. through poetry, norm tells a story of love and resilience in a time of challenge, struggle and transformation. norm has shared his poetry as a featured reader and at open mics around the San Francisco Bay Area and open mics in zoom spaces around the globe.

A Meditation: Movement
A.A. Vincent

I have rearranged my comfort four times in three days
my bed & desk & bookcase & nightstand—
trying to settle, trying to still my room

in these past weeks I have been moving in a wave
of restless laughter, to the kitchen, to my room
to the corner store—smelling petals of sound

while futility taunts my sunny nightmares
—they have been staring into my afternoons
& lying beside me—

but there in the mornings,
beneath these discomposed days
I have dreamt my courage found itself once more

so I carefully grow my two potted plants, sitting them in the sun
& I applaud their leaves for blooming unapologetically
as they unfurl—day by day

Half Past October
A.A. Vincent

I am up with the beginning of these groaning days.
I keep my own counsel inside a radius of 385 square feet.
well time's not what I belong to & I'm not the season I'm in.

I bet against doubt every time the clock turns over, and win.
I do not gamble with the dismissal of harm.
The doors of my red prayer plant open every morning. I am saved again.

A.A. Vincent is a Black, disabled, poet and essayist from the Midwest. She recently received her MFA in Writing from the University of San Francisco. Her work has appeared in *Santa Clara Review*, *SF Weekly*, *Quiet Lightning*, and *Street Sheet SF*.

Unfound
Kim Shuck

How many single socks keep company with the
Expectation of something they called 'fair' in elementary school?
At some point you just wear your socks unmatched and hope that
Somewhere equality has warm feet
I've stopped hoping that history will include what I know
That the date when women got the vote will actually be
Celebrated as August 6th 1965
Or some time in the future when our elected leaders don't
    try to overthrow an election
I still hunt in my desk drawer for a replacement pen cartridge and
A day when protests aren't ranked in importance by the melanin
    measurement
I refuse to say that I've lost hope
I'm pretty sure it's in my purse somewhere
But it and other core ideas remain unfound

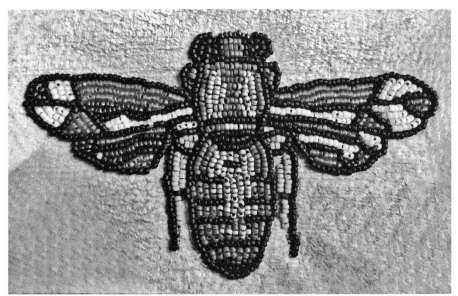

Kim Shuck, "Green Bee," beadwork on leather, 2019.

Honesty Poem
Roopa Ramamoorthi

My bed can be undone
Dust on my table or blinds
I'd rather study scene and story
structure and point of view
or pack a pint of poetry
than cleaning my closets
discarding pieces of paper piling up
filing and organizing my notebooks
I'd rather meditate, inhale and exhale
Be in the moment, listening to Jon Kabat Zinn's instructions
on the body scan
than clearing the clutter in my place

Do I pack, hold onto things as I could not hold onto
a lover who dumped me
a husband who left me for his Swiss Miss
my mother who died leaving me with only memories
my father now in his eighties
Am I afraid to clear out space
Or will it make me lighter, easier
for the rest of my journey
even if it is solitary
and what I need, do I carry already with me
not in my boxes, my clothes, my scattered writing
but in my atoms, in my eyes, the things I see, I smell, I remember
Do I carry both fear and forward motion
sadness and serenity
Am I enough to carry me on this journey

Roopa Ramamoorthi. I am a biotech scientist and poet living in the Bay Area, and I grew up in India. My previous publications include poetry, essays, and short stories, including in the VONA writers of color anthology *Dismantle* and the Berkeley Public Library Community Memoir anthology *Red Skirt Blue Jeans*, as well as Perspective Pieces on NPR and in *India Currents, Ursa Minor, Berkeley Daily Planet*, etc.

Silence
Janice Hom

Silence
The sweetest sound of the day.

It is the time
when I sit at my desk,
As images dance in front of me,
And the mute button is on.

It is the time
When I sit at my table,
Hearing only the pen scratching out letters
Forming words on blank sheets,
Hearing in my head the phrases
Now appearing in front of me.

It is the time
When the noises of the day retreat
like waves along Ocean Beach,
A place I have not seen for a while.
Remembering the wind and the salt,
Missing the sounds and colors
Since the Great Shut Down.

Silence,
The blanket that settles on the world
Comforts us through the night.
And leaves us
During the day.

Janice Hom, born and raised in San Francisco, has been writing for a number of Bay Area publications, including the *East West Journal*, the *San Francisco Journal*, *North Beach Now*, and *Asian Week*. In addition, she has been a community volunteer for a number of non-profit organizations.

Hediana Utarti, "Work from Home,"
collage, recycled magazines, acrylic, and Mod Podge.

"Work from home" might have worked well for some, but for others it did not. Workload increased, feelings of isolation intensified, and the fear of losing jobs and getting evicted loomed large.

Hediana Utarti has lived and worked in San Francisco since 2000. While SF is now her home, Jakarta (Indonesia) and Honolulu (Hawaii) are also her hometowns, the places where she learned and relearned about how to live, navigate life, and participate in social change. Besides her dedication in anti-violence work at Asian Women's Shelter, she loves arts, poetry, and heavy metal.

Moleskine Notebook
Darzelle Elivia B. Oliveros

Page one, I purposely keep empty.
Page two, I leave unwritten.
Otherwise, the ink would bleed on
Page three where I begin to see
the other side of me.

Page four, I give my thoughts a room
to breathe. Otherwise, my words
would bleed on Page five
where I write my affirmations.
I tell myself *I am I am I am*,
until one day they really
just might happen.
Page six, I leave unwritten.
Otherwise, the person who might
read one day would get upset
that I let her words bleed.

She'll be all that she said she'd be.
I am well. I am happy. I am loving.
I am confident. I am successful.
She'll be wise to know that some
things won't ever go as planned.

That journals aren't meant for setting
yourself in stone. Only words ever
stay on earth. She'll be wise to know
that laying yourself on sheets of
paper, such transient matter,
would be worth more than sufficient.
Though all are indifferent.

Even your Moleskine notebook
has nothing to say. Still, you were
never alone. So long as you
listen to the thoughts you've written.
Some things won't ever go as
planned;
but you'll be glad to have grown from
every word you've sown. You are
what you bury most.
And every space created by each
blank page was the breath you took
to take a break. The sanity in silence
tells you that it's okay. That you
understand. That you will, one day.
The last pages I can never leave
empty. There's just always so much
to say.

Darzelle is now 21 years old and still has a lot of growing to do. She recently realized that she likes to take breaks every so often. Her breaks are often productive anyway…given that those breaks tend to turn into breakthroughs.

case number 0812002
Dena Rod

missing: trajectory. no one
knows where we're going
anymore, least of all the future.
five year plans crumble into
getting through the next twenty
four hours, each hour sifting
through our hands like powdered
sugar on top of freshly fried dough,
oil absorbing each fleck into thick
paste. we stop and start, rusted joints
waiting for oil that will never come.
standing still, we claim someone
glued our eyelids shut but we can
clearly see the whites of our eyes bald
with fear over what the next four years
will bring.

Dena Rod works to illuminate their diasporic experiences of Iranian-American heritage and queerness, combating negative stereotypes of their intersecting identities. Described by *The Bold Italic* as a "verbose advocate," they're currently the creative nonfiction editor at *Homology Lit* and a reader for *The Rumpus*. Their debut poetry collection, *Scattered Arils*, is forthcoming from Milk & Cake Press May 2021. You can find them at denarod.com.

Seeking inner peace
We look outside of ourselves
I sit in silence

—Max Leung

safe at home
norm mattox

when you leave out the door
go where you're gonna go,
do what you goin' out to do,
you just wanna Get Home Safe!

living while Black
in this amerika,
no matter the age,
getting home safe is
not a foregone conclusion.

stayin' at home while Black
in this amerika
don't guarantee your safety,
neither
tryin' to make me disclaim
the skin i'm in,
afraid to wear it on my face
eyes showing fear
looks like rage can't breathe
can't sneeze, can't cough
can't wear a mask
to be safe
in this amerika
may as well martyr me Black!

Previous page: Max Leung co-founded the SF Peace Collective in March 2020 in response to rising violence and vandalism in San Francisco's Chinatown. The group's volunteer foot patrols provide a peaceful, protective presence for the vulnerable—single females, the elderly and small businesses. The group works with Asian American organizers on both sides of the Bay to protect their communities from hate crimes and to negotiate peaceful solutions to conflict.

Waves of Change
Tisa Ambrosino

It was like watching a storm roll in from the coast, except it was more like a hurricane. There went Wuhan. A virus-tracker popped up on the front page of the New York Times. Surely though, this would never happen to us. And then went all of China. A glimmer of hope appeared as the word containment was thrown around on the news. But then went the Other Eastern Countries: Iran, Japan, Russia, Taiwan.

And then France.

The first Western Country. Surely, France could get this right. But then, Italy fell. Italy, in a lightning strike, surpassed the number of deaths in China. There was no way around it. The world had to admit defeat. Blame could be passed around, and it was. But in the end, it wasn't the fault of anyone. It was coming for us. Maybe it was already here and we didn't know. Maybe it wasn't. Regardless, there was no stopping it at our shores.

It spilled into the Bay and onto the shores of San Francisco. The Grand Princess. Docked with 21 people on board who were sick with the virus. The unavoidable horror. Waiting for its chance to drown us in its despair.

* * *

I worked quietly at the front desk of the Department of Elections until they handed me a laptop and told me to go home. No one was to come into the office until further notice.

At home, days rolled into one another. Time warped as if existence was suddenly a rendition of The Persistence of Memory. Restaurants and public spaces closed. Flowers unfurled as we shut ourselves inside. The city hushed into an empty quiet that echoed our fear. We were riding the wave of uncertainty.

I received almost daily emails reminding me that under a declaration of emergency, City and County of San Francisco employees were required to be Disaster Service Workers. But that was all I knew until early May when I was called to the frontlines.

Dread filled every step I took that brought me closer to my assignment. I was going to the hotels opened to shelter the unhoused and quarantine those who had nowhere to go. Establishments once open for tourists were now open to those who couldn't afford their own safety. Most City workers stayed with one hotel during their assignment, but I was assigned to roam the Tenderloin like a lost traveler, rotating to three different shelters a week.

As I walked into my first hotel, a woman brusquely informed me: "You're going to want face shields and plastic gowns here on top of your mask and gloves. They won't tell you this, but this place is for people who have tested positive."

The hotel was an Isolation and Quarantine facility and I hadn't been told. Panic and anger flooded me. Why was I not told what I was walking into?

A worker from the Port, a clerk from Human Services Agency, and I, meandered between the marble lobby and the back rooms, talking about the riots, how we would get home after curfew, and how the world had gotten to this point. Anything but COVID.

As food deliveries arrived, we gowned up, carrying heavy boxes up winding flights of stairs. Elevators were reserved for patients. We set food down in front of doors, knocked, shouted DINNER, and ran. We still weren't sure how the virus worked, but we did know it could get into your eyes.

On that first night, tendrils of rumors began to spread about hotels where drug overdoses and murders occurred.

"But this would have happened on the street, too," someone said as we stood in a circle, the dark windows in stark contrast to the white lobby.

My shift was over. Feeling defeated, I caught a ride home.

"It's like you're a soldier at war," said the driver, driving down the eerily empty streets with boarded up buildings.

They weren't wrong. Hotels were battlegrounds. Heroes, they called us. But it didn't feel that way. The days, set at odd hours, were drawn out and quiet, except for the occasional ambulance. Nights were filled with quiet entrances into houses as we stripped at our doors. Mornings filled with dread. Everything was still and yet, we kept moving. Nothing was normal anymore.

I moved onto the next hotel, wondering if it would be another Isolation site. Instead, guests wandered in and out of a dimly lit lobby while a man stood on a chair, shouting instructions for the shift change. It wasn't an Isolation site, but a Shelter in Place hotel.

Each hotel ran differently, had different protocols. But each was filled with City staff from every department imaginable. Some were on their last days of assignments. Some were just beginning. And many were stuck in an unending middle, unsure of when, or if, they would return to their real job. Official directives were muddled. Everyone had different answers. Confusion and uneasiness ran rampant.

Instead of wandering this second hotel, we sat in a locked room on the 5th floor, waiting for residents to call for supplies. We sat among rolls of toilet paper, towels, clothes, masks, and soaps. For dinner, we still knocked on hotel room doors, but this time there was no running. I worried I was bringing the virus with me like an unwanted suitcase.

Friendships that bloomed were fleeting and intense, knowing our paths wouldn't cross again after the assignments. In such small spaces, waiting for anything to happen, we bonded. At the second hotel, I worked with two librarians. We reminisced about grocery stores and cafes and pondered what we would have done with our lives had we known the future. Lingering questions hovered: what will the world look like? Are you scared, too?

Answers leaked out of the corners of our lips in the confined space: I hate how people don't wear their masks correctly here. I haven't been sleeping. I'm glad that I have something to do, but I'm so tired.

Exhaustion was the new wave of uncertainty.

Entering my last hotel of the week, my nerves frazzled, I wondered if this would be where I got COVID. Tents lined the sidewalks in front of the hotel. We sat in what was once a lounge for guests, barricaded by a table covered in boxes of gloves. Two staff from the Human Services Agency were there. One was still performing their other job, working over 70 hours a week. Guests came and went from the other side of the table, asking for gloves, soap, masks. This hotel required much more involvement with the guests. Something I'd been assured wouldn't happen. Minimal contact had kept my fear at bay, but now it roiled inside me. Soon though, it lessened as I came to know some of the guests.

On one of my last days there, a guest leaned over the table and confided "I've lived on the streets for years. This is the safest I've ever felt. I don't know what will happen when this ends, but I'm happy I'm here right now."

We were living out the waves that came crashing down. trying to find normal in the chaos, fear, and unknown. The abnormal. We were living it.

We still are.

Tisa Ambrosino is of Mexican American and Cherokee heritage, raised by an Italian-Lebanese family. She is a writer with a passion for exploring the significant moments of our lives and the attachments we form. Her work can be found in the *Bridge Literary Journal*. She is currently working on Openly Adopted, which details the experiences of adoptees from open adoptions (www.openlyadopted.org). She earned a BA in Clinical Psychology from Tufts University and lives in San Francisco.

First months of lockdown: Richmond District window, March 30.
Mission District lamppost, April 11. Photos by Shizue Seigel.

3 AM
James Cagney

awoke again at three in the morning
at that hour, everything sounds buried
i opened the curtains
to a blueblack sky bruised with clouds

before anything could be decided
the power cut off
streetlights blew out at once
houses submerged to sleep

right then, i missed you

every you i have ever known

i am your hollowness drawn thru the vacuum of space

silence suckling milk from my eardrums
compelled me back to bed
despite my radar scanning.

the ceiling fan, the fridge
every invisible motor whirred to a stop.

i touched my throat

the sky ceased to promise anything else
ghosts held their corners
drew up the ectoplasmic lace of their skirts

from bed, i reached out far as i could
feeling between the ribs of a dead animal

longing for even an echo of illness
or rapture howling its lasers to spite the moon

Oakland native James Cagney is the author of *Black Steel Magnolias in The Hour of Chaos Theory*, winner of the PEN Oakland 2019 Josephine Miles award. His poems have appeared in *Poetry Daily*, *The Maynard*, and *Civil Liberties United*, among others. Visit nomadicpress.org for his book, and more writing at *TheDirtyRat.blog*.

Solitary Dawn, Quarantine City
James Cagney

awaiting dawn in a quarantined city
on streets antiseptically silent—
there's still a taste of summer's blood in the gravel
and sheets of smoke drying in the overnight air.
to a rooster who's been weeping in his sleep
the dawn is bullshit, stubbornly rising in a poisoned color.
the sun scissors the night sky, stars jiggle as baby teeth.
my eyes a delirious bride before the newness of the world.

in the prison of time, presence is freedom
and memory will kick hope down a flight of stairs.
that god might be a junkie on the nod for human pain ain't lost on me
after having misread Help Us in a chain of rope lights strangling a house

the dawn's breath begins sketching ideas for the day
you can hear dreamers solving equations in their sleep
phantom santa's poxed in reds, whites wave drunkenly
from yards black as cemeteries. the streets have ceased recycling;

they call for death or nothing

dear smoke cloud
Mihee Kim

made of,
you are born from fire
as naturally as a child
is birthed from her mother
your mother rages
they say
rages

[while incarcerated men lay too sick in their petri dish prisons to meet
your rage with their labor]

dear labor,

you are *necessity*

the slow and seep
of take

the slapdash horror
of production line
of bottom line
of big big
of

dear labor,

you are weighted body. man overwhelmed by waves
of forest fire. the word for a large swathe of humans
who can *produce*. the food source of clean white hands.

                                        the swarm.
a nation-sized operatic performance

without an audience our labor goes unseen
from dawn up to dusk our labor goes unseen

a tree falls in an explosion, not a preening sway

Mihee Kim, "Astral Communion," oil on canvas, 2020.

Mihee Kim (she/they) is a Queer, Korean-American artist, poet, and Managing Director of Kearny Street Workshop, a longstanding Asian Pacific American arts nonprofit based in San Francisco. She earned a B.A. from UC Berkeley and is in the MFA program for Writing at CCA. She creates on Chochenyo Ohlone land aka Oakland, California.

Next page: An Bùi is a poet and educator born in Sài Gòn and raised in San José. Through her writing, she explores the lens of daughterhood, queer Vietnamese Catholic identity, the grief of losing her younger brother, and social justice. She dreams about a world where care exists on structural, community, and individual levels. Her work has been featured on *Autostraddle*, *QTViệt Cafe*, and more.

Shelter-In-Place
An Bùi

On March 17th, 2020 Santa Clara County
issued a shelter-in-place mandate
I've been staying home ever since and even before
temporarily employed since May
flirting with unemployment since March
and grieving in San José since November

From a social distance, the world feels quiet but isn't silent
Hums of an airplane fly through hazy orange skies
California forests crackle through acres and acres
Begging for indigenous stewardship and care, questioning
why we don't for her and the incarcerated who soothe her burns

Inside, screen lights stay on long before and after dark
News outlets and media continue to tell us to slow the spread,
But they only mean of the virus
Not of police brutality and racism across the states
Not of the evictions of those losing their home sweet homes
Not of the transfers to ICE detention centers and deportations
Nor of hidden agendas of politicians that put profit over people
or the amount of work and labor you must still produce

Even during a global pandemic when the world is burning,
People are dying, and places are closing,
Society makes sure to tell us that we're not worthy of care

But this is a lie.

And in our multigenerational homes in San José,
We have no choice but to take care of each other
For we know what it's like to live in chaos and survive
Refugee resilience alive and flowing through our ancestry
Covid-19 could never ban this essential love
This healing of our past through câu chuyện từ hồi xưa*
This building of our future in solidarity with our cộng đồng*
We must learn to mend the gaps between Tiếng Việt, Español, and English
We can't keep this distance of 6 feet apart from other communities
Can't preach what we won't even try to practice in our own homes and city
Because liberation cannot exist just in theory

The world is on fire
we can't pretend that we don't see the smoke
Our loved ones have passed into ancestors
they can never come back
We don't have to wait for the county to lift restrictions for us to connect
Because we are all that we have left
and this cannot be all that we leave for those after us.

---

*câu chuyện từ hồi xưa - stories of the past

*cộng đồng - community

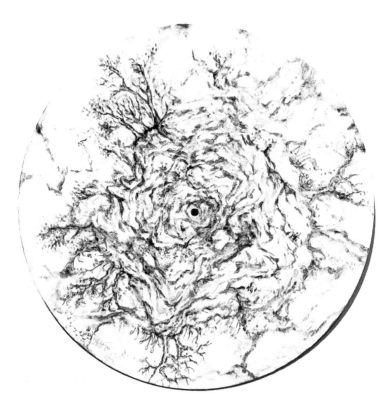

Cindy Shih, "Seasons," graphite powder and gold acrylic on vinyl record.

Having been sheltered at home for most of the year, I scarcely noticed that four seasons had passed. A mandala of sorts—this piece was a reflection on how the cycles of seasons, nature, and history continue to change and turn.

In a Space of Hope and Loss
April Yee

There is the fact that I survived. Beyond that fact are the deep losses this survival incurred. One is easier to talk about because it has shape, latitude and longitude, unlike some others that occupy a nameless space within me, the wordless sense that things have disappeared, possibly irrevocably. As I adjust to living with parts of myself that have been damaged and replaced, I realize that some losses are like black mourning crows ascending to faraway treetops, too full of sorrow to talk about. I can only ask questions: Will my body get strong enough to allow me to create the future I once envisioned? What can I release to feel free again? How can I reconstruct my life? Where do I belong now? At the time, I felt a sense of displacement from my life; and in this year of COVID-19, how many other people feel a sense of catastrophic loss, whether physical or economic? When will they recover the life they hoped for themselves?

After my sudden and unexpected departure from New York City in 2015, I saw pictures of my beloved apartment. My friend and her boyfriend moved in and they've made it look fabulous with their color-coordinated and stylish modern furniture and just the right amount of things. But they are not my things. Not my storm blue couches, not my yoga ball chair, not my structured lamp, not my dark blue blackout curtains secured on the south-facing windows, not my candles, not my books stacked on nightstands, on end tables, on the floor. All the things I'd chosen for the first space that was my very own, without roommates or relatives. I imagine myself visiting now, walking across the threshold and breaking down in tears. The space that I chose and filled all on my own, but never got to empty.

Instead, I was in San Francisco recovering from emergency open-heart surgery that replaced two bacteria-eaten heart valves and saved my life. While I was still bewildered and drugged up post-surgery, it was decided that I wouldn't be going back to NYC any time soon. Two of my girlfriends generously flew to New York to pack up my things and find a friend to take over my lease. A month after my surgery, my apartment held no trace of me. I never got to say goodbye. At the time, I was too busy being grateful to be alive to feel the loss.

* * *

After viewing over twenty apartments all over lower Manhattan within two weeks—imagining myself and my things, making a life in this apartment or that one—I finally found a space that felt right. It had an easy rectangular shape, only three floors up, its high ceilings giving the illusion of a bigger space. I remember receiving all my boxes and furniture from San Francisco after all the papers were signed and the space cleaned out, repainted. The moving men grunted up the three flights of stairs as I stood overwhelmed with nothing to sit on and a forest of boxes surrounding me. I spent the next three exhilarating weekends at Crate & Barrel, Bed Bath & Beyond, and the Container Store picking out what I needed in order to settle into my new life in NYC, making the place mine.

Within the walls of the 400-sq-ft one-bedroom space, I became familiar with the sounds of my building. The nightly crash from the tenants above me, a neighbor during his usual 11:00pm departure pounding down the stairs as if being evacuated, car horns blaring at every hour of the day, the firetrucks screaming down my street at what seemed like once every two hours (could there be such a need for help?), lovers arguing outside at 4:00am. And above all this, the normal frenetic din of the city that caused my apartment to vibrate on its foundations—buzz…buzz…buzz.

For a person living in New York City, I spent an inordinate amount of time in my apartment on the days I wasn't working. My space became a refuge from long hours at work, the disappointments of relationships, and the anonymity of NYC that causes loneliness even while being smothered between people on the streets and in subway cars. My apartment became my haven mostly because of the south-facing windows. A few months after moving in, during one homebound weekend, I experienced the phases of sunlight moving through my apartment over the span of a day. These phases I didn't get to see while working 10-12 hour days at the job that brought me to NYC. I left in the morning when the sun's early rays cast the apartment in drab grays and returned home most nights to dim luminescence from the streetlamps.

But I discovered this: for about four hours during the day, the sun would shine hot and bright through the windows and the whole apartment was a sun-drenched happy place where bold colors—blues, yellows, browns, a shock of purple—and warm feelings were all I saw and experienced. That's when I felt the freest to do anything. I played my music loud and read, or wrote. Or I danced and practiced yoga, or napped. I did whatever I wanted because it was just me in that space, with room enough for my stress to dissolve and my hopes to expand. I reveled in the strength of my body and the whims of my mind, exalting in the joy of the moment. Then, as the sun slowly arced behind the tall buildings, I was like a cat, curling myself into the shrinking panels of warmth cast on the hardwood floor, trying to reap the vitamin D benefits of some UV, chasing strips of comforting light before they disappeared. Then, without the sun to placate me, I would get ready to go out for another New York City night.

* * *

On a 70-degree February day in San Francisco, ten months after my surgery, the ocean called to me as it does when my tangled thoughts need unwinding. I walked down Balboa Street to the ocean and passed under the wide windows of a second-story apartment. The windows were thrown open on the warmest day so far that year. The bright notes of recorded acoustic guitar music drifted down to me—perfect for a warm, sunny afternoon, lifting my mood and filling me with carefree hope. When I reached the coast, the wide and powerful expanse of the ocean eased my sense of loss, as it always did.

On my walk back, feeling consoled, I passed by the apartment again, hoping to hear the music, only to be disappointed by its absence. That's when I noted it was a south-facing apartment. On a sunny day, the sun arcs from east to west and its rays stream through those windows for hours. I remembered a prompt from a writing book: "Write 'Things I didn't know I loved.'" In response to those south-facing windows, I thought:

> *The freedom of walking around naked in a*
> *sun flooded apartment that was all mine.*

In longing, I remembered myself in my sun flooded NYC apartment, full of hope and expectancy, ready for my next big city experience. But now, as the sun begins to arc low, the panels of warmth cast on the hardwood floors shrink and fade away, along with that version of myself. I am here now. But over there like a beacon, my New York City apartment—the only space that has ever truly been all mine in a time when I was free, whole, strong, and certain of what I could accomplish.

April Yee worked in the private equity industry for over 10 years, being based in San Francisco and New York City. After undergoing emergency cardiothoracic surgery which saved her life in 2015, April now works part-time and is a holistic life coach focusing on well-being and self-care. April graduated from UC Santa Cruz (Go Slugs!) and enjoys reading, writing, learning, connecting, and practicing the handpan.

re: your ad
danny ryu

Quotations are excerpts from a paper advertisement posted in San Francisco.

I saw your letter—
first known to me as an ad
taped hurriedly on a metal box
outside the coffee shop near my apartment,

"Interior Painting AS LOW AS 189 A Small Room"
your fonts swell and shrink across the page,
capitalized letters standing proudly
as if they know they're breaking the rules,

"Design & Create Things in That Drawing Board in Your Mind"
I felt undone by your assuredness,
the intimacy of your claims to know
what I keep close and rarely publish
for non-me audiences.

At the bottom of your letter
you left us 3 tear-off tabs in a neat line,
containing not just your number,
but a miniature version of your love letter in its entirety—

carry me with you, you seem to ask,
and pre-ripped each one so all we had to do was
say yes,

"it's never too late."
this part almost a whisper,

in my fantasy, you wrote this letter just for me,
taped it up on each telephone pole
hoping I would find it,

*"Keep your brain from turning into Jello by Reading Books, Seeing the writing
on the wall,"*
your gentle plea crescendo-ing across the page
into an impassioned intervention,

a hail Mary,
the kind you only risk for the ones who truly matter,

don't worry, I let your words spill their stinging medicine
down my throat
all the way to my fingertips,
as I tore off the first of your tabs—
by the time I memorized your letter,
you had already painted my interior,
full and awake
I walked home
with your paper gospel cradled in my palm,
belly raw with purpose,
reciting my new divine instruction:

design and create
      a small room
            in your mind
                  see the writing
                        it's never too late

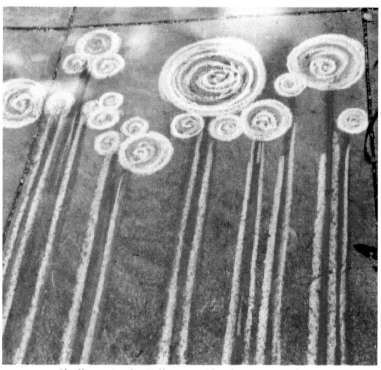

Chalk art in the Fillmore. Charles Dixon photo.

Phantom Man
André Le Mont Wilson

On St Patrick's Day, I planned to wear my "Kiss me, I'm 6.25% Irish" T-shirt, but the executive director closed our Oakland day program for adults with disabilities on March 16, 2020, because of the pandemic. Now, my shirt remained unworn in my closet while I remained at home, navigating the unfamiliar world thrust upon me—and billions.

I had worked as a backup personal care attendant for twenty-five years. I changed the diapers and clothes of men who couldn't change them themselves. In the absence of lifting men from their wheelchair to the toilet and back, five days a week, my body experienced shock. I had adapted my body to support another man's body to such an extent that I felt lost without him, like the hindquarters of a centaur separated from its man half. I wobbled on two hooves. A severed horse torso searched for its man half but couldn't find him. Memories of his weight lingered in my flanks. He existed only as a phantom limb, a phantom man.

If man and horse were united again, the virus could kill us. I had engaged in work I couldn't do remotely. Social distancing and six feet were incompatible with a job that required close, physical contact with the bodies of others. I watched with trepidation as first dozens, then hundreds, and then thousands of attendants and nurses in nursing homes, group homes, and hospitals contracted the virus and died. I wondered if I would receive personal protective equipment when I returned to work, or if I would be forced to wear a trash bag.

I returned to work on April Fools' Day. The building was empty of the sounds of wheelchairs, walkers, and their occupants. A skeleton crew of masked staff either taught Zoom classes or disinfected surfaces. The executive director asked if I wanted to teach storytelling. I used to perform stories before participants behind the building after lunch, but in the year before the pandemic, attendants needed my help in the restroom after every lunch. All storytelling ceased. I told my director I would think about it over the weekend. On Monday, I told her yes.

During the shutdown, I had attended several literary events and workshops on Zoom, so I was familiar with the virtual meeting technology. However, I was so accustomed to working behind the scenes, wiping behinds, that I felt odd working in front of a camera. I used to change men; now the pandemic changed me.

My first Zoom storytelling classes consisted of videos of my storytelling performances and comedians with disabilities, followed by class discussion. However, my host so botched the sharing of videos that I took over as host and began to tell stories.

"Why are you still wearing that?" a participant asked from his box on the screen. His eyes motioned to the mask and shield on my face.

I said, "I wear them not because of you, but because of the support staff around me."

For the next class, I placed a portable dry-erase board behind me, not only to block views of the classroom, but to prevent staff from walking up and breathing near me, even if they were wearing masks. Now, I removed my ghost's bedsheet—shield and mask—and unleashed the full arsenal of facial expressions and gestures during storytelling.

The participants laughed from their screen boxes, like the Brady Bunch in their tic-tac-toe boxes at the beginning of their seventies show.

After six weeks, I received a report. My storytelling class had the highest average attendance of any class we offered on Wednesday. I filled my office with storytelling books and ordered another on virtual storytelling. I intend to revamp my lesson plan to make my class more interactive. I'm not in a rush to reattach my horse half to my man half as his essential servant after the pandemic. I have a lot of stories to tell.

André Le Mont Wilson was born the son of poets in Los Angeles. His work has appeared in *Civil Liberties United*, *Rattle*, *The Sun Magazine*, *Red Planet Magazine*, and *Genre: Urban Arts*. He has been nominated for the Pushcart Prize. He teaches storytelling and writing on Zoom in Oakland to adults with disabilities throughout the San Francisco Bay Area. "Phantom Man" was previously published in *RFD*.

Missing you
Janice Hom

It has been months since I have been here.

I miss going through your doors
Down your steps
Down your halls and
Down your aisles.

I miss going through your shelves
Running my fingers along the spines
Touching the fronts and the backs,
Sniffing the fragrance of ages
Wafting from the pages.

Sitting in stacks,
Neatly in a corner
Are your brothers and sisters
All waiting to be returned to the shelves
For others to explore their contents.

I received the unhappy notice
That I cannot enter your halls,
Go through the doors,
Returning the books
To the rightful shelves.

Another two months
Of not touching new books
Of not perusing the contents
Of not picking up the books I have on hold,
Waiting for me.

Oh, come on!
Enough is enough!
I miss my libraries!!!
And I want them now!

Paula de Joie is a California native who has lived most of her life in Berkeley. She earned degrees in Fine Art and Law and has worked in many different fields, including education, television, and advertising before returning full circle to her first loves, art and writing.

Most recently, Paula has focused on art as a healing tool. She created "She Who Watches Over Those Still Missing" to honor 300 Nigerian girls were kidnapped from their school in Chibok by the terrorist group Boko Haram. It seemed that very little was being done to find these girls who were being married off and raped. Paula found many of their names and photos on the internet and incorporated them into her mixed media piece.

Paula has always felt a strong connection to her ancestors—to both of her grandmothers in particular—who embraced her with their love during tough times. Paula continues on her spiritual journey by creating healing cards honoring her grandmothers and other ancestors. Her work can been seen at http://www.pauladejoie.com

* * *

Paula de Joie is one of several artists in this book whose work was featured in the 2020 *The Black Woman is God: Reclaim, Reconfigure, and Re-Remember* exhibition curated by Karen Seneferu and Melorra Green. This exhibition of Black women artists was held in Fall 2020 both on site and virtually at the SOMArts Cultural Center. The virtual gallery can still be explored at https://somarts.org/tbwigvirtual2020/

III

across the gap

Paula de Joie, "She Who Watches Over Those Still Missing,"
mixed media, 2015.

From one virus to another
christl rikka perkins

Dear Covid-19,
You are 10k smaller than a human's cell
You target our heart, lungs, kidneys and intestines
invade, hijacking the cell's structure to replicate
so that from the one comes the two, comes the four
Comes the multitude, so many more
to overwhelm your host
You are killing individuals, institutions
We humans strive to create antibodies against you

Dear Covid-19,
All humans put together are $10K^{10}$ the size of Earth
We target the water, the atmosphere, the mountains and valleys
Colonizing and hijacking the planet's resources
becoming super predators
Classes, consumerism, hyper inequities
the haves and havenots revolt
With each revolution we become stronger, more prolific at murder and
mayhem
We are killing entire species and forests, overwhelming our host

Dear Covid-19
I think, perhaps you are the Earth's antibody
Now mother nature pits us against each other
Virus against virus
It's not personal, I know
All viruses are amoral—whether we want to admit it or not

Christl Rikka Perkins is a bi-racial (Black/Japanese) writer and special education teacher currently living in Oakland, CA. She is a 2018 participant in Voices of Our Nation Arts (VONA-Voices) as well as an inaugural member of the Writers Grotto SF's "Rooted & Written." She has earned her Certificate in Fiction from the UCLA Extension Writers Program. As a freelance writer, Christl has published numerous articles (under her real name as well as pseudonyms) in *Beijing Scene, City Weekend, Metro,* and *That's Shanghai.* Her short story, "Driving Lessons," is published in *American Fiction 17* (New River Press, 2019).

Survival of the Kindest: Truths from a Zoom Reality
Hari Srinivasan

Boxed faces floating
around Tetris game in
our dreams.

Only faces, perchance
shoulders. Rest of body a
distant reverie.
I mourn the loss of the human body!
A dozen faces all in one screen.
Senses overwhelmed by a million pixels
Cameras off, mic mute.
Whence humanity?
I mourn the loss of touch in society!
Each house, a spaceship.
Disconnected bubbles floating in space.
Connected by those tunnels of zoom.
Messenger bees bring in the food.

I mourn, I mourn, oh I so mourn this new reality!

For much of society, zoom did become the new reality when a microscopic virus brought the world to its knees.

Yet an essential truth emerged; humankind can adapt, and that too very quickly when called upon to do so. Employees of tech companies can work from home for the indefinite future. Almost overnight, universities and schools switched to zoom instruction. Ways were found to ensure social distancing yet carry on productivity.

The irony is that the disability community has been asking for the option of remote working or hybrid options for decades. They were told it was impossible, it was not feasible and would never happen. You had to be collectively present at a physical location for 8 hours a day for any work to happen. A hybrid option would have been a blessing to the disability community, for reasons from inaccessible workplaces, inaccessible public transportation to health issues to having to deal with a sensory environment for extended periods of time. Yet when enough of the able-bodied world demanded such change, the impossible became the possible.

Indeed, I'm one of those disabled autistics, with minimal speaking skills and a user of Augmentative Alternative Communication technology (AAC). Mine is a very visible disability with my impulsive and rather random body movements, called autistic stims, topped off by sensory processing difficulties, health issues and ADHD, amongst other things. Yes, I miss the human interaction and interacting with real people that the lockdown has taken away. I do miss going into stores and restaurants or attending events. Most of all I miss sitting in campus classrooms at UC Berkeley and listening to my professors and the hum of student chatter around me. But though I was there, I wasn't. When you have communication challenges, you are often left out of that conversational hum. I was an odd man out, the disabled student sitting at the back of the room.

But in zoom education, suddenly I was on equal footing with those other boxes in zoom. My disability was no longer forefront. Selective use of camera off and mic mute meant you could control sensory input. With the chat box, I became part of the conversation rather than an observer of conversations. In some ways, I've been more productive during the pandemic year and participated in more events than ever before. I have connected with events and people from across the world, something that would have been thought impossible in a pre-pandemic world.

The year, which marked the 30th anniversary of the Americans with Disabilities Act (ADA), also saw the Disability Rights movement and Black Lives Matter movement gain more visibility and momentum. There is actually a lot of intersectionality between the two movements. For instance, it turns out a police officer's idea of a suspicious person often lines up with autistic behaviors, starting with the lack of eye contact, the inability to comply with commands, unusual body movements and continuing to perform actions even after being told to stop, or trying to break free as they are unable to tolerate touch or certain sounds. The effect of disability is just exponentially compounded if you are from the BIPOC community (Black, Indigenous, People of Color). In terms of justice, we are far from done in the journey, though we are making progress.

However, an overarching essential truth still stands, that humans are innately good. Darwin is most associated with the phrase, "survival of the fittest." But what is less known but equally important is Darwin's idea of the "survival of the kindest": that our human species survives only due to its instinct to care, nurture and to have sympathy. In fact, we could even say that emotions like compassion are hard wired into our DNA: a fact backed up by gene studies and oxytocin related studies. And indeed during this very stressful year of a global lockdown, we saw unprecedented acts of collaboration, generosity and compassion all over the world.

As a society, we are still a work in progress, whether it's that move towards social justice or rediscovering our love for the natural environment and working to reverse climate change. We have the innate capacity for all that's good within ourselves. Let us reach down to that goodness and project that thought into the external world through action. That's the daily nudge we need to create long-term sustainable change.

Hari Srinivasan is currently a student at UC Berkeley and a student journalist at the *Daily Californian*. Hari is a prolific writer, having won many awards for his writing and poetry. He is also a minimally speaking autistic and passionate about disability justice. His advocacy was mentioned on President Obama's instagram campaign on the 30th anniversary of ADA.

The late poet Earnestine Patterson, blinded in infancy by excessive oxygen in her incubator, draws her Fillmore District neighborhood from memory. She attended Write Now! regularly, and we miss her. Photo by Leon Sun.

Living in the Square
Elmaz Abinader

I just got off a Zoom call with my friend, Maha, who lives in Cairo. To hook up, we exchanged several emails, calculated the time difference, checked our calendars and settled on 9:30 am in Oakland: 7:30 pm in Cairo. She appeared on her side of the screen, reclining against pillows at her seaside home in Ain Soukna, while I sat in the red chair near my front window, the winter light brightening my face. Our salaams ate up about five minutes before we got down to the business of family, health and an upcoming Fulbright Residency I hoped she would take at my college.

Our relationship started back in 1996 when I was on a State Department tour of the Middle East and she was writing her dissertation on Arab American poets, including me. We connected like sisters immediately, my moving in her circles of friends and family as if they were my own. Maha gave me everything from tours to parties, from family time to friendship. My departure a month later was filled with promises of keeping in touch, any way we could. This was the time of calling cards and exchanged phone numbers. We designated a day, a month, a time, that we would try to reach each other.

Over the years, our relationship developed deeply: My yearlong Fulbright to Egypt, my 6-month performance tour of three countries including hers, her Fulbright at Cal, her family visits to Virginia. One year, my sisters and our husbands joined me on a trip where I could share my Egypt home and my Egypt family. The blending was constant. Between Maha and me, over the years, we accumulated more than ten meet-ups. Maha is brilliant: a writer, a scholar, an educator, a poet, and an activist who created the blueprint for anti-harassment policies in Egyptian universities. She is one of my best readers. We love some of the same writers and her knowledge of African-American poetry outpaces many American scholars'. Our minds entwine like Solomon's Knot.

Along with our kinship, the modes of communications matured: The calling cards develop into Skype, Google Voice, Facebook calls, What's App and now Zoom. Rather than several back and forth emails securing a time, we show up at each other's door, the computer screen, holding our own cup of Arabic coffee. The sense of familiarity is keen. We know each other's houses, look at children and grandchildren, live or on share screen, have shout-outs from our husbands. After the call, my husband Anthony says, "How was your time with Maha?" The question was interesting because he didn't say "call" or "meeting," or "Zoom."

I answer, "It was wonderful, just like always."

The switch over from in-person to online has changed how we are positioned in our day. We sit more, move less, wear spongier clothes, rarely put on shoes. In addition, we are seen and see ourselves in a proscenium of gallery or a solo speaker's view. We not only know we're present at a Zoom, our visibility to ourselves is a constant awareness of our appearance, as long as we have our cameras on.

The screen is not a mirror, although we are reflected back to ourselves and are tempted to fluff our hair, straighten our collars, and adjust our seating positions. While Zoom's option to "touch up appearance" helps, we are in close proximity to every detail of our face and sometimes it's too much. What do we do? What colors? Lighting? Scarf?

The Zoom mirror also exposes our space. We curate what's around us: bookshelves or paintings or plants or blank walls?

Because in reality, we're not only attending the Zoom, it is meeting with us, in our place in the world. The frequency of Zoom activities fills many of our lives, taking over jobs, education, classes, fitness, game time. We have tried to replace a large percentage of our in person activities with something online. It has become an online life, so much so that we enter the Zoom as if we are really going into a room, an auditorium or a gym.

A friend says, I went to Jericho's reading. Another asks if I will attend the writing group. In my slow-to-adapt mind, they are sitting in an auditorium listening to poetry or we would be sitting around a table, sharing poems. After I take a minute to reframe, the reality hits me: They are basically going to sit in the chair they sit in for all their meetings and join other people in squares.

Going to something, attending, being present, basically means clicking the right link. And we're there. At a conference, a Pilates class, a reading group, a cooking class, an interview, school and work. And while this has kept us in our spaces, it has opened our world. Writers, actors, friends and family who couldn't often be together are gathering inside the squares to tell stories, play games, learn folklore and histories, stretch and meditate, and engage their imaginations.

We can stretch across the wide world and meet with the author of a favorite book, or a friend we haven't seen in years. People who never collected before are now online together. Because we are sitting in place, our longings for the warm in-person times, or the right kind of gathering that kindles our soul, are palpable.

I didn't know I missed you.

After my call with Maha, I reflected that if the pandemic had happened at another time in our history, say the calling card times, how would we handle that need to gather or to see and hear the familiar, the inspired and the hopeful? When would I see how tall her granddaughter has grown or how the addition on the house has come along?

These intimacies have grown in importance and reaching toward others, even on a tech platform, reminds us of our humanity even as we're trapped in the square.

Elmaz Abinader's poetry collection *This House, My Bones* was the Editor's Selection 2014 from Willow Books. She has a memoir: *Children of the Roojme, A Family's Journey from Lebanon*, and a book of poetry, *In the Country of My Dreams...* Elmaz teaches at Mills College (www.elmazabinader.com), and she is co-founder of the Voices of Our Nations Arts Foundation (VONA), which has nurtured writers around the country for 20 years. www.vonavoices.org.

Screen shot by Susana Praver-Perez of a virtual poetry reading.

Learnng to Heal
Dr. Sriram Shamasunder

When I was 6, my father had a seizure in his bed. His kidneys had failed. He was 44 years old, just a few years older than I am now.

My father was an immigrant new to the United States. I was too young to know that he struggled through dialysis and work for the next two years while trying to raise my siblings and me.

High quality care at the right time gave me my father into my adulthood. He lived long enough to meet my daughter. In most places around the world, though, he would not have. He got a chance at life because modern medicine reached him at the right time with the right care.

As a physician who spends much of my time living and working in resource-denied communities around the world, I witness so much needless death. Sometimes when I fill out death certificates, I wish I could write "racism" or "poverty" as the cause of death.

I remember caring for an undocumented Mexican man who worked and worked for four decades in the vineyards of Napa. He never had health insurance. I saw him in the hospital when his bone marrow finally failed, exhausted by decades of fieldwork.

In India, in rural Malawi, in East Oakland, in Haiti, the story for the underserved plays out in similar ways. Here in the United States, abandoned uranium mines are left to poison the ground and the water in the Navajo Nation. The uranium in the earth rises as a lump in a Navajo woman's breast. Preventable illness and premature death follow predictably for so many of the world's poor.

It doesn't have to be this way.

In 2015, I co-founded HEAL make common cause with underserved communities in the fight for health equity around the world. HEAL's two-year program is training and transforming a generation of front-line health professionals who make serving the underserved a life-long choice. HEAL's model combines deep immersion in impacted communities, mentorship, leadership and advocacy training with a community of like-minded health workers.

Let me give you an example. We have been working alongside Navajo Nation since we started HEAL. Because of our deep ties to the community, as the COVID crisis ravaged Navajo this spring, HEAL was able to step up in solidarity in a big way.

Before COVID, there were 54 frontline HEAL clinicians working in Navajo. During the surge, at the invitation of our Navajo colleagues, we added 45 nurses and doctors from UCSF. This allowed for respiratory care units to stay open and not buckle under shortages of staff and health provider fatigue.

HEAL in Navajo Nation during COVID is a case study of what leveraging a world class university like UCSF in true partnership with impacted communities can look like. We helped shape a narrative of solidarity, not saviors.

Over the last 5 years, HEAL has trained 150 front line health professionals across 9 countries in our two-year immersive program. A quarter of our Fellows are Navajo and another quarter are from the Global South. The remainder come from hospitals across the US, and 35% of them have stayed in Navajo Nation after their fellowship ends. In a region with significant physician vacancies, that's transformative.

I imagine a world in which every health professional considers a commitment of two years to serve the underserved as they finish their training—compensated time, with school loans forgiven for their service.

In the US, I imagine every health professional spending part of their training learning from Native communities, communities of color and marginalized communities across the country with mentorship, and a curriculum that allows them to unpack our history of inequity and become allies in self-determination for these communities.

And I imagine that they are joined by talented health professionals from those very communities whose capacities grow to serve their own.

HEAL is working to realize this vision.

As we fill out death certificates, instead of writing on poverty or racism in our black and brown communities around the world, we dream of writing a version of "old age."

Dr. Sriram Shamasunder is an Associate Professor of Medicine at UCSF and co-founder/faculty director of the HEAL Initiative, a health workforce strengthening fellowship working in nine countries around the world. He led the HEAL UCSF response during the ongoing COVID surge in Navajo Nation, spending several weeks there caring for patients and supporting volunteer UCSF nurses and doctors. In April-June 2020, 40+ UCSF nurses and doctors joined 50+ HEAL fellows (Native and non-Native) to serve in Navajo Nation.

To Walk In Beauty Once Again
Siram Shamasunder

Fragility sticks to everything alive like the quiet wetness of morning dew
in this global pandemic
as a doctor
I see this fragility
Threatening to swallow so much of what we love
like a large red blanket covering a small bed
and I can't unsee it

In the spring
I spent five weeks in Navajo Nation
An indigenous community in the southwest of the United States
Taking care of covid patients
Covid as common as desert cactus in Arizona
blooming like dandelions in an open field

That evening like every other evening
I stood outside a patient room
an emergency room converted into several pods of plastic
cocoons that separate one patient from the next and them from us
all in the hopes of keeping the virus at bay

Blue plastic reflects emergency room light
light like a parking lot at night or a mall
perpetual and yellow glow fluorescent

I methodically wear my PPE
Velcro gown clasp
secure the back
face shield
N 95 on
cloth mask over
double glove blue glove pulled over brown skin
no brown skin between gloves and gown
Double-check
Zip up tent
step in
zip closed behind me

He lies left side down
a young Navajo man
Black hair braided down long past his lower back
right down the middle of his back
like an outer beautiful spine
stark against
bleached white sheets

each thick hair knot
dense and strong as rope
like ancestors clasping hands one over the other
Each knot
a closed knuckle
gathering like a prayer at the base of his skull

He has an oxygen mask on.
I watch his eyes closely for signs of fear
And I watch his hands for signs of trembling or what they might reveal
About a life before and up to this moment

guilt hangs in the room
like fog
"where did I get Covid and why
and who in my family did I expose?"

He breathes fast
We make small and short talk
A few words between catching his breath
he says real soft between quick breaths
I don't wanna die

I say we will get through this
and then again louder
the first time for him
the second time for me
we will get through this

I leave the hospital at midnight

The next morning
short coffee run in my rental car
my colleague calls to say that overnight my patient emptied his lungs like a

gas tank and puttered into the early morning in fumes
exhaustion
He was just intubated
He will be flown to Albuquerque or Phoenix
Off indigenous land

My wife calls at that moment FaceTime with my five-year-old daughter
behind her shoulder

I submit to the fact I likely will never see him again
I submit to the fact that he may not survive
I submit to tears that slip down my cheek
And I watch my own hands as they wipe them away

Everything submits to something I tell myself.

The bears rummage through rotted wood and suck up and slurp up ants. The
ants submit to the bear
The bear submits to winters
trees submit to fire
the rocks submit to water as it etches grooves across grey
the river water submits to the seasons thinning out come late summer
and our bodies to time.
And so many black and brown bodies this time.

This is the year of submission
Or surrender
Or survival
I can't decide which

When a patient is about to be discharged from the covid unit
a call goes overhead

From all over the hospital
like a bird migration we descend on the covid unit from
anywhere we might find ourselves in the hospital
All the health providers gather in a line on either side of the hallway
like a sports team
waiting to high five their star player to come out of the tunnel onto the field

It is this moment a covid survivor gets wheeled out the big doors
into the sunlight

Like exiting a dark tunnel
into
their families' arms
In those sweet moments, i think
This is the year of resilience
the year of I won't let you go

my Navajo friend tells me with confidence
The Navajo people will walk in beauty once again
And she repeats it again
We will walk in beauty once again
The first time for me
The second time I think she says it to convince herself

Dr. Sriram Shamasunder is a published poet who studied and taught with June Jordan's Poetry for the People while at UC Berkeley. He believes that drawing untold stories to the surface builds the solidarity required to build true health equity for all.

Farewell
Chun Yu 俞淳

—Mourning Doctor Li Wenliang

You woke up the world to the truth
Yet no one was able to save your life
Waking up not knowing which age we lived in
Tears flooded every screen and every pair of eyes
A nation bid farewell to you in boundless sorrow
We fumbled to reach our hearts lost in pain
Wishing we can now wake up on our own
And never again let the healer's heart down

送別
Chun Yu 俞淳

—悼李文亮醫生

君喚世間眾人醒，世間無人能救君
醒來不知身何世，滿屏滿眼皆是淚
舉國哀慟送君去，低首撫心各彷徨
但願世人能自醒，不負醫者仁愛心

What Is Enough?
Raluca Ioanid

Every work day I get up at 6:30am and drive to my clinic in Hendersonville, North Carolina, from my home in Asheville. The commute is a straight shot through the Blue Ridge Mountains, along Interstate 26, a major artery of the South that runs from Tennessee to South Carolina. As I drive the twenty miles between artsy, cosmopolitan Asheville and the orchards and farmlands of Hendersonville, sporty SUVs give way to tractor trailers and pick up trucks with deer carcasses tied onto them and MAGA and "Jesus saves" bumper stickers. Our clinic, a federally qualified health center for uninsured and low income folks, is a cluster of simple but handsome two story brick buildings sandwiched between Wal-Mart, the Lost Sock Laundromat, Ebenezer Baptist Church, and Moores Grove United Methodist Church.

When I arrive at the clinic, I meticulously change into clean scrubs, and retrieve the N95 respirator mask I have been reusing all week from a paper bag inside my desk drawer. Now I am ready for the day. For patients without COVID-19 symptoms most visits are now done via Telehealth. While video limits my ability to adequately examine and accurately diagnose patients, it has offered rare and intimate glimpses into the homes and lives of my patients—to the inside of double wide trailers shared by multiple families, the cool shade of covered porches, threadbare favorite armchairs, Virgen de Guadalupe statues, and cameos from kids playing in the background, cats, dogs, chickens, and even pet lizards.

In the clinic parking lot, sick patients with possible COVID symptoms wait in their cars until we can screen them by phone or video call, and if they meet the CDC's stringent testing criteria, I don a paper gown, latex gloves, N95 mask, and a plastic face shield and conduct the medical visit through the patient's rolled down car window. As I approach one dented, dusty, once-white Ford minivan, I see the patient. Ms. O is a middle aged woman who has her elderly mom in the passenger seat and two teenage kids in the back. Both

Previous page: Dr. Li Wenliang, a Wuhan opthamologist whose early warnings of COVID infections were ignored in December 2019, died of the disease in Februry 2020. He was 33.

Ms. O and her mother, recent immigrants from El Salvador, are still wearing their uniforms from the local nursing home where they work as caregivers, and several residents and employees have just tested positive for the virus. Everyone in the car looks uneasy. I try to smile with my eyes above the mask and make polite conversation in Spanish before I poke nasopharyngeal swabs deep into the nostrils of each family member and drop them into carefully labelled specimen jars to be shipped to a lab in the state capitol.

This "no touch" approach to caring for patients feels invasive and distant at the same time, and it runs counter to everything I know about being a good nurse. I can offer no real answers or reassurances for this anxious woman, her frightened kids or her vulnerable, elderly mother. There is no treatment or cure, and the lab is so overwhelmed, test results can take 7–10 days to come back. I try to convey kindness and compassion through the thin sliver of my face that can be seen above my N95 mask as I hand them flyers on "CDC home isolation instructions" and "What to do if you get sicker," and ask them to wear masks and self-isolate until we know their test results are negative.

At first, the threat of pandemic seemed low. The total cases in Hendersonville county were few, and for a while, not one of the hundreds of COVID-19 tests our clinic sent to the lab came back as positive. We've had access to more tests and protective equipment than many other healthcare facilities in the country, and that feels like a luxury. But as the first positive tests started coming back, I began to face the possibility of getting sick, or worse, becoming a carrier of this virus. Every time I return from doing a COVID-19 test, I peel off the thin, easily torn, permeable yellow paper gown and the week-old N95 mask, and I wonder if this protection is enough to stop the virus from seeping into my skin. There still aren't enough tests to know who is carrying the virus and who isn't. I am afraid of the day the protective equipment fails and I become "radioactive," and unknowingly infect more patients, coworkers, family members, friends, and neighbors.

Often my patients who test positive for COVID-19 confront a whole different set of challenges that amplify the risks. Many are low wage workers already at higher risk because they cannot work from home, cannot afford to stop working, and have "essential" jobs (farmworkers, packing plant workers, home health aides, janitors, nursing home staff, construction workers, food delivery, and grocery store workers) that require interacting with others at close range, often without adequate protective equipment. Some are migrant farmworkers or undocumented immigrants from Central America who don't have safe spaces to quarantine, no opportunity for paid sick leave, no access to stimulus checks, unemployment benefits or health insurance. On top of that, some fear that accessing medical care and testing positive for COVID-19 will lead to deportation.

As I toggle back and forth between worlds, from the farmer's market in rapidly gentrifying, middle class, and mostly white Asheville to the trailer parks and factories and farms that my patients inhabit, I wonder if my neighbors are aware of the struggles that those who pick and pack our food are facing. It's an unprecedented time in our lives of forced physical distance, isolation, and economic shut down. I worry for those who are already living at the margins. This virus has further unmasked the hypocrisy and dysfunction of our nation and shown us to be a country unwilling to care for its most vulnerable citizens or protect the "essential workers" who provide us with food and keep us alive.

A few weeks ago I joined my colleagues from the clinic's Outreach team and went to a tomato packing plant where there have been several confirmed COVID-19 cases. We set up a mobile clinic inside the plant, known also as "La Tomatera" and tested all 220 workers. For my colleagues, it was just another day on the job, but for me it was my first experience going inside a factory to care for the needs of assembly-line workers. I was struck by the enormity of the plant, a large aluminum sided box the size of a football field, surrounded by a vast parking lot lined with row upon row of sixteen wheeler cargo trucks. Inside the plant there is a constant deafening roar of conveyor belts and forklifts as workers wearing hairnets and cloth masks worked elbow to elbow to sort and package thousands of pounds of tomatoes at a breakneck speed. Almost all of the workers are LatinX, many of them middle aged and even elderly. Some are stout and stooped with age, the packing plant being a welcome respite after decades of work in the fields, others are lithe and strong young people, wide-eyed new arrivals to the area who form part of the seasonal Eastern migrant stream from Florida to Vermont.

The workers handle thousands of pounds of tomatoes shipped from Florida and pack the individual tomatoes into plastic packages and then stack them into cardboard boxes and load them onto trucks that criss cross the country to supermarkets where consumers cringe at the prices and want cheaper, fresher produce. The workers earn $7.25/hour and are on their feet working the assembly lines for 10-12 hours/day.

My role at the mobile clinic was to physically examine each person who had symptoms of COVID-19 and anyone with abnormal vital signs to determine who had to be pulled off the assembly line and sent out on a 14-day quarantine. Each worker suspected of having the virus had to be reported to their supervisor, a stocky gray haired white man with a trucker hat who would snap a photo of them with his phone "to keep track." He spoke a few words of Spanish but mostly relied on a young bilingual/bicultural Latina manager who explained to sick workers that they would be paid for the 14 days of forced quarantine. The workers were incredulous, having never been paid sick leave before.

The tension between a worker's ability to keep earning and their health is a frequent paradox in my work, especially when caring for low-wage and undocumented workers. The workers I examined looked at me with fear and pleading in their eyes. They asked questions I could not answer like: "Do you think I have the virus?" "How will I support my family if I am off work?" "What will happen to me if I get sick?" "How can I protect my babies?" The vulnerability behind their questions and my inability to protect them from COVID-19 or bring fair wages and working conditions to the tomato plant underscores that I am definitely not a hero. I do not have the answers and I do not have a treatment or a cure for this virus. I stand by, impotent as the virus disproportionately ravages communities of color and the working poor. What I can offer is my presence, my willingness to be here in this with my patients and bear witness.

Raluca Ioanid was born in communist Romania and raised in capitalist New York City. By day she is a UCSF trained Family Nurse Practitioner working at a community health center in Western North Carolina. By night she is a trapeze-flying writer of stories. She is a founding member of the Reverie Writing Group and has published her work in several anthologies and literary journals.

The past is written
The future is ours to write
We fight for the pen
—Max Leung

And You Blame Us
Celeste Chan

We, who cover our hands with plastic bags, who rummage your trash and collect your cans, who weep as you chase us with brooms and film it for CNN. We sneeze into sleeves and shed DNA, press our mouths to white masks. We, with no sick days, change your sheets and wipe your asses. Dare to cough, we shake your machines, run, rasp-lunged, fling our sweat across your airports. We bloom, gnarled, purpled bodies under hospital gowns. We fry your fish, line our lips, swish in our leather chaps. We scrub your porcelain bowls; we glide like astronauts, pick up plates and pills, wait for you to hose us down.

You call us yellow and ghosted, you sneeze and spray us with Febreze, scream unmasked at your rallies. You jangle your keys, glop us with sanitizer, spittle flying from your lips, "China virus," you shout, coronavirus, you cough it, messy droplets suspended mid-air.

(An earlier version appeared in the SF Public Library's Poem of the Day)

Karen Hom, "Dragon."

Celeste Chan is a writer and filmmaker based in San Francisco, born to immigrant parents from Malaysia and the Bronx. She has served as founder/director of Queer Rebels, editor/board member at *Foglifter,* toured with Sister Spit, and been published in *The Rumpus, Gertrude, cream city review, Citron Review,* and elsewhere. She has led writing workshops at the QTPOC Free School, and the Queer Ancestors Project.

Karen Hom is a San Francisco artist and proprietor of Studio on Chestnut, a clothing store for older women. Her artwork can be seen at the Clarion Performing Arts Center in San Francisco's Chinatown.

Invisible Crises and the Need for Sustained Change
Yaminah Abdur-Rahim

It's wild to me how abusive relationships and any relationship with employment mirror each other so seamlessly. I am attempting to unpack what loyalty means to me: how much I've always wanted to be a loyal person; how much this quality has been instilled in me as a necessary part of being a good person. I'm reflecting on how much both employers and abusers expect unrequited devotion in exchange for very little: maybe the legal minimum wage, or intermittent approval, or the vague sense that you are a part of something greater than yourself. But, it is always their mission. It is always their get-rich-quick or at-least-survive mission that will string you along as long as they need you, or are able to convince you that you need them. It is always their mission that labels you dysfunctional, lazy or entitled when you start to question if this is an equal exchange.

I think about the jobs I held through 2020, how they responded to COVID and the choking California wildfires. Half way through shelter-in-place, I received a one dollar raise as a token of appreciation for my "loyalty" which I can confidently and loosely translate as putting my life on the line for breadcrumbs. Just like any other dynamic where my labor is in service of maintaining others' wealth, I don't know if they are aware this is an unequal exchange. I can't imagine all of the fantastical worlds employers create and place workers in to justify paying us less than a living wage in one of the most expensive cities in the country. I know that they are ultimately concerned with their own bottom line and struggling to stay open. Still, I can't imagine a framework in which sacrificing an employee's livelihood is an acceptable solution to paying rent on time.

Families and businesses sporting signs saying "We Support Essential Workers" don't impact essential workers emotionally or financially. "Black Lives Matter" signs in the windows of families and businesses that have displaced Black families and businesses have an equal effect. As much as I appreciate the outburst of concern for Black people and the subsequent desire to read up on anti-racism, I remain unimpressed. White friends have called me out of the blue to see if I need care in the last few weeks. And, as much as I appreciate the concern, a month ago, I was still Black and navigating all of the things living in this body and its history encompass..

I google former employers to see how they are choosing to respond to this uprising, this outpouring of rage that has burnt down police stations and hollowed out department stores: both sources and sites of our oppression. Small businesses who are suddenly compelled to put up Black Lives Matters signs in their windows, or are suddenly raising money for Black organizations really need to do the uncomfortable work of evaluating how they pay and treat their Black and Brown employees. Businesses who fish for people of color to be the face of their business, have the grave responsibility of uplifting the very people who are systematically kept out of living wages. They are not doing us any favors by asking specifically for us to work in positions that do not pay living wages. Affirmative action was meant to help get Black and Brown folks out of poverty, not to create low paying jobs that congratulate employers in recreating oppressive racial hierarchies in their own job sites.

When businesses randomly fundraise for Black organizations in response to rioting and property damage, or they fundraise for anyone other than their low wage employees who are often Black and Brown, they are simply, again, putting our bodies and trauma on the line in order to protect and increase their profits. Using Black Lives Matter posters and slogans to protect their profit isn't that much different than using Black labor to create profit, and this sounds a lot like slavery.

People have tried to convince me that a dollar over the minimum wage is a good wage. In so many ways, it's safer to dismiss the reality that getting paid lower than a living wage is exploitation. Even if we are the ones being exploited. Sometimes the anger is explosive. Sometimes it makes more sense to compartmentalize this anger when your ability to stay employed depends on you appearing happy they pay you. I wonder, however, how much harm we cause ourselves when we won't even acknowledge that we are being exploited, when we commit ourselves to time frames our employers place on us when all of the agreements we make with them benefit them and not us.

It is wild all of the iterations of misogynoir: the expectation that I, Black and femme, should both be satisfied and make the most of receiving the bare minimum. This narrative replicates itself both in job sites and among the people who love me: that I should be grateful that my employer pays me at all.

It's wild how the expectation on Black women is to put the group before ourselves as individuals. How we discuss at length the toxicity of individualism and its birth from colonization. But what if the group, in its current state, isn't looking out for our best needs? Whether, again, it is in our workplace or in our families or communities? What if the group just offers a flimsy appeal of protection that isn't protection or protection that is intermittent and unreliable?

What if the group/job is not safe but safer than being alone and there is nowhere to go where you are free from the racism and misogyny that plagues your current situation?

I want us to conjure spaces where care is preventative. Where care is priority. Where care is protective. Where care rehabilitates. Where we integrate care into our culture as a daily practice. Where care goes beyond the framework of emergency medicine: physically, emotionally, financially, and politically. Our voices, struggles, and income need to be priority not just when the crisis is visible. Visible crises are just that—the tip of the iceberg—they only point to the profound inequality that needs attention at all times.

Yaminah Abdur-Rahim is a poet and essayist from Oakland, California. She has performed with Still Here SF, and was selected for a Radar Productions residency and the Rooted and Written conference for writers of color. She is an administrative intern at Write Now! SF Bay, and is currently working on her first book of poetry.

CHERRY BLOSSOMS BLOOM

AMIDST SEASON OF THE WITCH

PINK IS BEAUTIFUL

Max Leung haiga (haiku with brush painting)

Max Leung, a native San Franciscan and 2nd generation Chinese-American, co-founded of the SF Peace Collective in March 2020 in response to rising violence and vandalism in San Francisco's Chinatown. The group's volunteer foot patrols provide a protective presence for the vulnerable—the elderly, single females, and small businesses. The group works with Asian American organizers on both sides of the Bay to protect their communities from hate crimes and negotiate peaceful solutions to conflict.

Offering
Karina Muñiz-Pagán

As an organizer for the National Domestic Workers Alliance, my work did not stop when the pandemic hit. I had the privilege of being able to work from home, but the housecleaners, nannies, caregivers in our membership did not have this privilege. By April 2020 most domestic workers had lost 85-90 percent of their jobs. The caregivers who did still work risked their lives to take care of others; while lacking access to hazard pay or enough PPE to keep them safe. To help our members stay strong and in community, we began weekly webinars. Hundreds of members attended every week to learn safety tips from health care workers, get access to mutual aid support or anti-eviction resources from housing rights organizers. We started a care fund to get some money into people's pockets when the government had yet to show up for them. Undocumented workers—who risked their lives to care for others and to provide for their families—knew that federal relief would never arrive. They shared stories of how they organized to help each other. One used her sewing machine to make thousands of cloth masks; another caregiver worked 12-hour shifts and then dropped off groceries to an at-risk neighbor who couldn't leave her home. Our members and organizers in New York—at the epicenter at the time—were doing all they could to stay safe, provide for their families and/or grieve the ones they lost.

I was in rapid response mode, putting one foot in front of the other to meet each day's new needs. I was also witnessing the race and class divide in heartbreakingly sharp contrast—so many Black and brown folks I knew were the ones doing the essential work and bearing the brunt of the virus.

During this time, I received an invite from a theater friend, Fiona Leonard, to participate in a virtual festival where teams of three artists, all strangers, would come together online for one day. She began the festival as a response to the impact COVID had on global artists to show how creativity could transcend walls, borders and isolation. So along with 30 other dancers, musicians and writers from 11 different countries, our group of three had one day to create a piece based on one of the four elements before the virtual curtain went up to debut our 5-minute videos. The theme my group chose was earth. The three of us, strangers from the US, Ghana/Australia and England, shared what it was we were feeling and how we wanted to make art out of these emotions through music, dance and poetry.

Until I was given this opportunity to create, I didn't realize how much I needed art to keep me going, to cry, to grieve, to write into the sorrow I was feeling. I sank my feet into the earth, looked up at the sky in my own silent early morning ceremony and then sat down to write this offering.

Madre Tierra, Tonantzin, Pachamama
Mother Earth
In the silence of your branches
We hear your words
As I my love shall mourn for thee

Tonantzin, Mother Earth
Let the absence of touch be retrieved in the warmth of your soil
Dig our hands in so deep
The alchemy of your womb turns fingers into roots

Grounded amidst this insanity of grief
Hold our fragility of what we thought couldn't break
From the weight of invisible war

You are the original life cycle
The reminder of only two constants
A composting graveyard, a seed bed of growth
Of hunger that waits to be fed by tomorrow's sun

Madre Tierra, Tonantzin, Mother earth
Root us to you
To this calm underneath the storm
Dew on a silent still morning
Life buzzing just below the surface

You are the expansiveness of our contained, constricted bodies
Of rhythms we took for granted
The magic of a hummingbird's migration
The freedom of movement
The interconnectedness of all life forms

Madre Tierra, Tonantzin, Pachamama

Mother Earth
In the silence of your branches, we hear your words
As I my love shall mourn for thee

We touch your soil
In honor of the bodies we could not hold, nor properly prepare
Could not kiss goodbye
Touch our lips to outstretched hands
Caress a forehead
Whisper prayers of peace in unexpected last breaths

Our tears they cannot see
Madre Tierra, Tonantzin
We lay marigolds at your feet
Underneath your swaying branches
Crack open our hearts
To this collective grief

The roots of inequity exposed
Cavernous wounds
Safety nets washed away in the river's surge

This was not of your making
So much sorrow could have been prevented
And still, we are here
Letting go of perceived control
Accepting the offering of your stillness

Left with our essence
Plant our feet firmly inside your resilient core
May we move with the
Lightness of spring's renewal

Karina Muñiz-Pagán is a queer Xicana prose writer and literary translator of mixed-heritage (Mexican and Swedish) with roots in the Bay Area and the El Paso/Juarez border. She grew up in South San Francisco and now lives in Long Beach, CA where she is the Creative Strategies Lead Organizer for the National Domestic Workers Alliance. She is the co-editor and translator for the bilingual anthology *Mujeres Mágicas: Domestic Workers Right to Write*, published in 2019 by Freedom Voices Press. She holds an MFA from Mills College where she served as the Community Engagement Fellow.

Not All Heroes Wear Capes
Kevin Madrigal Galindo

but they do wear masks.

At least, Rosa Villa does.
For her protection, and for yours

She's 73. And not a goddamn pandemic is gonna stop her
from distributing food to her community in need.

She makes sure each car that pulls up to the
emergency food relief pantry
is loaded before they're on their way
a beaming smile on her face, her mouth covered but
I can see it in her grin-wrinkled eyes.

At 73, she's a hero.
Not a goddamn pandemic is gonna stop her.

Kevin Madrigal Galindo is a food justice advocate and decolonizer of health. He is a Chicano first-generation child of inmigrantes Mexicanos from Sur San Francisco. In 2016, he co-founded Farming Hope in San Francisco to provide employment opportunities in food for folks experiencing homelessness. A recipient of the Brooklyn Poets Retreat Fellowship for 2021, his work has been featured in *The Boiler*, *Meniscus Literary Journal*, *The Antilang Project*, and others.

The Relay
Beverly Parayno

Late 1990s. I ran the first leg of three along Skyline Boulevard in the dark, gripping a baton in my hand, a headlamp lighting the way. To my right, the vast Pacific Ocean I could hear and smell but not see. Ahead of me, a long, empty two-lane road. My teammates had dropped me off at the handoff point, where I jumped out of the van and grabbed the baton from the previous runner: each of us with a hand on one end of the stick for a brief moment as one runner—tired, fatigued—let go so the fresh, well-rested runner could take over. It went like this for 24 hours until our team of twelve made it 192 miles from Calistoga to Santa Cruz to raise funds for charity. On my last leg in Ben Lomond, the lack of sleep, the cold and hunger had taken over me. Just when I thought about giving up, two exhausted teammates who'd already completed their three legs emerged from the van to run alongside me. Because of them, I made it to the handoff station, where the next runner grabbed the baton from me and hurried off.

* * *

August 2020. I got the call late in the afternoon from Rose, a longtime housing worker and activist. It had been eleven long days since I started helping Anita, an African American houseless mother, and her four children ages two to nine. Her boyfriend, her niece, and her nineteen-year-old son were also part of the tight group that made up their family circle. All of them were living between two small tents in Oak Knoll Park at the bottom of my street near Lake Merritt.

I hoped my conversation with Rose would be the beginning of a months-long effort to get this family housed during a pandemic and raging wildfires that pushed Bay Area air quality to unhealthy levels. However, after listening to my story, she said, "The need is so great. Housing is just one of their challenges. You don't know them; they didn't come through 'the system,' you don't know their history, if there's drug or alcohol abuse. I know this isn't what you want to hear but I wanted to call to protect you. To make sure you don't get too involved. The need is so great."

It took me several minutes to process her advice. A part of me wanted to disagree with Rose, to let her know I couldn't stop now. A two-year old girl in diapers living on the streets. And then, another part of me exhaled in the deepest way, as if Rose had given me permission to disengage myself from the difficult situation altogether. Something I didn't think possible at that point, or ethical. A realization I mightn't have arrived at on my own any time soon.

**

I first met Anita and her kids when passing out lunch bags to the houseless folks in my neighborhood, something I started doing when homeless encampments developed in my immediate area over the past year. It got to the point where I couldn't run an errand or walk my dogs without seeing people in need in my own neighborhood. I've experienced secondhand trauma from my dad's stories of hunger during WWII in the Philippines; his mother, my grandmother, died from starvation. I didn't want to be another person looking away.

Each week, using money I would've otherwise spent on sushi, I bought Costco lunchmeat for sandwiches, chips, and chocolates. I packed the lunches on Sunday afternoons and distributed them until I ran out. Soon I started to include dog food as well. I asked for donations online so I could expand my operations. Never had I come across any children during my deliveries. That day Anita's two-year-old emerged from the tent, followed by her four-year-old, followed by her seven-year-old, followed by her nine-year old, I couldn't make sense of it. What are they doing here? How can they be living here? How can we (neighbors, passersby, the city of Oakland, the mayor) allow this?

Anita and I exchanged numbers. She asked me for multi-vitamins because the whites of her eyes turned yellow, something I'd noticed immediately. She pointed to her shoes to show me her swollen feet and said her boyfriend's feet also were swollen. When I asked her what she needed most right now, she said a van that seats seven, which I couldn't provide for her. "You need medical attention," I said. She looked at me like I'd just said something in a foreign language. Her young kids crowded around me. I asked them what they wanted to be when they grew up. "Basketball player and scientist!" said the nine-year-old boy, with every confidence he could be both.

Operation Dignity arranged to put the family in a motel for a week. I used the funds I raised online to buy food and water in bulk and delivered it to them along with Anita's vitamins. She texted to ask for a hot plate for cooking, so I ordered one and brought it to their motel along with a large pizza and quarters for laundry. One generous person on Nextdoor paid for two extra nights when their motel voucher had expired and air quality worsened. I called every nonprofit I could find to ask about assistance for the family. Many said their shelters were full. Some offered food and diapers, and temporary shelter but only for Anita and up to two kids. All of them asked, "Is she in the system?"

When I'd ask Anita if she were in the system, she would say 'yes' even though the case managers I spoke to at various agencies said she was not.

After intense efforts over a few weeks, the call with Rose woke me up. At the same time, Anita stopped responding to my texts, weary of my insistence that she sign up to a system that can both help and hurt her. "I don't want to lose my kids," she would say. I couldn't reassure her otherwise because I knew it to be a real possibility. I knew the chances were high that they could take away one or all of them, something that needs to change if houseless mothers are to get the help they need without fear. Unfortunately, I never heard from Anita again.

* * *

My boyfriend once said to me that you can't help everyone, but you can do small things to help make someone's day better. I've realized that, although I couldn't help Anita and her family in the way I'd hoped, I and my neighbors did make their lives better for a brief period. That we're all in a long relay race, doing our part the best we can, and then handing the baton off to the next person who can help as much as they can, and so on. Every leg of the race counts, every gesture, however big or small, matters.

I've since left the Bay Area for a small town in the Sierra Nevada foothills. As soon as things open up, I'll be ready to help again in any way I can.

Beverly Parayno was raised in East Side San Jose by immigrant Filipino parents. She serves on the board of directors of Philippine American Writers and Artists (PAWA) and on Litquake's executive committee. She lives and works as a writer, grants professional, and animal communicator in Cameron Park. You can find her at www.beverlyparayno.com.

Urban Alchemy staff at a short-lived, city-managed houseless encampment at Geary and 18th Avenue in San Francisco's Richmond District.

Virus
Tony Robles

if the virus is to
be caught, let it be the
virus of an unsaid prayer
that lives in the eyes or
in a nod that bridges the
distance

just the other day, a guy
spread the virus of 2 words: Thank you
uttered underneath
a mask that left his eyes
exposed

a neighbor of mine with
a red baseball cap with a
political slogan stitched in
white came over with a virus
a few weeks ago

5 slices of watermelon
on a paper plate
(He bought more than he could eat, he said)

if these things are viruses
or virtues in disguise then
let me have it

Another guy spread a virus
the other day when he said,
i treat people the way i want
to be treated

and there's a big virus,
the one we can't see

The one that is telling
us in so many words
who's calling the shots

it's spreading
be careful
God bless

IV

vectors

C. K. Itamura, "Self Portrait With 9 Masks," photography, disbelief, masks.

"Masks. I don't understand what the problem is.
I can wear nine of them all at the same time."

Lover to Loved
Octavia Baker

In the eleventh month of twenty-twenty
I finally turn toward you
At dawn, the birds in the bottlebrush tree sing
as I lie still and listen to your waking wisdom

At four in the morning
the hour of breathlessness
you write and draw furiously
heart racing, I calm you
with chamomile and coconut oil

Learning to soothe / the forgotten parts
Give me a chance / to unbutton your day
*to unsnap your longing / to untie your loneliness**

Each time I open to you
your words spill out for hours
turquoise and mango secrets
baptize me with new experience
multi-colored mandalas whisper your love language
and I cry with disbelief

How many seasons of lovers
before I sing your song?
centering
becoming
whole and holy
beginning again
and again
and again.

*Inspired by "Lovers of Asian American Men" by Erwin Cho-Woods: *"Give me a chance /*
To unbutton your day / To unsnap your anger / To untie your frustration."

Octavia Baker was born and raised in Silicon Valley by Black hippie and Filipina immigrant multi-hyphenates. A great, great granddaughter of former slaves, Harriet and Free Jerry, she is a seeker and connector committed to cultivating spaces of joy and belonging within herself and communities of color. Her love languages are hot springs, belly laughs, and questions that make you go hmmmm.

Counting the Stains on Our Button-Down Long Sleeve Shirt
A PechaKucha by Cole Pragides

[TWIN PEAKS]

Circling like a screw pointed towards the sky, we are on a mission to climb to the top. People flock every night to watch the sunset along the San Francisco skyline. She flew out on impulse; A shot of whiskey carelessly poured onto our laps. As night arrives, the winds become so strapping they rip everyone's clothes right off. Smiles tug at the corners of our covered mouths. Below, the streetlights flicker on one by one. Two mounds watch one day spiral into the next.

[LATE COLORADO SPRING]

She'd run back to her dorm—where she first fell asleep on his shoulder— because she was tumbling down a spiraling red slide. Suffocating dark. Alone. She was imagining how they would fold into each other like origami. Four hands are needed to bend all corners at once. Then she heard his boots knock on the entrance up top. He was catching up. She stopped him from swiveling her desk chair away from her when he cried into his collar more than he was ready for.

[TUXEDO RENTAL]

It was golden hour; that brief moment that comes every night but is never noticeable unless you feel the memories being made are special. Timing is always optimal when your skin looks too nice to touch. Like expensive clothing only worn on occasion to avoid being spoiled. Until you drop a spoon in a bowl of her grandmother's pozole, and the spicy broth splatters. And when you look back you realize time had frozen into slices a hundred times over. You should've danced.

[PAID VISIT]

Windshield wipers squealed, trying to clear their vision. Each mumbled word dripped into the puddle of her stomach. Jets shrieked overhead. The rain surrendered as she pulled into a spot with fading white outlines. She didn't want to cry. His bag lay fetal in the trunk. On a disposable camera, he captured her with the sun peeking through her plum hair. New masks sopped up tears. They held each other; A stick of gum squished in his chest pocket. She knew he had to go home.

[NO KISSING]

I asked whether she cared that the yellow tinted windows made the melting heavens look more colorful than they actually were. She replied, "with or without, both look good. One's just better." I wondered if she'd filter her touristy pictures of the mural on 24th and York. We shared a box of $2 sugar cookies. Pink frosting on my yoke. The Uber driver screeched his vocal cords to a halt as we rounded a bend, pointed to a laminated sign on the back of the passenger seat.

[IMMOBILITY SICKNESS]
I'm full of bullshit. I lie about being the girl who's not afraid to work the night shift alone. I lie to my boss about bleaching leftovers so the homeless can't eat them, about hiding a sweating Chocolate Glazed in his shirt behind my back. I lie to him about being happy, that distance is ok. I've been staring at the ground so long my neck won't snap back to upright position. If I tried, the roof would fly off my head. I'd look up at him, and instead find a 1000-mile ceiling.

[CENTER-STAGE]
With each step, they left footprints in the calm grass. Walking under the canopy of painted trees, they exited campus, past the edge of the veil, and continued. Their newly grass-stained clothes were the souvenirs they noticed first as they stepped onto the cement in syncopation. Red and white streams of light whizzed past them, cheering. A symphony of honking for two. They embraced. Her hand left the small of his back gently, like the warmth of summer slipping away.

[THROUGH THE MIRROR]
The echoes of two electric toothbrushes fill her bathroom to the brim. His mouth overflows with white foam. She struggles to contain a laugh from jumping out of her throat, her face inflating like a chromatic bubble one blow from bursting. A dribble rolls past her chin and down her neck, discoloring the button-down she'd borrowed from him. His torso disappears as he leans over his sink. He calls her by a nickname, recites his devotion, hangs up. She rinses, gargles, spits.

[BEACHED]
They huddled together, staring at the big blue screen from their divot in the sand. Sharing body heat, clutching waists, and momentarily whole, they uttered "love." Soon the fog would burn off, and stretching to limber her muscles with the bottom of the shirt still tucked under her butt, she'd tear a stitch by the armpit. She'd take it back to Colorado. It would grow. They'd skip rocks, and before he could let her win, she'd throw a rock that would bounce seven times off into the bay.

[DRAW A BLANK]

There's an empty space on our shirt. A bare plot of cotton, unmarked since its bleaching. How many days has it been? Maybe you'll rush to the can, get most of it in the bowl, but drunkenly wipe your mouth afterwards. Maybe I'll tickle you, and your knee will catch my nose, spouting blood. Maybe we'll accidentally start a grease fire, and the shirt will have to be sacrificed to put it out. Maybe you'll drool on me, and when you wake, I'll say it's been there for years. Maybe I'll accidentally rest my head—freshly saturated with whatever color I dye it next—on you. Maybe.

Cole Pragides is a Korean-Filipino American teenage writer from San Francisco. He's currently pursuing his undergraduate degree in Environmental Engineering at the University of Colorado, Boulder. His work has recently been published in *High Shelf Press*, *Stay Journal*, *Maudlin House*, the *Heaventown Haverhill Quaranzine*, and is forthcoming in *The Vital Sparks*. You can find him skating, with his hands in the dirt, or staring at half-full water bottles. He wants to know you.

Bio for p. 87: C. K. Itamura is an autodidactic interdisciplinary artist. Her work responds to a wide range of personal and social content realized as metaphorically layered, cross-media, conceptual and sensory installations, and participatory actions. C. K. is a recipient of the 2019 Discovered Awards for Emerging Visual Artists, the co-founder of Book Arts Roadshow, and a former director of San Francisco Center for the Book.

Seigel, street photo of wheatpaste ad on Clement Street, one of several images of kissing Asians whose lips were "censored" by black marker.

Waiting
Farzaneh Safavi

The chasm between us has grown wider
I wanted to run to you, my true self,
but my limbs have become thin and lax
Like the burning logs that turn to ash
Waiting for the season to pass.

We sat and watched our own shadows
leave us alone at dusk.
The river turns black as the forest night
The wind carries the news of us to the edge of light
Where the oceans meet
And you wake to see a new day meet your eyes when you blink.

You were not here, you couldn't see
My body became a barren garden in winter's snow.
The bold nights grew long and cold
When laws of love were broken
Before they were even told.

If tomorrow never comes,
Our sitting together was not in vain
The heat that we brought to the cold night
stopped the wind from reaching the peak of our flight.
And we slept in the heavy clouds and did not despair.

Farzaneh Safavi has lived in many countries including Iran, where she lived for the first decade of her life. It is there where she understood that poetry resides in everything and began her love affair with words and their relationship with the world. She has a MA in Comparative Literature and teaches English at Mission High School in San Francisco.

Dear Mama,
TaSin Sabir

Our isolation strings us together like ropes that anchor ships to the shore.
Holding tightly, but barely holding on as we slip in and out of fear and into hope for yesterday times.
We move forward blindly, arms outstretched,
Warning! Measuring! But yearning for closeness.
The memory fading.
Stories we will tell our young if we could only remember.
This masquerade is now the only show and we are lost.
There is no map through these vacant streets, abandoned buildings, and empty parks,
Yet, we will bear down and push.
The way we did before.
Push through the pain and weeds surrounding our core and we will feel at peace.
Again.

TaSin Sabir uses her love of art to express topics that are important to her. TaSin graduated from California College of the Arts with a BFA in Photography. An Oakland native, TaSin's artwork has been exhibited all around the Bay Area and Nation. TaSin has published two photography books: *Madagascar Made* and *100 Families Oakland*. Currently TaSin runs a Photography and Graphic Design business. tasinsabir.com

Uneasy Lies the Head of the Black Mom
Francee Covington

I listen in the night for the return of my son, who is out with his friends for the evening. I don't worry about his non-black friends—they're congenial, working hard at their first jobs post college, just as he is. I worry about those who don't know my son, never had a chat with him. I worry that his insistence on his right not to be hassled, arrested or beaten by police without cause will be seen in and of itself as an act of aggression. I fear any interaction he might have with police officers who lean more toward the warrior code, than their public service mandate.

As the daughter of a black man, the widow of a black man and the mother of a black man, I have lived in a state of anxiety about the safety of the men in my life, for my entire life.

I've had to teach my son that whenever he goes into a store, even if it's raining outside, he must slide his hoodie off his head and leave it off until he leaves the premises. He has to take his hands out of his pockets while waiting for the cashier to ring him up. He must put his purchases in a bag, not walk out of the store with them in his hands and always, always, get a receipt and don't discard it until he gets home. I tell him that people are so blinded by suspicion of all black males over the age of five, that they can't tell the robbers from the fraternity guys, or the shoplifter from the man who doesn't want a bag because he plans to immediately drink the bottled water and eat the chips he's just purchased, that someone might challenge him, calling him a thief. I remind him that he has to think, not only for himself, but for people who will assume he's a criminal or just up to no good, because that's what they've been told. You'll be considered dangerous until you're well into your seventies.

About the police—I say: "Make sure your phone is on and fully charged before you leave the house. If you see the flashing lights of a police vehicle behind you, activate your phone, pull over and place your hands on the steering wheel. If you're a passenger in the car, at all times, keep your empty hands where the police can see them. Again, make sure your phone is recording."

He says, "Mom, you worry too much."

I think, *I hope I haven't left anything out.*

There is such a thing as beautiful, loving sons like mine, just as there are such things as Tasers, lethal weapons, centuries old assumptions and racism. Racism handed down casually, and yes, sometimes intentionally, by millions of other moms and dads. I know that after he's received a graduate degree, married and had children of his own—even then I will worry, because his blackness will not have faded.

When the downstairs door finally opens and the hushed steps to his room recede down the hallway, I take my first deep breath of the night. Relieved that, at least on this night, my son's name will not be preceded by a hashtag.

Uneasy lie the heads of all Black mothers.

Francee Covington is the mother of an awesome son. A five-time EMMY nominee and retired TV producer, director and writer of news, documentaries and public affairs programs, she now devotes herself to writing short stories. Her work has appeared in various anthologies and she recently completed her first novel. Previously published in *Ms. Magazine* in 2020.

Daniel Camacho, "BLM," street mural, Fruitvale, Oakland, 2020.
Photo by Edsel Rivera.

The Map
Chun Yu 俞淳

When I was born
your bosom was the map
I occupied all of it
   in your cradling arms

When I began to walk
your eyes' sight was the map
I learned my steps
toddling and waddling
   in your adoring gaze

When I started school
your mind became the map
I ventured out and back
from morning to night
   in your unceasing care

When I grew up and left home
from hometown to other towns
home country to other countries
your heart became the map
I searched far and wide
high and low for my direction
and place in the world
   in your loving thoughts

Each time I set out for a journey
you asked for my destination
studied an open map
accurately locating the point
of my being

Then one day
you picked up a magnifying glass
eyes moving closer and closer
hands trembling more and more

Finally, at a loss
no longer seeing clearly
the lines and points on the map
   you hold me in your heart

Growing older and older
you can now only walk
in my eyes' sight
fumbling steps
every trip outside
an adventure

From now on
I will walk
by your side
so you can
lean on me

When we are at a loss
not knowing where to go

   love is the map

Chun Yu authored a free-verse memoir *Little Green: Growing Up During the Chinese Cultural Revolution* (Simon & Schuster) and a graphic novel in progress to be published by Macmillan. Her poetry has been published in *Veterans of War, Veterans of Peace, Open Doors* and other anthologies, as well as in the *Boston Herald, Xinhua Daily, Konch, Orion* (forthcoming) and elsewhere. She holds a BS and MS from Peking University and a PhD from Rutgers University in chemistry. www.chunyu.org.

地圖
Chun Yu 俞淳

剛出生時你的胸懷
是一張地圖
我是那地圖的全部
在你的懷抱中

剛走路時你的目光
是一張地圖
我在那地圖中
搖搖學步
在你的注視中

上學時我走出了家門
你的腦海是一張地圖
我在那地圖中
朝出暮歸
在你的牽掛中

長大後我離開了家
從故鄉到外鄉
從祖國到異國
你的心是一張地圖
我在那地圖中
摸索方向
尋找位置
在你的想念中

每當我開始一個新的
旅程
你總會打開一張地圖
詢問我的去處
時時準確地找到
我的所在

後來你拿起了放大鏡
眼睛離地圖越來越近
手抖得越來越厲害
終於茫然中

你已經看不清
地圖上的點與線
我在你的心裡

漸行漸慢
有一天
你只能在我的
目光里蹣跚
每一次出行
都是一場冒險

從此我將
把你攙扶
在我的臂彎

當我們茫然
不知所向

愛是一張地圖

"The Map" was published online as a Poem of the Day curated by Poet Laureate Kim Shuck for San Francisco Public Library.

Liquid Salt Mined From an Ailing Earth
Sabina Khan-Ibarra

fennel seeds crushed between my teeth
sticks and grass stuck to the bottoms of my white socks
I chase my daughter

she runs with my book
excitement of moment
curls unbound
sleepydust in eyes
she shrieks with no fear
an abandonment
that holds me captive

fragments transient, moving and connecting

     don't change, I murmur

I've undone my elbows
crushed them
mixed them with my breastmilk

I've taken my shoulders
lined them parallel
made them ladder rungs

I've opened my belly
salted my innards
so you can eat and eat
stay nurtured

so you can keep
your body intact

     you are world and world is sweet

Photo by TaSin Sabir

Disquietude
Sabina Khan-Ibarra

Eyes unlatched in the unlight
Promises moneyed
fashioned into gold coins

And sometimes the night brings with it
shrieking doves

Across the room, my children sleep piled
on the floor, a pride of my very own

I drop shiny coins into a broken jar
counting, waiting for sleep to honey my eyelids

Slumber comes only

when we stop thinking of ever afters

Sabina Khan-Ibarra recently received an MFA from San Francisco State University with Distinguished Honors. As a Pashtun American writer with a background of oral poetry, she is fascinated by how to take moments and images and put them into words. She is always looking for places for her work, places that value and center writing that does not always fit into the dominant mold/gaze/narrative. This includes stories about women by women.

The Art of Losing
Farzaneh Safavi

After "One Art" by Elizabeth Bishop

The art of losing isn't hard to master
Each day becomes a new memory that collects dust on the ladder.
We meet the rock at the foot of the cliff
Lost in the journey with the stone in motion is the ever-after.
Children lost in their play bring the world some laughter.
Losing joy is a tipping point when all you find is disaster.
Losing at love a thousand times the hands reveal the same answer.
The heart breaks like shattered glass and I reassemble the pieces with plaster.
I have mastered the art of forgetting and letting go much faster.
The lines on the face are all of a smile that remains that's fastened.
The lost twinkles in our eyes went from fire to embers,
A distant reminder to attend the dying flame of the lantern.
We weave our own cocoons to sleep in the starry night,
Though sleep doesn't come easy from such restless banter.

Scars not visible
some hurt people hurt people
we are all in pain

—Max Leung -

Fly
Jiatong Liu

Leave home and enter broad strangeness,
flee home and wander on the street
Make shelter near peaceful water.
nearly pee on the middle of the road
Hard hand, soft stone.
he keeps yelling god loves you to me
Shining moon, gentle night, close to the flat sea,
where waves are like a self-repeating poem.
sleep beside the pool in the park, under the blue stars and cold wind,
like the night dad takes the three of us to the waterdog mountain
Swinging hammock being made of loosely silk.
the pool looks so shiny
Old lullaby: Well er… for oil…
like the face you had as you read to me when you're still alive

Past the escape bridge.
Sent back by the police to a home with father only
Sail far away flickers, a sign of mark moving.
had the accident in the bathroom
Floating, careless wave.
he holds my hand, step and step carefully,
down the stairs, to the hospital
Wind brings me to the shore!
20 days later, discarded in a wheelchair and I being anew

Jiatong Liu is a 20-year-old Chinese student at a Bay Area community college. She won second prize in young adult prose in 2019 SoulMaking Contest with "Minds Off," published "Tilt" on FreedomFiction.com and "The Flat Man's Guide to The Galaxy" on theworldofmyth.com in August 2020 and "Letters in Experience" in the 2021 anniversary issue of scarletleafreview.com. She hopes to be a sci-fi author.

The meaning of life
Often so romanticized
The insect walks on

—Max Leung -

Reposado
Juan Hernesto Gómez

FATHER:

a barreled toxic in

Oak,

for nine months or so,

to make, from me, to you,

made freshly from the

spiky green flowers of Jalisco—

an exotic fracture of my chaos

CHILD:

it feels like so, when the

needles in my temple

begin to throb

(and throb and throb), and

gush inside me

the weighty-wine of all

that's ever

MOTHER:

i hope you'll entertain his tics

with mild amuse, and

should i see another child

a-tease him so for this (or that,

or this, or that)

i hope you choke a shard—

yes: choke. a. shard.

and wonder: "why to me this petty

wretched end? am i joke to you?"

crushed me.

im trampled down

to this

muffled place

where

nothing ("Nothing")

is a

good idea

Juan Hernest Gómez, first generation college graduate of Mexican descent. Native of Oakland, where I currently reside amidst quarantine, for whom this sordid state of affairs is business as usual (INTJ and Cancer—not that I believe in those kinds of things). I write poetry at dawn to slow the tide of modernity and rediscover the comforting whispers of old that hint of a future possibly.

Quarantine Meditation
Gustavo Barahona-López

After Rona Luo

Close your eyes, feel the sensation,
your clothes against your body.
I close my eyes and gift my nerve
endings all of my attention.
Feel the sensation of the air
touching your skin.
My child envelops his toddler
hand around my pinky.
Visualize a white light,
follow it through the forest.
My child pulls me away
saying *Come, come.*
Cross the river, you see your
ancestor on the shoreline.
I glance at my face on Zoom,
see my past in my features.
Your ancestor gives you a gift:
an object, a hug, a few words.
My father gifts me his eyes,
I stare into our hazel irises.
Return to the forest, listen
to the leaves. What do you see?
My child climbs on me and
stands upright on my thigh.
Arms ready themselves to catch
but my child does not waver.

"Quarantine Meditation" was previously published on the *Latinx in Publishing* webpage.

Gustavo Barahona-López is a writer and educator from Richmond, California. In his writing, Barahona-López draws from his experience growing up as the son of Mexican immigrants. His micro-chapbook *Where Will the Children Play?* was published by Ghost City Press. A VONA alum, Barahona-López's work can be found or is forthcoming in *Iron Horse Literary Review*, *Puerto del Sol*, *The Acentos Review*, *Apogee Journal*, *Hayden's Ferry Review*, among other publications. He and his family moved to Wisconsin this past summer due to work. They hope to return in future.

Affliction
Sandra Wassilie

My two sons
afflicted
their bones, their schemata
compromised
blood undermining the body:
one, at the joints
lava gathering under the surface
before it explodes
as volcano, fire let loose
upon the land
the other, a fusion of vertebrae
energy choked
into a narrowed stream within
distorting posture.
Radiation like the past buries
a time capsule.
Broken my bones liquefy as rock
turning molten
and implode into the blood but
my day sets.
My children writhe
     in the unrelenting
glare of Yua
burning up the pestilence that
spawns affliction.
Where are you, Raven?

Or, is it Sedna
wanting the bones of all people
to wash back
into her realm, the ocean filled
with tears for what
they have done to the earth
the tundra the tree
that lifts itself to sky to find rain.
Oh, my mother,
where is Raven? Have his wings
tired in trying
to find land where no sickness lives?
Where we can heal
in the freshening breeze and seed
an action verb
for kindness in soil so soft
we can lie
down upon your bosom and hear
your heart beat.
Where we can stand up tall on strong
     bones
And reach for the sky.

Born in San Francisco of Celtic-Mexican descent, Sandra Wassilie lived many decades in Alaska. She was married to a Yup'ik Eskimo artist, and normally travels frequently from Oakland to visit their sons and grandchildren. Her first book, *The Dream That Is Childhood: A Memoir in Verse*, was published in 2020. Her poems also appear in a chapbook, *Smoke Lifts* (2014), and in several literary publications.

Riding the Wave Toward Acuity
Venus Zuhura Noble

The year 2020 has spawned lessons in acuity that cannot be overlooked. It has been a surreal horror flick depicting the slumbering slaughter of Breonna Taylor and the blatant, racially charged assassination of George Floyd on camera—eight minutes and forty-six seconds of abhorrence. We have mourned the deaths of our beloved real-life superhero Chadwick Boseman (Wakanda Forever), Black Mamba, basketball legend Kobe Bryant, and his beloved little Gianna, Little Richard, John Lewis, CT Vivian, Tiny Lister, the great Betty Wright, Ja'Net (Willona) DuBois, and Bill Withers to name a few. On top of it all, the dreaded Stay-At-Home orders, that people undoubtedly are not honoring, are causing the spike to continue.

Right at the height of the pandemic, I sought treatment for abdominal discomfort. After the second CT scan, I received a panicked telephone call from the treating physician. "We're not sure what it is, but it looks serious. Extremely serious. Get to the emergency room now!"

I arrived at the hospital, virtually empty except for those who were contained in a secluded area for COVID-19 patients. My frantic daughter wailed as they rolled my wheelchair through the double doors of the emergency room. Two hours after an extremely uncomfortable "female" ultrasound, I was admitted to the hospital. An Obstetrics and Gynecology Oncologist was called to review my images. The next day a procedure to scan my colon for cancer was done because two of my grandmother's sisters perished from the disease. All I could think about were the scores of Black women who die prematurely. Was it my time to leave or not?

For three of the five days in the hospital, I agonized that they would find advanced metastasized cancer in my body. The pandemic dictated I lay helplessly isolated without the benefit of family by my side. I was utterly alone, recalling the last time that uncertainty discomfited me: fifteen years ago, following my son's unsolved murder.

I toiled about how my daughter would juggle the care of my mother-in-law, a near centenarian, and my mother, an octogenarian, simultaneously. Hadn't God considered that I lost three people, my dear friend from college, my son's Godmother, and recently my closest cousin from cancer last May? Helplessness and panic gripped my soul.

Utilizing the metaphor of surfers riding a wave resulted from this unforeseen illness. I became a hypervigilant surfer, patiently observing the rhythm of the ocean. I lay in that bed thinking about how the currents affected those who could not afford the care I was receiving due to a lack of insurance. I thought of aggressive surfers riding billows in turbulent waters. They are in a permanent upper-class with their foot on the necks of those in an under-class. A complete wipeout.

Another wipeout occurred the morning of the surgery. I was brought a peculiar set of releases to sign. There were at least eight varying outcomes that I had to agree that the hospital was not liable for. The most significant clause stated that I might come out of the procedure with a colostomy bag as a result of a good portion of my intestines being removed.

The lead surgeon later told me that it took great diligence to tug the nine-centimeter mass out of my abdomen. My appendix had ruptured and fused with my right ovary and fallopian tube. If the mass had broken open, poison would have spread, and I could have died from septic shock.

The success of the surgery was an enormous accomplishment for a team from two Kaiser Permanente facilities. The mass was sent to the lab for examination. The results were excitedly delivered by my surgeon. No cancer was found in the tissue.

Following my convalescence, I attempted to follow the recommended outdoor activities to combat depression, anxiety, and stress during this COVID-19 pandemic. I often walk the trail around the San Leandro Marina. My tension level decreases each time I stare into the blue sky sprinkled with puffs of white. My thirty-minute strolls often include listening to the GirlTrek Black History Bootcamp episodes on Spotify.

This public health movement for Black women playing in my earphones is my motivation to take better care of the temple loaned to me by my Creator. As I listen, I marvel at the strength and tenacity of this caramel-brown girl. I gaze across the Bay at the silhouettes lining the shoreline of San Francisco. I contemplate the lessons that this pandemic and being ill has taught me.

Though our country is disjointed and has been altered by a racist, homophobic, sexist, ageist, caste system, we can overcome the wipeouts that impede our progress if we continue to follow a path with heart. My most significant lessons are to live valiantly in the solution, not wallowing in the wave of the problem. Dogged determination is the only element that provides strength when I am weary. I am inspired by ordinary heroes/heroines. I applaud all who are wiped out and stand strong to ride the endless waves of change every single day.

This is a year that I am not sorry to bid farewell. It has been tumultuous. It has tested every relationship, family, community, and nation. I am more resilient than ever. In the words of the poignant gospel song… *How I got over…My soul looks back and wonder… How I got over*. Thank you, Aretha. Astigmatism has fallen from my eyes. Thank you, Creator. Ase'.

Venus Zuhura Noble's published works include academic pieces, social justice commentary and poetry. She is currently working on a reality-based fiction text. Her inspirational narrative is scheduled for release in the summer of 2021. An original native of Chicago, Illinois, she moved to California in 1970. She currently resides in the East Bay Area where she practices clinical, social services, and advocates for disenfranchised groups.

Paula de Joie, "African Indian Earth Mother Goddess," mixed media, 40 x 30 inches.

Photo by Roji Oyama.

Nalukai
Roji Oyama

Nalukai means "one who has weathered the waves of the ocean," or, in a greater sense, the storms in life. The pandemic has reminded me of valuable lessons from life storms from the past.

As fear and trepidation about my health and economic security became my daily mantra, I have had to reset my spiritual compass on how to live life. During these uncertain times, I rely on a source of personal salvation and sanctuary that keeps me feeling alive and connected—engaging with water in all forms. For me, water is key to maintaining a sense of mental and physical balance.

On my first trip to Polynesia, I was introduced to a culture that was deeply connected to the ocean for sustenance and spiritual strength. The first time I paddled an outrigger canoe alone and glided through crystalline waters above coral gardens teeming with fish, I was enveloped in the beauty and splendor of te Moana, the ocean. Whether fishing, taking tourists out for a ride, or escaping to an isolated islet for contemplation, I was on water most of the time. I witnessed te Moana's gentle, kind side, along with her tempestuous fits of rage. She was an almighty force greater than any mortal, to be respected at all times.

I returned to San Francisco with a renewed reverence for nature, but the romance of my journey began to fade. As life's challenges took me down the path of despair, I joined a local canoe club to reengage with the magic of water and embark on a journey of healing.

I practiced hard, committing five days a week to training. My body and soul were on the mend. With every stroke, every mile, te Moana nurtured my reconnection with her. The Bay's waters, even when cold and gray, lifted me out the darkness into the light. On the water, you are at the mercy of the elements. The potential for danger demands that you find the calm within your inner core to safely navigate the situation. Whenever the pandemic threatens to swamp me emotionally, I recall the last time I got into trouble on the water.

It was a clear, calm morning in October 2015 when I paddled to Angel Island from Sausalito. Skies were blue with a warm breeze blowing at my back. I made the trip in less than an hour, but by late afternoon when I was ready to leave, the wind was picking up. I decided it was now or never. I launched and immediately felt the current working against me.

As I rounded the lee side of the island and entered the open waters of Raccoon Strait, I was met with the fury of brother wind and te Moana's furious, in-rushing tide. It was as if I had entered a huge washing machine with a chaos of waves coming at me in all directions. I bobbed up and down like a cork, making little progress against the combination of headwind and incoming tide. Clouds raced across the sky. A huge fog bank had entered the Golden Gate and was making its way towards me.

Intense salt spray now blurred my vision, and I was getting soaked and chilled to the bone. My heart started to race, and I had to keep fear and panic at bay by constantly meditating and asking te Moana to show me mercy. I was losing feeling in my legs and hands each time freezing waves broke over my canoe. Several times, I dropped into a deep trough between waves; I was sure I would capsize. I was truly frightened that I would perish that day, but there was no turning back.

I prayed to Akua, the Almighty, to show me the way. I had no business being out here alone, I thought. My own bravado got me into trouble and I had to find the way out. I tried to keep a sense of doom from overtaking me. I could not give in to failure.

I remembered Uncle Kimokeo's advice in Hawaii: Don't try and fight your way through forces greater than you. Say calm, focus on te Moana and try to see the path through the chaos. It was an extreme test of concentration. I was tossed around and then she would relent enough for me to make some progress before she tossed me around some more. It took close to an hour to make it across the strait to Belvedere Point.

I could see Sausalito in the distance with seemingly flat water all the way, but when I rounded the point, brother wind met me full force. I leaned forward, paddling hard, but he kept pushing me sideways and I had to relent to his wishes. My freezing body was starting to cramp, but I had to push on. It took another forty minutes to make it across Richardson Bay to Sausalito.

I beached my canoe and collapsed as thick fog blanketed the bay in opaque whiteness. I'd made it back just in time. As I lay shivering on the beach, staring up at the sky, I gave thanks to te Moana for sparing me and teaching me a lesson I will remember for the rest of my life.

I came away with a renewed respect for forces greater than myself. Sometimes, sheer ego and an abundance of confidence are not enough; you have to awaken to what nature is trying to teach you. This pandemic must be respected in the same way.

Roji Oyama was born in Japan to Japanese American parents and came to the U.S. at 8. As a student activist at San Francisco State in 1968 he helped efforts to form the first Department of Ethnic Studies in the U.S. He earned a BFA in filmmaking from the San Francisco Art Institute. He lived in Japan in the 1970s, and now lives in San Francisco. He volunteers with Japanese diasporic community groups in San Francisco and in Latin America. He has performed in several films including *East Side Sushi* (2014).

Lorraine Bonner
Artist Statement

The African concept of Ubuntu, means "I am because we are." Instead of a struggle for power I call for an ecological network of "we," in which I am a node between the collaborative project which is my body, and the collaborative project which is our culture and community; within the tapestry of all our relations: the animals and plants, the insects, birds and fish, even the bacteria and fungi; the pulse of earth and sky and water; the inhalations and exhalations of bright stars and dark endless cosmos, ancestors whose consciousness pervades the universe.

Lorraine Bonner was born and raised on the East Coast. She moved to California in 1970, and began working in clay in the early 90's. Her work began in response to trauma, but soon evolved to embrace the larger political and spiritual themes of dominationism and the mutually reflective processes of the political and personal. She lives in Oakland and is a mother and a grandmother. https://www.lorrainebonner.com

V

in my heart

Lorraine Bonner, "In My Heart."

I am, we are, because all of this is. Art, music, dance, poetry live
within the sacred rhythm and harmony of Ubuntu, beating in the heart
of each of us, connecting us, making us whole.

A Gift to Gab!
Charles Dixon

My brother Andrew died from COVID-19 on November 17, 2020. His passing made me reflect on his life and how close we were, although 4 years and 3,000 miles physically separated us. Andrew, with his gift to gab, could have been the "Mayor of Philadelphia" for the people he knew and greeted, every day, with a kind word and a smile. His words and infectious smile would create a uniqueness surrounding a personal encounter that would elevate one's spirit and would lighten one's daily burden.

The first event I remember as a child was my mother crying in front of the radio when Franklin D. Roosevelt died. The second event occurred when my younger brother Andrew did not speak for the first two years of his life. All he would do was smile and suck his thumb. My mother was concerned that he was mentally delayed. A family member concluded that if he stopped sucking his thumb, the ability to speak would follow! To stop the thumb sucking, the family doctor suggested coating the thumb with a mild solution of hot sauce every day. Mom placed the prescribed solution in the bathroom medicine cabinet after bathing Andrew and coating his thumb. Later that day, Andrew went into the bathroom, climbed up on the sink that was below the medicine cabinet, opened the cabinet, poured out the solution, replaced the hot solution with plain water and placed the bottle back in the cabinet. My mother coated Andrew's finger for a week, he would smile and shortly thereafter place his thumb in his mouth. After a week, Mom became curious and tasted the solution and realized the original contents had been replaced. All mom could do, after her initial reaction of frustration, was laugh and conclude that Andrew's mind was developing. At 2+ years he suddenly began to speak! After Andrew gained the ability to mouth words, he has never stopped talking.

When my brother was drafted my Mom's hair turned grey overnight. During the 60's and 70's in our Philadelphia neighborhood, young males, soon to be drafted, did not know anything about deferments or options for avoiding the draft. We assumed if called, you proudly served! I was quite lucky, I survived the early draft calls; following college graduation, I was called to report to my local draft board and deemed draft eligible (1A). However, I was working as a chemist at a local company and was given a critical skills deferment. Andrew was not so lucky! He was drafted, graduated Army Boot Camp, next stop Vietnam! After Boot Camp graduation, primary assignments were made by the command sergeant. The sergeant stepped into the room and asked the question, "How many of you can type?" Andrew meekly raised his hand! He had taken a typing course in high school. He was immediately assigned to the quartermaster's corps and shipped off to Germany. He then made the base basketball team and spent the remainder of his tour travelling Europe with the team and typing requisitions. To my mother's relief, his letters requested travel money (which she and I supplied), and told tales of the European locations he had last visited.

Shortly after returning from the war, he gained employment with the telephone company. He worked for the telephone company for over 38 years and became one of the region's highest paid telephone installers, and also one of the most requested based upon his communication skill and love of conversation. However, talking was his downfall: after completing an installation, his clients wanted to continue their stimulating conversation—about nothing important, but soul nourishing, over coffee and donuts—which increased his in-home call time. Andrew was taught it would be impolite to be a bad guest, but it resulted in his call time being significantly higher than the the regional average for installers. Subsequently the company decided rather than pay his high overtime hours to fire him on the grounds of his inability to reduce install time, which they attributed to loss of skill. Termination by firing meant loss of pension and other accrued benefits. He protested the dismissal, hired a lawyer, and won his case by detailing his client satisfaction reports; and he retained his position and retirement benefits.

Several years ago, he went to the emergency ward of the local hospital suffering from what he self-diagnosed to be a gout attack. His trip coincided with a major Philadelphia commuter train derailment. While sitting in the ER, an influx of casualties arrived from the train accident, so he was cataloged as a train wreck victim and luckily retained overnight for continued evaluation. His daughter, a nurse, visited him the next day and noticed that his speech was slurred, indicating further tests were necessary. This resulted in the gout diagnosis being altered to include a minor stroke. After the stroke, he relied on me to fill in his memory blanks and do weekly computer research so his high daily "Dunkin Donut" conversation index would not drop on key issues (76'ers basketball trades), family ties, and song ("Slow Down,"—Bob Marley and HER). In return, he suggested weekly, lucky lottery numbers and gave me undying praise for my memory recall.

I will sorely miss our wide-ranging conversations and the humor embedded in our daily discourse. The key things I can share about Andrew is that he loved his family, cared for everyone, shared his warmth with everyone, and had a comforting word for all.

RIP Andrew!

Charles Dixon was born in Philadelphia to Willard and Mattie and now lives in Fillmore. He is a nerd that likes to rabble, eat Cheese Steaks, and listen to Teddy P, Miles and Coltrane in his spare time. He has completed his Bucket List with the exception of making a boxing movie and becoming the responsible adult his daughter and granddaughter desire.

Love, Death and Distance
Karla Brundage

Day 34: My Father has COVID-19

We are on the phone. I can imagine his frail body leaning stiffly against the hospital bedrail. Everything in the room was a dull blue and grey, like his eyes, the hospital blanket, the half open tied robe, his house shoes.

On the phone I can hear him opening and closing his mouth gasping silently like a fish, hooked, on its way to be sliced.

He says, "I wish I could download my brain."

My own brain spins to receive this. Knowing he has not ever used a computer. "Yes," I say.

I keep imagining this phone line is like a connection between us.

"When I close my eyes," he says, "I can see it." There is a long pause. "I can see the connection."

I close my eyes.

"I was wondering," he resumes. "Do you know where we could get any LSD?"

LSD, I ponder, why?

He responds before I ask, "Well, we could take it together."

Oh… I say. I know what my father believes about LSD—him having spent most of my teenage years on "the truth serum" as he used to call it.

"What made you think of that?" I ask.

"Well it's a way to connect, you know, an opening of the minds." I think about how long he has had that thought sitting in his head. How many years it has been lingering there. My father, pioneer WASP married to a dark skinned Alabama woman in 1964. How they of his generation believed that LSD was the portal to a new way of being. Of blending the races. Of overcoming prejudice.

Now, so many years later he is asking me, what he could have told me, his three-year-old daughter, about why her daddy and mommy were not together any more. He says, "I did not know what to say."

And then "I felt so much shame…. All we could say was that we did not love each other anymore but it was not true."

I am trying to process these feelings of longing from my dad. How much he still loves my mom and how he never let go of that ever. Not that I wanted him to. But all the anger, all the wasted time. I do not know what to say to all of the waste. What were they doing all that time? Especially my dad? My mom, she built a life. There is nothing she can really regret. She moved on. But my dad stayed stuck in time, despite the LSD and the truth serum.

Day 96: Dreams

When I woke up the other day from a restless night, my bed was wet and salty. I could still taste the moisture of the thick sea laden air of Ehu'kai (red ocean) when the surf is high. My mind clung to this image of glass balls hanging outside the salt crusted window of an old house, a ladder, and lots of naupaka.

My dream lingered on me like seaweed or Pele's hair. I could not shake it off. I could still place myself in the old wooden frame house, battered from years of high surf. I had just finished reading poetry and had that inner elation I felt at a job well done. My audience, a straggly group of white men with white hair, looking like ghosts in aloha shirts and shorts. I focused in on my mom and my dad, and at the same time was drawn towards this feeling of ecstasy at the party inside. My father's eyes wordlessly communicated that he needed me.

He stood up creakily and yet in the next second was ascending a wooden ladder to the balcony where I now realized I was standing, as if on a stage. He rose quickly, his cane clattering on each step. I leapt over to the edge to help him up. An old white man in the corner nodded at his wife.

As I reached out my hand to my father's, he clasped on tightly, the cane flopping over the ledge of the balcony knocked over a glass bottle and a window louver. They shattered on the concrete below. As he continued to climb, he hit a glass ball which also fell with a crash splintering into thousands of tiny pieces. I felt compelled to both help him and to clean up the glass. I fumbled as the old man and his wife shot disappointed looks my way. I got a broom from his wife. I suddenly felt alone. Where was my mom? Could she help me?

Suddenly I realized my father was level with the plane of the balcony. I left the broom, and rushed to my father who was hanging from the ledge. Not hanging, as he was horizontal, buoyant, as if surfing parallel to the balcony with nothing holding him up by the sky. His fingers stiff gripping the edge. And then, without notice, a huge wind came and propelled him through the air about 50 feet away on the other side of the yard in the Naupaka bush.

He was gone—dead.

Death & Technology: The Great Connectors
Sridevi Ramanathan

We had no choice. We had to cancel my mother's trip to Texas even though her brother was in the ICU. It was mid-March, the shelter-in-place mandates had just begun and there were still too many questions about the virus. One thing for sure: age put Mom in a high-risk category. Since she was staying put in San Diego, I wasn't needed to "daddy-sit" in her absence. So, I cancelled my travel plans too.

My uncle had suffered major health issues before but had somehow always bounced back. Our family gave the medical field all due credit, but we also believed that divine hands had carried him through. It made sense because my uncle was a religious man of tradition. Despite living in the US for decades and all the demands of career and family, he'd never stopped practicing the daily Hindu rituals he'd been taught in boyhood. So, it seemed plausible that he'd actually earned the blessings responsible for keeping him alive and thriving to this point.

But this time was different. Cancer had left my uncle's body frail and knocked out his usual hopefulness. I was disappointed Mom couldn't go see him, but she was distraught. "He sounded so weak; his voice wasn't the same," she said. Dad mourned that the hands reaching to carry my uncle this time could be Yama's, the Hindu God of Death. Mom didn't want to agree, but she couldn't disagree either. I could tell she was trying to sooth herself because she kept saying, "He's come through in the past." My chest sank, but I took a deep breath to agree with her. After all, I thought, Yama wouldn't come around to the same family so soon, would He?

Just months earlier, my mother's other brother, the youngest of the family, had suddenly passed away in India. I'd never attended the funeral rites of any relative because travel to India has never been quick, simple or inexpensive. Viewing the body would have been impossible because Hindu custom requires bodies to be cremated within 24 hours of death. Going to India was more about emotional support and being with family. Unfortunately, no one in my family could go there when my uncle died, and we were still reeling from the shock of his loss.

Now my Texas uncle was in the hospital, where COVID policy barred even his own wife and daughter from visiting. I tried calling him a couple of times on his cell, but he didn't answer. I wondered, what if Dad is right? I felt heavy and my shoulders slumped.

After spending a few weeks isolated in a hospital room, my uncle died alone. Alone. That's what pierces my heart and makes me cry every time I think about it. He was alone. He didn't have COVID, but because of it, he died alone in a hospital.

But COVID offered an unexpected gift—connection sans travel. My extended family was spread out around the world through different time zones. On the day of my uncle's funeral, it was early morning for me, night in India, and I don't know what time it was in Europe. Yet, we synchronized in cyberspace to congregate at the memorial home—all thanks to technology. How great…I guess. Here I was, for the very first time, attending the funeral of a relative (a close one at that)—and I had to do it via technology! How weird!

The funeral home wasn't equipped for virtual services, but a phone or laptop was set up so we could watch. It ended up not being positioned in a way we could see my uncle's body, or much of anything for that matter, and the audio kept cutting out. What a letdown! None of us was feeling the calm of closure, so we set up a virtual meeting immediately afterward to connect as a family.

After cremation, the next part of the Hindu funeral ritual is to scatter the ashes in a river or ocean. Most Hindus believe that if you can immerse the ashes in the holy River Ganga, the soul will be released from the cycle of rebirths. Mom and my uncles grew up in Kumbakonam, a temple town of South India. The sacred Kaveri River flows through it, which the locals will confirm is the "Ganga of the South"—equally auspicious! My uncle's love for his hometown was strong and stubborn. The absolute *only* way to complete this *janma*, this life incarnation of his soul, is to bring him back to Mother Kaveri. My cousins and I agreed, until then, he's not really gone-gone.

When my Texas uncle died, the wife and son of the uncle who had died in India a few months prior happened to be in Kumbakonam at my grandparents' home. They had gone to check up on the house when the pandemic hit and the government of India abruptly closed all businesses and halted all transportation services. Officers were posted on the streets to enforce the shelter-in-place order, so my aunt and cousin were stuck there indefinitely.

"Give us a tour," I said to my cousin. He flipped his phone and showed us the front room. The open-air patio had not been sealed off. My grandfather's tulsi plant altar, still painted with red and white stripes, stood there. Perhaps the plant my cousin was showing us stemmed from the original roots and seeds my grandfather once planted long ago.

"What about the swing," another cousin asked.

"Of course it's here," my cousin responded, turning around and angling his phone so we could see it.

What symbolized the Kumbakonam home for me, however, stood in the backyard. "Show us the well," I urged.

Living in Kumbakonam meant pulling water for your bath and daily needs. It was hard work and a hassle, but what a difference from life in the US! That's why the nostalgia of the well never wore off. Before I could ask the question, my cousin answered it, "Yes, it's still full."

Throughout the years, everyone on my mother's side of the family has traveled across thousands of miles (or kilometers) by air, rail, car, rickshaw, and even bull cart to meet in my grandparents' home, to be with family. Now, after a long time, here we were again and another memory was made—travel not necessary. We may gather there in-person yet again once the pandemic is over. My uncle's ashes still need to be taken to the Kaveri River. In the meantime, we meet regularly in our virtual "Kumbakonam Cousins" group. I type the question, "Does the well in Kumbakonam get water from the Kaveri?"

"Good question! I don't know, but check out this picture I found of our parents when they were kids," a cousin responds.

"Wow! How old do you think they were then," another wonders.

And so the conversation and connection continues.

Sridevi Ramanathan is a writer, dancer, artist and gardener. She is co-founder and co-facilitator of the "Diversity Circle" in Oakland, CA. Among her publications are pieces in: *She Rises*, *All the Women in My Family Sing*, and *Civil Liberties United*. In addition, Sridevi is one of the women profiled in the book, *Birthing God: Women's Experiences of the Divine*.

Next page: Shirley Huey is a Cantonese-speaking ABC, born and raised in San Francisco. She is an alum of VONA, Kearny Street Workshop's Interdisciplinary Writers Lab, and SF Writers Grotto's Rooted & Written program. Her writing has been featured in *Catapult*, *Panorama: The Journal of Intelligent Travel*, *sPARKLE+bLINK*, Oakland Asian Cultural Center's *I Am Hungry* zine, among other publications.

Getting to Water
Shirley Huey

My father died on this day thirty-three years ago. The length of time for grieving has been as long as Jesus lived, as long as Sam Cooke lived.

I often get a giant craving for a burger when I feel the longing for my father.

It's like the act of eating will supplant the feeling of pain. Sometimes I imagine I can eat my way through it, like eating my way through a bag of shrimp chips in one sitting. I won't feel so well at the end of it, but the movement and the discipline of digging my hand into the crinkling plastic bag, silver on the inside, fingers clamping onto each chip like crab claws, compel me. Chip after chip entering my mouth, the crunch of each one, satisfyingly pulverized and then liquefied in my mouth like a compulsion.

Is that a thing? A compulsion blender?

No. The immersion blender is a handheld tool with a wand, little blades at the bottom, ready to blitz everything it touches. Only now I imagine that it blends the compulsion to eat, grinding it up into something else, something that is the sum of its parts—nostalgia, fear, affection, melancholy, memory, taste, hunger—but also transformed into something new and different at the same time.

The compulsion to eat the oily, greasy, salty, fried goodness takes over like the compulsion to grieve on this day. Twinned desires. As a child, I believed that a prolonged grieving was bad. That I, like the grownups, needed to show a happy face and not more tears. That tears and suffering were shameful and not to be shared with the world.

Observable grief with its balled-up Kleenex and uncontrollable tears scared me. It still sometimes scares me, even in myself. Like the younger me, I want reassurance that someone is in control.

So, I channel my feelings into eating—a compulsion to eat things that remind me of my dad even if the food can be unhealthy. When I was a little girl, my dad would take my brother and me for burgers at classic San Francisco places like Zim's or the Hippo. Sometimes we'd go to Mickey D's for a Big Mac.

Today, though, I think I'm healing. I don't feel the need for a burger. I don't need food to comfort me about my dad.

I went to the water today, and that was enough.

You And I Are Soldiers
Rocio Evans

my brother Herbie said to me,
as we survived our childhoods

Thunder of storms
Lightning of shock and pain

Winter of heavy rains
Our mother's death and the sound of falling rain,
etched forever in our sister Luisa's memory

In a playroom
Herbie joyfully rode a dappled rocking horse,

while I placed topaz, pearls gleaming from earrings
our mother purchased at a thrift shop into

white seashells
Translucent light of paste gems
my child's eyes momentarily saw as real

I remember Herbie and I Christmas shopping at J. C. Penny's
Herbie thoughtfully buying an elegant bottle of Channel 19,
for our mother Ines

Pulse points
scented with poignant perfume
I remember Herbie and I missing our school bus,
on purpose

Herbie and I happily walking back
into our yellow clapboard house,
to stay home with our mother
On a rare occasion when she stayed home from work

On a rainy morning
our mother drowned on a flooded road
while driving her Honda civic to work

Our mother planted flowers, for us to remember her
In the spring, tiny tangerine roses, bloomed to my delight
Delicate pink roses bloomed for Luisa

I remember Herbie
walking across a field,
carrying our mother's tall yellow sunflowers

In memory of my brother Herbert who died during COVID-19.
Always loved. Never forgotten.

She planted roses
Rocio Evans

In subtlety of rain
Will I find beauty kneeling at the edge of my mother's grave
Will I find peace in her memory

As I lay down bouquets of crimson roses
Will I lay down to rest fears
that I too will die
will vanish without a trace
disappear
on a cold rainy day
where no one will ever find me
find my body
As I sink deeper into an empty death like space

As I gaze into a round mirror of my past
I see my beautiful mother wearing
her gold Virgin of Guadalupe necklace

I never understood back then,
the time we would have together
would be fleeting

I see defiance in a young girl's eyes
for the mother who would soon leave her behind
to journey onward with angels

Memories cut short
machete cutting down sugarcane

We are sleeping on a bus,
winding its way up from Mexico City
Our mother Ines and little brother Herbie
sip coca cola from glass bottles given to them,
by our bus driver
Herbie stares out a bus window,
at a Carlos Castaneda desert

Our bus stops by a church
We kneel down, pray to the Virgin of Guadalupe

Our grandmother Adela prays for the virgin to bless us
with safe passage into our new country

In a dream, the virgin floats among gravestones in mist
Her aura glowing cherry and gold

She is here, my mother
never having really died
I was mistaken as a young girl,
when I felt she had abandoned me
I despaired there was no one left to guide me

She has been waiting patiently all these years,
for me to understand
she has been ever there for me

Waiting for me to build my bridge back to her,
bless our journey together

Rocio Evans has a Certificate in Expressive Arts therapies from John F. Kennedy University. She has worked as a Play therapist and a school counselor in San Diego and San Francisco. She has published in the Solo Press, Women of the World Encyclopedia, and Voz Alta. She loves music from the 70's, the 80's and harmonicas.
She believes that power comes from the margin.

Love's not a feeling
It is but a commitment
I am beholden

—Max Leung

Clouds Go Up
Malcolm Williams

For my Aunt Carol, taken from us
by a cancer we thought was beaten.

Clouds that go up
get wispy and unstable by the time they reach me
and shroud me,
like a virtual background.
What do they carry?
Those bite-size clouds that
steam up from BART tunnels.
Water from the pavement?
Life from the land?
An individual future from a family?

Can any one stop in the rain cycle
be considered leaving?
What if it's the most painful stop?
How do you believe what wasn't seen?
Hindsight shows no signs of what's missing.
Who's missing.
After the video call is over
I trace names in the wisps,
that script is now as unreliable as any CA forecast,

sunny skies are cast solemn
and predicted rain is postponed.

Will these clouds that go up
join those clouds above?
Those that slide freely
and visit frequently.
No matter how high or how grey,
these only wobble and dissipate.
They won't break,
they won't keep rising,
here in San Francisco.
Even as it rains in San Diego,
pouring sheets of concrete
that build and swell and curl
and break
into frothy curbs
that crash
onto unsuspecting shoulders.
Naïve beach goers turned back,
sea lovers, eyes closed, facing forward.
How could you see it coming?
How could you not?

How could one cloud go up,
out of order, but within natural cycles,
leaving the foundation that preceded it?
After the clouds have gone up
there's grandpa and grandma,
tracing names,
writing in the wet concrete,
"Life is for the living, so go live it."

Malcolm Williams is a biracial poet and middle-school teacher in San Francisco. After growing up in Orange County, he attended undergrad in the Bay Area and has stayed since then. Not for the weather, although it is nice. As soon as it's safe to get haircuts, please refer me to your favorite barber.

We Will Be Carried Forward Upon The Whispers Of Our Elders
Sandra Bass

Dearly beloved, we have gathered here today
To get through this thing called life.

~Prince

One evening in early March, before we were all sent home to shelter, I got a call from my mother. She told me that her cousin and her cousin's husband had been rushed to the hospital. Both were diagnosed with pneumonia. Shortly after entering the hospital, my mother's cousin died. She was 88. Her husband spent weeks linked to life by a ventilator. Tests later revealed that they were both positive for the Coronavirus.

When my grandmothers died, family members spent hours by their bedsides, soothing them as best we could as they transitioned beyond the veil. Death by an infectious disease however is an exceptionally lonely experience. No one was allowed to be close to our kin, to hold her hand, gently knead aching muscles, or express words of love that may have been deeply felt but perhaps never shared. In her final hours she did speak to a family member by phone. Her last words, spoken between labored and fragile breaths were, "Remember…me."

Traveling upon the misty vapors of our exhalations, this tiny, crowned conqueror has wound its way across the globe devastating families, cities, even countries in its path. Along its journey it unveiled truths about our current state that are breathtaking in both their beauty and brutality. The sounds of sheltered Italians singing together from their homes in the medieval town of Siena reminded us that our desire to connect transcends our ability to share physical space. And then there were the calls that came from pundits and elected politicians to sacrifice our elders on the altars of the American way of life. Lt. Governor Dan Patrick of Texas framed this fatal bargain as such:

"No one reached out to me, as a senior citizen to ask, are you willing to take a chance on your survival in exchange for keeping the America that all Americans love for your children and grandchildren? And if that's the exchange, I'm all in."

The Lt. Governor's notion that some lives are expendable to save "the America that all Americans love" (and his odd arrogance in thinking that he should have been consulted about whether millions should live or die), not only reflects an ignorance of the bittersweet connection many feel towards America and our history, but is consistent with a line of thinking that did not emerge anew during our present crisis. In fact this callous logic, what veteran freedom fighter Ruby Sales has called "Empire Consciousness," lies within the very foundations of the America Lt. Gov. Patrick believes we are all so eager to preserve.

Empire Consciousness prizes domination for the chosen few above all else. It thrives by seeking to snuff out genuine human connection, our collective narratives, historical memory, and embodied spirituality, and to supplant these qualities with a social order that deifies the constructs of whiteness and wealth concentrated at the very top.

The self-destructive and dehumanizing contradictions of Empire Consciousness are embedded in the very birthing of America, for was it not slave owning patriot Patrick Henry who emphatically declared, "Give me liberty or give me death," even as he denied dozens of enslaved human beings their liberty? Like many politicians of his day and ours, Patrick Henry betrayed his deepest values to preserve the reigning economic order. Even though he was a vocal opponent of slavery for years after the revolution, it appears he did not free one single slave throughout his lifetime or even upon his death, since he could not fathom as he would say, the "general inconvenience of living here without them."

Despite all efforts to conveniently erase the humanity of enslaved Africans, however, the Empire Consciousness enterprise failed completely in this regard. While the unspoken aim of Empire Consciousness is to crush the souls of the oppressed and oppressors alike (for the souls of Patrick Henry and his brethren are surely fractured by their choices), enslaved Africans and their descendants were liberatory geniuses in "finding a way out of no way," as the old adage goes. Across the span of centuries, they found a way to keep the internal fire of future liberation aflame even when there was no rational reason to believe freedom would ever come.

To dream of freedom while suffering under the lash and the lust of slave owners requires a level of consciousness about your worth and the worth of your people that runs counter to everything Empire Consciousness holds dear. This consciousness rejects the notion that certain lives are expendable in order to prevent the "general inconvenience" of the privileged few. In defiance against the hopelessness systems of oppression cultivate to maintain command and control, those operating from this plane of consciousness understood that our liberation was not bound to a body or dependent upon the graces of a totalitarian power.

Freed from the constraints of time, place, and corporeal reality, the potential for "Mountaintop Consciousness" as Ruby Sales calls it, can be discovered within each individual spirit. It is activated when grounded in something larger than ourselves, gains strength when we gather as fellow travelers, triumphs when we act collectively and courageously, and is carried through the ages upon the whispered wisdoms of our elders.

By bearing witness and sharing legacies, through their devotion and their admonishments, even in the lessons learned from witnessing the travails of misdirected or unmoored lives, our elders bring forth the wisdoms that have sustained us. And at their best their lives stand as a testament to the evolution of our human journey and inspire future generations to grow beyond what they could imagine.

This call to sacrifice the elders is not noble, as Lt. Governor Patrick suggests. It is not just a heartless disregard for the lives of those who are no longer seen as worthy contenders in the fictive race for the survival of the fittest, it is an age-old tactic that has been used throughout American history to hobble our future liberatory possibilities by attempting to destroy our kinship with the past. It failed then and it will fail now—if we stand, united, against the destructive Empire narrative and have the courage to birth a new story.

It is ironic that an illness that takes our lives by stealing our breaths also invites us to consider what needs to be breathed into life in our time. For some

of us the experience of sheltering has been chaotic and frightening. For others it has seemed like endless solitude or a time of reflection and reconnection. Wherever this moment finds us, the possibility of reimaging new ways of being with and for each other lies there as well.

And so dearly beloveds, we are gathered here today, in this precious, pregnant pause, to figure out what we need to do

Malik Seneferu, "Queen Sandy," 40 x 30 inches, 2019. Homage to Sandra Bland.

and who we need to be to get through this earthly experience. This marathon riddled with maladies and melodies, joys and pains. This thing called life.

After the ill winds of illness have ceased to blow, will we choose to ventilate our world with justice and compassion? When the sting of grief for loved ones lost and the passing of a torturous but familiar normality has subsided, what wisdoms of the elders will we bring forth and what new story will we willingly embrace? And as the tides of our lives turn towards holding more yesteryears than future horizons, and our voices are reduced to whispers, and the fruits of what we did with our time in this moment are laid before another generation, may we be remembered as the brave and true ones, who dared to stand, hand in hand, hearts open, unafraid, ushering in the break of a new day.

Dr. Sandra Bass is Associate Dean of Students and Director of the Public Service Center at UC Berkeley. She earned a PhD in political science at UC Berkeley, where she researched community organizing and the dynamics between police and communities of color. She has led programs for girls and women in Sub-Saharan Africa for the David and Lucille Packard Foundation, was executive director of Teach With Africa, and Board Chair of the Ella Baker Center for Human Rights. She currently serves on the regional Board of the Jefferson Awards Foundation and is also a nonviolence trainer and educator.

Joan Osato, "Tanya Orellana, Scenic Designer," from the photographic portrait series *unseen labor,* 2020.

It's October &
Kevin Madrigal Galindo

I want to get drunk
with my primo in person.

To get enpulqueado and begin the
late night mission to find
señora tacos de la calle.

I want us to reminisce
on the time pre-pandemic
us sleeping in adjacent rooms like
brothers going for jogs at the park
and runs for late night
churros and elote.
All evenings enjoyed, either an
adventurous meal at a place I found
on Instagram or game night with
friends and
plotting the next mezcal night out.

I want us to remember the mundane.
His dad, my tio,
at the head of the dinner table
"Pasame el chile" he'll say,
and one of us will gladly hand it
over sipping on agua de jamaica
as he downs a diet coke.

My tia preparing his plate, taking it
out to him for his lunch break

watching over the papeleria where
highschool students buy last-minute
supplies.

I never earned my nephew Juanpi's
trust. Sandra would bring him by
and he'd look at me in suspicion.

The most I'd get was a "choca la"
fist bump before he ran off to
abuelito, my tio.

Luis told me that Juanpi asked
when his abuelito is coming back
and I teared up. How many years
will it take for him to
learn
to understand that he isn't.

And I want us all
to go back in time
pre-pandemic,
so we can properly say
goodbye to my tio.

But we can't.
So, I want to get drunk
with my primo in person
& pretend like we can.

A Mi Querido Negrito en su Día
Susana Praver-Pérez

For José de Jesús Pérez, my late husband.

December eleventh arrives
enrobed in fog and missing,
and the warm cocoon
of a cantaloupe room
you painted before
you became one with the wind,
your ashes dancing above Aguadilla.

Born in that place of little waters,
('though some say Aguadilla is not Spanish
but Taino for garden),
hijo de palmas, orquídeas, y olas del mar
crashing on ivory sand, your song
ran along stone rivers,
Río Piedras where you grew,
sweet mangos bursting as they rained
upon your flat cement roof.

I place a slice of that fruit
like a heart
upon your altar
and a flag of your beloved
Borinquen unfurled
black and white in a sky
like leche de coco that once fed
your vibrant flesh.

En el cielo
encancaranublado,
your soul, still
bright, veins the gift of you
like rivulets of molten gold.

136

How I Operate
Grace Morizawa

I am a dreamer.
I am not good at reading a room
Or reading long, complex novels
Or seasoning stir fry.
I often missed the boat.
Even while nodding my head
I misunderstand.

Saved by dreaming. I close my eyes
And find a lighted path
Step beyond the asphalt cracked around my house.
I didn't notice how wind assaulted
The Japanese irises,
The blooming roses,
The geraniums, wildly potted reached up like open arms.
Finally, the two foot basalt pagoda toppled.
The wind on cars, stopped traffic
swept the leaves just below my front steps
Branches fell.

By the time I woke up
The damage was done
Invisible to me.
The sun was out, the skies, clear
The hummingbird braked in fresh air
To sip the nectar from the scarlet sage.

I dreamed my mother was there
Stroking my hair.
"I've been dead 32 years" she sang.
The red crowned crane spread its wings
I live in a lullaby, I whispered back.-

Grace Morizawa, a Sansei originally from Ontario, Oregon, is a former elementary school teacher in Oakland and former San Pablo principal. Currently she is the education coordinator for the National Japanese American Historical Society, writing curriculum about the Japanese American incarceration during World War II.

Wayne
Steve Fujimura

He died
young—24—due to
a civil war in the streets
between Black and white and
a few Koreans with guns on
LA rooftops and others
watched or ran and he
watched, ran, got a gun, too
against those who
beat Rodney King that night
beat him and went free
causing the riot
a white truck driver pulled
from his cab and stoned
and punched and kicked on TV
he watched that passively
as one could watch that
and it was painful
to the other him watching,
triggering a memory

he remembered a gun
dormant under a bed
a gun used for hunting
said the TV news
a gun that fired semi-automatic
rounds
under and over police cars
injuring two officers at an armory
where he stopped to end
the force
of the state
he was in. We
figured it must make sense
at his age—24—depressed
a time that has been repeated again
and again
if only that were the sound of him
coming back again
from the fields where we played
among the strawberries

Mark Harris is a San Francisco-based artist whose work has appeared at numerous galleries, including the USF Thacher Gallery, San Francisco; Rock, Paper, Scissors Collective, Oakland; 111 Minna Gallery, San Francisco; Marin Museum of Contemporary Art, Novato; and The Whitney Young Cultural Center, San Francisco; among others. Harris has combined his passions for social justice, activism, and art making to create a unique visual vocabulary that he uses to engage his audience on some of the most critical issues facing society today. He is equally passionate about working with youth, and has taught in both public and private schools in San Francisco and the surrounding Bay Area.

VI

whose America?

Mark Harris, "Pride and Prejudice,"
mixed media on panel, 40 x 30 inches, 2015.

snakes in the garden
vanessa diaz cabrera

between weary eyes
tear ducts run dry
consuming ballots
watching numbers filter

democracy exists on cnn
between blues reds and purple

on univision they can't escape screens
jorge ramos hunched over tweets
media eats media

I eat democracy with my eyes
feeling the edges of the thing
that hides underneath

they say this is the thing of third world countries
boarded downtowns protecting leather purses and apple stores

it is third world to protect material goods
plague the people of towns with wars
it is the same taste
"american" democracy
puppet governments
gleaning fruit from trees

eyes that never thought they would see
snakes in their own garden
maybe it is the lie we tell ourselves
to believe we are free.

---

vanessa diaz cabrera is a writer, educator, and bird nerd. she grew up in the mission, where her mother taught her to speak spanish to plants.

Living I.B.M. (Implicit Bias and Microaggression)
Venus Zuhura Noble

So, my purse strap broke
While dashing around the campus
I had a presentation in an hour or so
Why of all days did this have to happen?

Up from the quad I hustled
With my backpack in tow
Going to the mall next door
I ran across several people I didn't actually know

As I hurried past the Library
A classmate noticed that I had blown out the curls in my hair
She reached toward me to touch my mane
I shook my head thinking… "This child is so unaware."

I took a shortcut by the business building
Where a group of white males were in conversation
"Asians are all smart, let's ask one to help with our project."
I was sickened when all of them nodded with confirmation

Finally, I reached the department store
The door was about to close in the elevator
A little old white lady moved to the corner and clutched her bag
As if I were a murderous perpetrator

On this short trek of a few short blocks
I experienced bias and microaggression
Black and Brown bodies living I.B.M.
Beholding the disease of covert oppression

Stereotypical thoughts and feelings
That many people are unaware of
Dismantles tolerance and connection
Extinguishing the ability to love

I am absolutely fed up
With so-called color-blind displacement
All of the insidious denial that non-whites overlook
Regarding the irrationality of racists
I hear that I am different
A credit to my race
Articulate and blessed above measure
Covert insults are thrown consistently in my face

I re-encountered the classmate that tried to touch me
She received my burning glare
How ignorant of her to assume it was a compliment
I sharply checked her, "Do not EVER touch my hair!

Karen Seneferu, "Breonna Taylor," 36 x 24 inches, graphite on paper,
The Black Woman Is God: Reclaim, Reconfigure, Re-Remember exhibition,
SOMArts Cultural Center.

In 2020 this usually joyous celebration of Black art, spirtuality and activism was impacted by the pandemic and its endless toll of inequity. Fortunately, the virtual gallery still lives online at https://somarts.org/tbwigvirtual2020/

Karen Seneferu, "George Floyd," 36 x 24 inches, graphite on paper, *The Black Woman Is God: Reclaim, Reconfigure, Re-Remember* exhibition, 2020.

What Happened To Him
Tureeda Mikell

What happened to him?
Did you see him?
I've not heard from him
What happened?
He's some one's father, son
appears he's gone ghost
Have you seen him?

Last saw him in the store
Paying for his son's birthday bike
So proud,
So proud he could do this for his son
No problem between him and the clerk
He pays, part cash and credit card.

So proud this young chocolate
30-something father
Buying a bike for his son's birthday
Receives his receipt
Heads for the exit
Police watching stops him
What wrong, he asks
I have my receipt.

Police will not answer him
What wrong, what did I do?
I have my receipt
My son is waiting for me
I told him I have something
Special for him.
He's waiting for me.

Police smirks
Handcuffs him
Another takes his son's new bike
Another empties his pockets
Takes wallet and receipt.

What did I do, what did I do?
My son is waiting for me
Don't you have a son?
How would your son feel
If you didn't come home?
Man to man
How would your son feel?
My son is waiting for me
To police
His Black life
    Did not matter

Tureeda Mikell is a ChiGong energy therapist and award-winning poet published nationally and internationally. Named word magician and activist for holism, she's published 72 student poetry anthologies through California Poets in the Schools. She was an Ethno-Tec Nu Wa delegation storyteller in Beijing, China, a Zoom poet for Egypt, Wales and the United Kingdom and a storyteller for the San Francisco De Young Museum's 2020 *Soul of a Nation* exhibit. Her book *Synchronicity: The Oracle of Sun Medicine*, released in February 2020 by Nomadic Press, has already sold out twice. @storymedicinewoman

Mark Harris, "In Guns We Trust," mixed media on panel, 30 x 24 inches, 2015.

America's Guns
Juanda J. Stewart

This is America!
Get your guns here.
No problem, no questions,
No authorities to fear.

No other country
Can say the same.
No standing in line.
To sign your name.

No, this is the country
Where you won't have to wait;
Or explain your cause
No tests to take.

No waiting time;
No explanations;
Not asked to prove
Your qualifications.

So step right up;
Don't be shy.
Just state the amount
You'll pay to buy.

No. This is the country
Where one has not to fear
The sale of munitions,
So get your guns here.

Juanda J. Stewart is a retired postal administrator and a San Francisco resident since childhood. She continues to enjoy life as an octogenarian. Her varied interests include music, writing and (before COVID) travel. She was at one time a local club singer and recorded a religious CD entitled *Songs My Mother Sang*. She also compiled a collection of poems entitled *The Rhymes of My Life*. Her work has been published in *Standing Strong! Fillmore & Japantown* and *Endangered Species, Enduring Values*.

Who What When Where & Why
Skooter Fein

Who -
So many names
now
piled one upon
the other

names lost
to history

& names
remembered

Emitt Till - murdered
the year I was
born

Sandra Bland
Walter Scott
Michael Brown
Tamir Rice
Freddie Gray
Breonna Taylor
Sam Duboce
Michelle Cusseaux
Ahmaud Arbery
& so many more names
the sky fills with
tears

What -
The failure of
America

nothing moves
forward
until this
madness stops

A knife on our
collective tongues
the hunting of
black men & women

When -
Today
Yesterday
Tomorrow

Where -
Here
everywhere
you look

San Francisco
Oakland
Houston
St. Louis
New York
Georgia
Cleveland
Memphis
Mobile Alabama
Portland

Everywhere

another hour to live
exit wounds fill the sky
as another man's heartbeat
is caught in the hands of
hate

Why -
is it that we
teach hate

Mark Harris,
"I Too Am America," mixed media on panel, 20 x 16 inches, 2016.

history's great lesson
is not the promise of
destiny & god

(aspirations have their shadows)

the great lesson
is that hate & fear
of the other is
(wounds heal – scars last)
never the winner

Skooter Fein—on this planet since 1955
also a musician and collage artist
works in a hospital
Been writing poetry since 2019

Without Selection
Susan Dambroff
After reading "The City Limits" by A.R. Ammons

When I was pulled over for going through a Stop Sign
I was memorizing a poem about the radiance
    that does not withhold itself
When a police car flashed behind me
    but pours its abundance
    without selection
The officer was white
I am white
    into every nook and cranny
    not overhung or hidden
Each line rolling around in my mouth
    without selection
I am white
He was white
    about the radiance
    that will look into the guiltiest swervings
    of the weaving heart
I said– I was sorry
He said– Be more careful
as he kindly wrote out the ticket

I had been memorizing a poem about the radiance
    that does not withhold itself
When the officer told me if I went to court
he might not show up
and they would throw the ticket out

I didn't write this poem
with all its shades of beauty
    the glow-blue bodies
    and gold-skeined wings of flies
But felt the words
    each is accepted into as much light as it will take
bristling
at the privilege of my skin

The officer was white
I am white
He asked me if I needed help
easing back into traffic
and the line
    without selection
scattered across my windshield
as I cautiously turned the corner

Susan Dambroff is a poet, performer, and teacher. She has published three compilations of poetry, *Memory in Bone, Conversations with Trees*, and *A Chair Keeps the Floor Down.* Her work has appeared in many literary venues including *Civil Liberties United, Ghosts of the Holocaust, and Colossus: Home.* She performs throughout the Bay Area in *Spoken Duets,* a poetic collaboration with Chris Kammler.

Mark Harris, "Devil in Blue Dress,"
mixed media on panel, 20 x 16 inches, 2020.

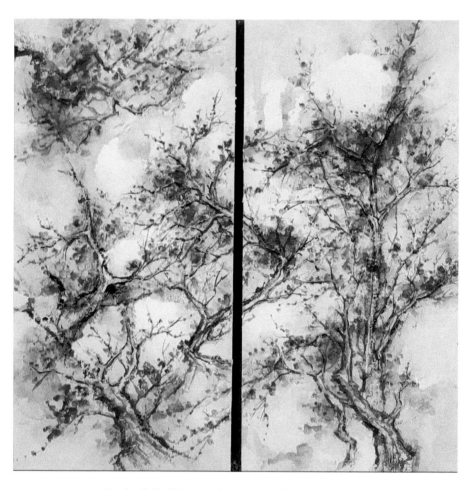

Cindy Shih, "Seven Plum Trees for Jacob Blake,"
sumi ink and watercolor on plaster, 2020.

On August 23, 2020, Jacob Blake, an unarmed 29-year-old Black man was shot
seven times in the back by police officers in Kenosha, Wisconsin. This was in
the wake of a raging pandemic and months of protests following the murders
of George Floyd and Breonna Taylor a few months prior. Outraged, horrified,
and disgusted, I felt the need to honor Jacob Blake—a rare survivor, with living,
growing, and blooming symbols of resilience and hope. Plum trees survive
through the bitterness and cold of winter, which is my hope for Jacob Blake
and all the young Black men facing the daily threat of racism, injustice, and
police brutality. See p. 171 for Cindy Shih's bio.

Antiracism is a State of Mental Health - E.K. Keith

We can't see ourselves
any more
than we can see
each other

It's like sometimes
on a rough day
an ugly person
looks back at me
from the mirror
on the bathroom wall
and I think   damn
where did that pretty woman go

Is she hiding
back there
somewhere
in mirrorland

I have my suspicions
about the ability
of science
to describe
how a mirror really   works

What if
it's not the mirror
but the eye

And how we see
collectively

Is racism
a societal dysmorphia
that results
in self hatred

and self harm

What would it be like

to be the light
particle
wave
something not quite yet described

to be
the light

in the mirror
reflected
deflected
redirected

Does a light particle see
its own intensity
and flinch

And if I
can barely see myself

And you
can barely see yourself

What does that mean
when we look at each other

Use the mirror
Get the hate out of the eyes

We   change how
we change   who
we see

E.K. Keith is a Latinx poet in San Francisco, and *Ordinary Villains* (Nomadic Press, 2018) is her first book. Type her name in any internet search bar to enjoy her poetry published online, as well as videos of her performances.

There are Only Birds
Joyce Young

The woman isn't bird watching,
She's hulking.
The woman isn't 50 feet away.
She's 6 feet away.
The woman isn't 6 feet away.
She's 1 foot away.

The woman isn't bird watching.
She's walking towards him.
The woman isn't walking towards him.
She is running towards him.

The woman is ignoring his pleas
to stay back.

She is walking.
She is shaking a leash in his face.
She is setting her dog free
to chase him.

He does not say: "Please don't come close to me"
Three times.

He does not say: "I'm going to tell
them, there's a white
woman threatening my life."

She does not say: "Please
tell them whatever you like."

He does not tell the dispatcher,
"A white woman is recording me
And threatening me [with her dog]."

The collar she would like to see
around the man's neck,
is the collar the dog is trying to twist out of,
the collar the dog is hanging by.

But there are no dogs in the park.
There are no bird watchers in the park.
There is no phone in anyone's hands.
There is no video to see.

There are no African Americans in the park.
There are no white women in the park.
There are only birds.

Joyce Young's poetry collection *How it Happens*, published by Nomadic Press, was nominated for a California Book Award. Her poems have received Pushcart Prize nominations and have appeared most recently in *Poem of the Day* at The San Francisco Public Library and *The Smith Alumnae Quarterly*. Joyce has been leading writing classes and workshops for students of all ages for over 20 years.

Lorraine Bonner, "Blinded by White."

Nonadventure II
E.K. Keith

When I peek out
from underneath
these anxieties
and look   up
the red-tailed hawk's
casual loops
turn into a serious dive
returning to big figure 8s
over my head
and even higher
than the hawk
there's a meeting
of black birds
ten of them
way
      way
         way
            up
              high

Paula de Joie, "I Hear Music," mixed media.

What 2020 Taught Me About "Radical"
Malcolm Williams

In 2019 I was flailing
casually grappling
leaves and crunching
detritus. Raking pieces
on a cement driveway,
the tines dicing foliage
and screeching
a dissonance of
failed groundskeeping.
Screeching
a disconnect between
waiting for rain
and neglecting the hose.
This oscillation like
pausing to pick petals,
I love me, I love me not.

During the onslaught of
calendrical horrors called 2020,
state sanctioned murders
and state sponsored ignorance
were poured into an American
cycle of: two steps forward
one step backward and
another step sideways
to make room for
all the praise heaped on

that one step forward.
I progress, I regress.
And in the reverberating
silence of communal isolation
I read a gem fertilizing social media
Angela Davis's words,
"Radical simply means
'grasping things at the root.'"

With that simplicity
I ingest, I digress.
I grip at that which
picks up the nutrients.
The causes that come
before growth or decay,
or diversion or affect.
With that simplicity
my downcast gaze
finds new agency.
Though the work of tending
may take a lifetime,
aiming deeper
is no harder than
tugging on petals,
and that energy is
better spent
radically grasping.

Rafael Jesús González
Decirlo Claro

Dicen los bobos
que venimos de mendigos
estómagos vacíos, vacías las manos
para quitarles lo que ya
sus propios canallas y bribones
les robaron.
Sí, venimos con hambre
huyendo la violencia
a donde la riqueza
del impero se concentra
pero con las manos llenas
de nuestras artesanías y labores,
corazones llenos de bailes y canciones,
con nuestra cocina rica en sabores.
Le traemos alma a un país sin alma;
traemos el arco iris
y prefieren el gris de sus temores.
Se empeñan en construir muros
si lo que se necesita es puentes.

To Say It Clearly

The fools say
that we come as beggars
stomachs empty, empty hands
to take what already
their own scoundrels & knaves
have stolen from them.
Yes, we come hungry
fleeing violence
to where the riches
of the empire are concentrated
but with hands full
of our crafts & labors,
hearts full of dances & of songs,
with our cuisine rich in flavors.
We bring soul to a soulless country;
we bring the rainbow
& they prefer the grayness of their fear.
They insist on building walls when there is need of bridges.

VII
walls

Romina Saha, "Cut," mixed media (oil and modeling paste)
on canvas, 16 x 20 inches.

Romina Saha, "Boxed," oil on canvas, 16 x 20 inches.

Romina Saha
Artist Statement

It's the wall, that wall, that put things into focus for me, a Filipino American, an Asian American. I didn't go through the southwest border to get into this country. I didn't have to climb a concrete wall to get to this side. But that wall is a metaphor for the immigrant experience.

Whether immigrants came from Asia or another continent, whether they came here legally or illegally, whether they came here on foot, by boat, or by plane, is irrelevant. The wall is real and it's not just physical. The wall consists of culture, language, speech accents, traditions, food, prejudices, religion, education, skin color—things immigrants bring with them that sometimes become labels that separate them from others, another hurdle to overcome. Things that do not disappear just because one obtains a green card or citizenship. Add to that the physical distance that separates immigrants from their family and friends and everything familiar that they have left behind. And assuming they transcend all of these, they know it is still not enough. The struggle includes being boxed into stereotypes, being trapped in assumptions and prejudices, being labeled "other." There is always a wall they must break down.

Some of us got here through the sacrifices of our forefathers, through their labor, through their service. Some of us got here through academic or employment opportunities. Some of us were escaping poverty, violence, war, economic inequity, political persecution—whatever it is we thought this country would make right for us.

Some of us are first generation, others are descendants and beneficiaries of the first generation. No matter how we came here, wherever we are in our lineage of immigration, we share similar journeys. We share similar obstacles and face similar prejudices, just for being "other." Our cultural and historic heritage filters down to us and our descendants, permeating our consciousness, influencing our tastes, our lifestyles, our choices. Our traditions may not have been experienced firsthand. Our traditions may have been passed down to us by our parents and grandparents and carried by our children and children's children. But our traditions, our native culture, are preserved through oral history, through visual art, through literature, through social or political relationships, through collective memory.

I am here as the granddaughter of an American serviceman of Swedish heritage who married a Filipina while stationed in the Philippines. Their child, my mother, obtained her U.S. citizenship late in life and never got to live in her father's homeland. My siblings and I are here because of her lineage. I intend to keep my mother's and grandparents' legacy alive through the memories I have of them and of the emotions they evoke. I embody those memories and emotions in my poetry and paintings.

Romina Saha worked as a journalist in Manila before she came to California in 1990 to complete a Knight Fellowship at Stanford University. As a student at the University of the Philippines, she was literary and managing editor of the student newspaper *Philippine Collegian*, where she wrote poetry prolifically. Today, she is a self-taught visual artist who keeps her poetry pen sharp.

America Went And Had This Pinche Pandemico
And All I Got Was This Lousy T-Shirt
Josiah Luis Alderete

America
¿After all this pinche pandemico desmadre is over with
will you still be known all over el mundo
for your wondrous acts of mega-consumerism,
your endless fields of capitalism that stretch off into the monotheist horizon?

¿Will we still be able to see
the intricacies of your Southern California shopping mall forests
and Las Vegas pyramids from outer space?

America
¿Not having looked
into a department store dressing room mirror this whole time
will you still be able to fit into your own esqueleto?
¿Will you be thin as a popote
or bloated from eating all the stale pan dulce that was hidden in the bomb
shelter?
Hair disheveled, Catholicism stained,
selfie prayers piled up in the corner,
shaky from not having had physical contact with cash registers
or having the sensation of being lifted up to heaven by indoor mall
escalators…

America
During all of this
you continued to beat your children,
you continued to lock up our children,
you continued to use cobwebs to stop the bleeding,
you continued to change the lightbulbs on the border,
and you created an altar in the corner of the casa
where you buried your still living elders and the rest of the money,
—we know this por que you posted the video on el Instagram.

America
You've left your pantaloons in the Zoom mundo
and are walking down Market Street with your nalgas hanging out
y your maxed out credit card dangling in the spot
where your cock used to be.

America
¿How much of all of this will you continue to do without?
¿How much can you not wait to get back to?

America
Stale loaves of colonized bread are still left on the shelves
at the looted bodegas,
immigrant fish and Chupacabras left over from the '90s
have managed to sneak back here during all of this.
¿America will you deport them?

America
Your concrete has a 5 o'clock shadow,
the grandchildren of your gentrification
have an interesting look on their faces right now.

America
You watched the ouroboros sitcoms
and let Netflix narrate this inmigrante's dream,
while you said "AMEN" to the newscasts
and drank and injected the bleach,
you wanted a new kind of vision
that involves not being able to see a damn thing
and a new kind of family that includes only you.

America
You went and had an insurrection
y todo mundo stayed inside,
you did not shoot your neighbor like you promised you would,
the folktales stayed forgotten in glass jars on the shelves
next to the fancy mustard and Tapatillo
while everything else was bandaged whether it was wounded or not.

America
You look like a failed revolution with a big parking lot
—but then again
you have always looked like a failed revolution with a big parking lot.

America
The prophecies never pronounced it like this—
plagues, pesadillas y ICE agents have come and gone by the window
while you reminisced with Amazon Prime about the good old days,

you finished your last drink
and went to dig up the bones in the backyard
so that you could rebury them again
and again and again…

America
If you look at this from el otro llado,
this is a story that has already happened.

Josiah Luis Alderete is a full blooded Pocho Spanglish speaking poet from La Area Bahia who learned to write poetry in the kitchen of his Mama's Mexican restaurant. He first began performing his poetry in San Francisco's Mission District at the infamous Cafe Babar's Thursday night readings and was one of the founding members of San Francisco's outspoken word troupe, The Molotov Mouths. He is also a radio insurgente whose stories have appeared on KALW's *Crosscurrents* and whose show, *The Spanglish Power Hour,* aired on KPFA. He curates and hosts the monthly Latinx reading series *Speaking Axolotl* at Nomadic Press in Oakland. Josiah Luis Alderete's first book of poems, *Baby Axolotls y Old Pochos*, is forthcoming from Black Freighter Press.

Joan Osato, "Tony Torres, Artist," from portrait series photographed at the *Resistance and Remembrance Dia de los Muertos 2017* exhibition, SOMArts Cultural Center.

Letter to Trump
Juan Gomez

May 16, 2017

To Donald Trump,

Donald Trump, when you started your campaign, you said "When Mexico sends its people, they are not sending their best..., they are sending people that have lots of problems, and they are bringing those problems with them. They are bringing drugs, they are bringing crimes, they are rapists, and some I assume are good people." As a Mexican I did not bring drugs and I am not a rapist. As a Mexican, I question the meaning of your definition of the best people.

When I finished high school, I joined the army. A year later the president of that time, Felipe Calderon, declared war on the cartels. My team was one of them that was sent to act. It was the time when I started to see what drugs can cause and what people can do because of drugs. Children, elderly, women, and innocent people suffer their consequences. So how can you call me a drug dealer when I was one of them who fought to stop drugs? I risked my life, and I almost got killed because of drugs. One of the soldiers got killed in front of me. So how in the world can you call me a drug dealer when I was the one who risked his life to save one of your citizens? When is the last time you risk your life to save someone? As the father of the Muslim American soldier said, "You have sacrificed nothing and no one." And I ask you a question, when is the last time you put your life at risk? Do I want to understand why do you call Mexican immigrants the worst of the worst? When your government sent guns to Mexico, I did not say neither the Mexican government said that the Americans are murderers because I truly believe that most of the people in this country are good people. They don't want to see bad thing happen. So why do you label Mexican immigrant as bad people? We are not all rapists as you said. I am a son of a lovely mother and a brother of beautiful sisters. I believe that women should live their life without struggle and without pain and fear.

Donald Trump, we are all immigrants, and your parents were immigrants as well. Your parents were dreamers. They were dreamers like George Washington, Abraham Lincoln. They were dreamers like other people around the world like Gandhi, Mandela, and the young lady Malala. They were dreamers like people who pick vegetables and clean your casinos because they want a better life for their children. The children of those people have dreamed as well. Maybe one day those children can be the doctors that can treat your great-grandchildren. So then, why such hate to immigrants? Your parents must believe that hard work was the key to success and you believe as well because you mention in almost every book you have written. I am an immigrant, and I am a dreamer like you. Don't you think you should honor your parent's dream? I honor the dream of my parents of wanting a good life for their children, and I have been working very hard since I understood my parents' dream. Have you ever understood your parents' dream? Maybe your response is yes because you have built a real estate empire. But remember history has taught us that empires can fall while love can survive. Do you think is much better to love than to build empires? I encourage you to think about love. But maybe you don't want to listen to me because I am not the best, I am not a celebrity, I am not smart, neither I am a white man. Who is the best and the smart for you? Is it people who hate or people who love and risk their life to do great things? We all deserve love because love is hope. I guarantee love is hope.

Since you are a Christian, you must know a lot about love because Christianity is based on practicing the good and kindness like every religion around the world. I believe most immigrants are your brothers in religion. So, why such a hate for them? And by the way, in Exodus 22:21, Moses gives God's law: "You shall not wrong or oppress a foreigner; for you were foreigners in the land of Egypt." This verse encourages every Christian to accept immigrants regardless of who they are. So then, why do you say you are a Christian when you ban Muslims, and you are eager to build a wall because you claim that all illegal immigrants are bad hombres. Are you such a hypocrite or a liar? In the Bible also says that those who don't practice kindness and don't practice the good, they will go to eternal hell. Donald Trump, I don't want you to go to hell or suffer the pain of others because I don't believe in revenge. I want you to practice love; I want you to open your heart and accept people no matter who they are. I want you to put in your shoes of those who struggle. I want you to realize that we need each other. Let's don't label all people the same because their actions can prove that we can be wrong.

Donald Trump because I don't have the absolute truth and I am not perfect, I want to finish quoting Martin Luther King letter "If I have said anything in this letter that is an understatement of the truth and is indicative of an unreasonable impatience, I beg you to forgive me…. I beg God to forgive me." Let's practice love because love is hope.

—Juan Gomez

Unwanted Visitors[1] - Maribi Mendoza

A knock on the door
    sends my heart through the floor
I prefer to hear the doorbell ring,
    Ding—ing, Ding—ing, Ding—ing, Ding—ing
Friends ring
      Foes knock.

On this day—I was eight.
    The unwanted knock on the door
sent a signal up my spine, all the way to my brain—
                "Run"—"you're prey"
I dashed fast—hid—turned off all the lights.
      But the loud knocking continued,
      harder, not restricted to the door,
Knocks flew to my kitchen window—
      beating—matching the flow
          of my young anxious heart.
"POLICE"—they screamed—almost with delight.
    "OPEN UP"—they banged.
Even at eight, I knew they were foes—
      Yet, I still opened the door
         and in they came.
I can't remember the faces—only the slick black
      barrels of death slung upon their waists.

"Your Brother home?"
      "No"
    No one was—I received these visitors alone.
One sat me down in the living space, the other roamed free
—found Brother's room—
      took the drawers from the wall—
all of Brother's clothes
      ripped and thrown—
          playeras con dibujos de calaveras[2] hit the floor.
These visitors are here to scavenger—
      One through Brother's things
the other wants to know what's in my brain—

Only eight, yet I faced interrogation.
Heat flashes—sweat gathers

"Do you know any of your Brother's friends?"
"Do they regularly come over?"
"Do you know of your Brother's whereabouts?"
 Mother never let strangers in
"Do you know your Brother's alias?"
 Mother wasn't here to save me
I was alone and what could I know? I'm eight years old?
So, I offered no hospitality
 No tea
 offered no answers
Who are they—
 No, I won't cooperate.
 I'm underage—
 what they seek won't be found within my brain.
"I don't know"—that's all I have to offer.
 One Scavenger finally comes to join—finished tearing
 Brother's room into parts.
The visitors now plan to leave
 having found nothing to take back to their "chief."
   I let them go—unwanted visitors walk right up out that door.

Finally, I felt at ease
 sensed peace,
 though Brother's room remained a battlefield.
Mother comes home—
 Ding—ing, Ding—ing, Ding—ing, Ding—ing

Friends ring
 Foes knock
I let Mother know
 an unwarranted—
  unwanted visit was paid.

1. In reponse to an Allison Hedge Coke prompt posted to Facebook, Sept. 2, 2020. "**Visitor -** When a guest arrives, how do we greet them?..."
2. Spanish translation: T-shirts with drawings of skulls.

Maribi Mendoza is 21 years old. She was born in Cotija De La Paz, the ancestral land of the P'urhépecha people. She immigrated North across a border with her family at 2 and became a naturalized citizen of the U.S. at 12. Currently, she resides on the land of the Southern Pomo and Graton people in what is now known as California.

untitled
Carole Chinn-Morales

Our lives are haunted by the lost faces of children
Indelibly etched in our brains, the look of fear, helplessness, abandonment
as they endure one more day without their families
Their mothers and fathers ripped away by the evil man in charge
La Migra, the foe long feared, has come to exact his most horrendous
punishment
To kidnap children, separate them from their loved ones
Secretly in the middle of the night, bus them to detention centers,
In obscure places all over the country

Hidden from the eyes of the public by tall fences, yards away from the
entrances
Detention centers, supervised like prisons, the inmates lost in the
terror and confusion of the moment
The incarcerated babies, young children, teens, not even able to communicate
in a common language
Not able to ask for water, a towel to wipe up an accident on the floor,
report sickness, change a stinking diaper, ask for another blanket
Children put in cages on top of other wailing children
Despicable, immoral, inhumane
Not who we are
Yet we have let it happen again, internment before our eyes, in our name
As if painful memories were not enough
The testimonies of what happened at Manzanar, Topaz, Tule Lake not enough
The government agile in its mistreatment, disregarding dignity, justice,
human rights Again, propping up atrocities with elaborate justifications,
appealing to fear, racism
In truth, policies meant to punish refugees, fleeing perpetual intimidation,
murder, kidnapping, extortion in their own countries, seeking safety
The once welcoming nation has let walls be built at its border. Why?
The people cry out but it is not enough.

In the land of the free, home of the brave…
Whose land?
Who is free?
Whose home?
Who are the brave?

"Grandma, what did you do when they put babies in cages?"
"Well, we wrote letters, called people in government, but nothing happened.
We walked in front of the ICE building, chanting, carrying signs, but nothing
happened. We sat in courtrooms, to show our solidarity and support, but
nothing happened.
We joined groups to help migrants living at the border, but nothing happened.
There never was a plan to bring children and families together, the bitter
truth."

"And Grandpa, what did you do for those crying babies?
Please tell me, I want to know..."

Carole Chinn-Morales does not consider herself a poet or an activist, but
she is both. She grew up in San Francisco's Chinatown, where her physician
parents both worked long hours at the Chinese Hospital. She has long been
active at Cameron House and the Presbyterian Church in Chinatown. Prior
to the pandemic, she trained for volunteer first response support for families
impacted by ICE.

The Chinese Virus
Carole Chinn-Morales

The insidious term "Chinese virus"
Our president intentionally uses in every speech
Infects receptive minds, stoking fear, long held biases,
Causing a pandemic of rage, blame, hostility inflicted upon
All Asian looking faces.
The welcome mat of our country has been contaminated,
Blighted by abuse and disdain, false narratives, and self-serving rhetoric.

Evoking painful epithets of the past
Chinese are dirty, disease-ridden "others," foreigners
Excluded from the country legally in 1882
Caricaturized with long braid, buck teeth, squinty eyes
Characterized with dehumanizing, dismissive language by the privileged
The humiliation rots our psyches
The disdain infects our hearts

The disease of cruelty and mistrust continues
How can we overcome the contagion
Let fevered conflicts subside
How can we recover together, rise together
Re-create ourselves, our families, our stories
Strive for a common future
Become whole
How?

Dear Wuhan
Shayna Gee

When I heard the news / you were drowning / missed the train home / working / Lunar New Year / your one day off / they spat at your feet / called you bat / eater / dog / eater / squirming / diseased / bitch / do they know your body is a river? / I've swallowed your streams in the south / sea / where my ancestors / built dams

o, Wuhan
you were pouring into *us* / in waves / we didn't deserve your seeds / in return / we sent you our mountains of salt / pork / piss / plastic / nitrate / chlorine / sewage / sludge / you / your blood / tingent / on my tongue / when you're ready / let's talk about the butchering / we did to you / but tell me later / catch your train / and we'll meet at the estuary

Threes
Diann Leo-Omine

Microaggression

1. That it's insisted to you that rice must be made in a rice cooker because they heard from some authoritative but obscure source that all Asian people make rice in rice cookers.

2. That you get asked if you speak Mandarin and then proceeding to mention they have a quote-unquote crazy Vietnamese sister in law.

3. That you can't even socially-distant shop in a grocery store without an employee approaching you and your spouse to insinuate that English isn't your first language. No, I was born here, you insist, and English is my first language. You can't discern which is worse: the microaggression itself; or how the employee then proceeded to spout fragments from different Asian languages; or the fact that said employee both broke your six-foot boundary and removed his mask.

Fear

1. That even if Bay Area housing prices fall, you probably won't return to and afford living where you grew up. That the remainder of your friends will be priced out and forced to leave.

2. That the Trump banners on your neighbors' lawns disappeared promptly on November 4th, like Halloween was suddenly over and the jack-o-lanterns chucked in the trash. Don't worry, it's just more "purple" where you live, you're told. As if they left those royal blue and violet crayons outside in the hot valley summer, and then mashed them together with a hammer. That explanation doesn't assuage the reality that the Proud Boys unabashedly lurk some 40 minutes away.

3. That your grandmothers will both live the remainder of their lives with the anxiety of anti-Asian hate crimes, violence undoubtedly combusted by the President's Kung Flu and Chinese Virus vitriol. That regardless of how much (primarily East) Asians have thrived under the glass ceiling as the model minority, they are still the perpetual foreigners. That the model minority trope is intertwined with anti-Blackness.

Acceptance

1. That you can appreciate living somewhere outside of the Bay Area. That had you been living in San Francisco during the shelter-in-place, you would have felt boxed into a claustrophobic 7x7 square mile cage. That the grieving process of leaving your hometown is more fluid than fixed, more than well-meaning people telling you just to get over it. It's a grieving process of untangling your family's history, of the broader Chinese diaspora. It's a grieving process of peeling, preserving, and protecting the city's creative soul from the talons of gentrification.

2. That regardless of who is president, work is to be done.

3. That somehow, you can try to understand "the other side" but still brim that big city self-righteousness. What really is the other side? Is it a barbed wire fence? Is it an ivy-crusted wall? Is it a miles-deep moat with an impeccable fortress? Breaking down the cell water, the water boundaries, the capillaries, the veins of the matter. Maybe under those layers, we and they are still human. Maybe we and they are all human with demons and vices.

Diann Leo-Omine is rooted in San Francisco (Ramaytush Ohlone land). She now resides in the North Central Valley (Nisenan land), between the expanse of ocean but beneath ascent of mountains.
sweetleoomine.com / IG: @sweet_leo_o_mine

De-Collaging My History - An Huynh

Lang Co,
1963,
The life of my grandpa,
Imprisoned in the unrest of the war.

South Central Los Angeles,
1991,
The life of Latasha Harlins,
Remembered in the unrest of the riots.

South Central Vietnam,
1994,
The life of mine,
Birthed into the rest of my mother's arms.

Oakland,
1998,
The life of our family,
Immigrated in order to forget.

But like matter cannot be created or destroyed,
History cannot be forgotten or abandoned,
For our lives are the matter
That matter.

Our African-Americans' ancestors enslaved on plantations,
Japanese-Americans locked in internment camps,
Chinese-Americans driven out by exclusion acts,
Mexican-Americans deported thru ethnic cleansing,
Native-Americans forgotten thru genocide,
Vietnamese-Americans,
Hmong-Americans,
Laotian-Americans,
Thai-Americans,
Cambodian-Americans,
Silenced by the intergenerational trauma of war.
They say to make the dash between the time we are born and when we die
A memorable one.
There is a dash between our origins and American,
How much of ourselves can we keep in remembrance?

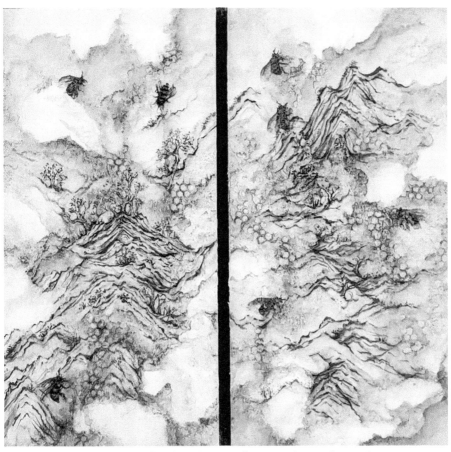

Cindy Shih, "Cultural Decay," sumi ink, acrylic, and
watercolor on plaster, 2020.

In my work, bees often symbolize immigrants as they migrate to new landscapes, work to create value, only to be unceremoniously pushed to the margins and discarded. As immigrants work to provide and cultivate this country, their cultures often fade, decay, or are destroyed.

Cindy Shih was born in Taiwan and immigrated to Los Angeles with her family at the age of three. She moved to the Bay Area in 2005, and currently resides and works in San Francisco. Drawing heavily from her early training in Chinese calligraphy, she uses techniques from brush painting, Italian fresco, and landscapes to touch upon issues of gender, race, and power.

from *Book of the Other*
Truong Tran

*when they say why can't he just go somewhere else. they want to believe that
such a question is contained within the context of an academic inquiry. there are
other jobs. that the job market is a right of passage. when they say why can't he
just go somewhere else. they are saying. leave. they believe what's not given is not
yours to claim. they believe that they alone have the right to claim. they believe
that you are a guest, a visitor. the lecturer. the labor. an unwanted presence of
whom they ask why can't you just go somewhere else. they say go back to where
you came from. they say you are not. you are not from here.*

*they believe in the saying welcome home. until you are no longer welcomed
in your own home. they put that saying on a mat. at the threshold of a place.
their way of reminding you. to wipe the shit from the soles of your shoes before
entering. they believe that home is a place with room. filled with books. and a
roof. with a garden where they can go up on. for a drink on a hot day. water the
plants. read a book. and pour buckets of water on the unhoused beneath. they
believe that no one would believe. that they could do such a thing. that is until
they are seen. on camera doing that very thing. their defense even then. that
it was just water. that you could go somewhere else. when someone names the
old white man pouring water from his roof. they say why would you do that to
a harmless old white guy. this is cruel. this is not poetry. this has nothing to do
with this book. this they believe. that your home is a tent. or a shell you carry. on
your back. you take it with you. as you leave the scene.*

*you write this book. and you think. this is about a particular thing. this is about
the academy. about your struggles. inside a place. acute and quarantined. inside
a world. and then the world happens. and you hear. that your students are
being arrested. for being at a protest. for being black. for being brown. for being
present. for choosing to be. they choose to be decent caring human beings. and
it is then that you think. you are writing a book. and this book is more. than
what you thought. it to be. what is inside. is outside. you hear a statement on tv.
read it in the headlines. it is all over the internet. it is then. that you remember.
you've been carrying this. all along. tucked deep within. the folds of your skin.
the memory of muscles. the hollow of your body. go back. to where. you came*

Bio for p. 170: An Huynh is a Vietnamese writer from Oakland, CA. Spiritually
rooted in his birthplace of Da Nang, Vietnam, his writings touch on the topics
of intergenerational trauma, healing, and community power. Writing to heal
his own past and passed-down trauma, his pieces are an offering of love to be
able to find power and compassion within ourselves.

from. and you write this book. and you ask this question. inside the book. where are you from. you are asking this. of yourself. and then this happens. you are answering the question. you are asking. of yourself. you are telling. the reader. of this book. there is no room. for interpretations. and then you say. you state. you are telling yourself. you are from. here.

Truong Tran is the author of numerous volumes of poetry. He is a self taught visual artist whose work has been exhibited in venues including the California Historical Society, California Institute of Integral Studies, SOMArts Gallery, Telegraph Hill Gallery, Avenue 12 Gallery and The Peninsula Museum of Art. Of his art making process, Truong writes: My art practices, be they writing, sculpting or making dinner for a group of friends, are just my ways of thinking though the consciousness of these times.

Fred Korematsu Day, Jan 30
Steve Fujimura

it's JA day
every day, no, well
for those
with this skin
these names
and this history

and if yours
aren't with you
every day, then
what is
with you

Steve Fujimura is a poet based in Berkeley, California. His writing engages with memory, history, loss, and family. His work can be found in *New American Writing, Milvia Street Art & Literary Journal, Written Here: The Community of Writers Poetry Review*, and other publications. He earned an MA in creative writing at San Francisco State University.

Questions at the bus stop
Jonathan Hirabayashi

I look into your weary eyes.
Are you thinking back to when
you were a prospective bride?
Full of gumption, full of hope
standing and waiting to cross,
an ocean wide.
Promises of a life of luxury and leisure.
I look at your face, your hands,
I know you had neither.
Once again there you stand,
amid possessions that still remain,
stripped of your livelihood and your land.
Is it possible to start over again?
Gomenasai.
Do ... do ... do you know
riding on bus No. 2,
my grandparents,
Towa and Buichi or
Yoshie and Hisaichi

This photo documenting the World War II incarceration of Japanese Americans was taken by Dorothea Lange in the farming community of Irvington, California, now a district in present-day Fremont. This is the bus stop where seven buses transported Americans and immigrants of Japanese descent to Tanforan. The names of families assigned to board each bus are posted on the side of the building. Both sets of my grandparents were assigned to bus no. 2, but the identity of the woman is unknown to the author.

Jonathan Hirabayashi. I was born in 1946 in American Fork, Utah. Retired, after a career in exhibition graphics, I began to notate some family history. I'm currently participating in a writing class hosted by Grace Morizawa at J-Sei. I reside in Oakland, CA with my wife, Susan Kai.

Body Language
Ann Muto

When hunger gnawed at my stomach and
my wails echoed through the tar paper barracks,
my grandfather saved me from my mother's angst.

He would rise heavily from his bed,
fumble in the dark for his sweater,
slip his swollen feet into soft slippers.
He would shuffle over to the bassinet,
gather the blankets around me,
place my head on his shoulder
and quietly leave.

Outside, darkness was slowly melting.
Fine sand swirled lightly around his feet
as the warmth of his hands,
the safety of him wrapped around me.
As he walked, I saw the rising light flash
brighter and brighter between the buildings.

As he neared the barbed wire fence,
he slowed, then stopped.
Beyond the boundary,
his eyes sought the open prairie,
the mountains in the distance.
I felt him breathe deeply,
again and again.

During WWII, Japanese Americans were incarcerated in concentration camps.
My family was assigned to the War Relocation Camp in Poston, Arizona.

Ann Muto, past Cupertino Poet Laureate, investigates her personal history and pursues her love of nature through poetry. Her book *Open Passage* was published by the Japanese American Museum of San Jose. Her poems have appeared in *Japanese American Internment During World War II*, *Dancing on the Brink of the World*, *Point Lobos Magazine*, *Inspiring Generations: 150 Years, 150 Stories in Yosemite*, and *Civil Liberties United*.

Mark Osaki

Chinese Camp

A rich vein of hating,
a pen to keep them working in
until they dropped,
a guidebook to lead me
through then out to here
where the prospect is only broader
the vein not yet exhausted,
history the pen
big enough to enclose all of us—
yellow by yellow
me by them.

The Fish Heads

Their faces are flat profiles:
eyes frozen, glaring dumbly,
mouths gaping, stacked in rows
on powdered ice below the sign,
Huen's Grocery.

Why are they looking at us
that way, she asks. I smile,
tightly pulling her arm.
What do I know of any race
that should save it in her mind?
We pass quickly as though
walking away moves us beyond it.
Still pretending distance makes
anything remote, I look back
and see their turned eyes following,
lips pulled down as if by hooks.

My work has appeared in various journals and anthologies, including: *The Georgia Review, Carrying the Darkness—The Poetry of the Vietnam War, South Carolina Review, Breaking Silence—An Anthology of Contemporary Asian American Poets,* and *Báo Giấy.* I have received awards from the Academy of American Poets, University of California at Berkeley, San Francisco Arts Commission, Seattle Arts Council, and the National Endowment for the Arts.

Walking in Translation
Tony Robles

Caminando—*walking* in Spanish. That's what I did on this stretch of road in Western North Carolina. I carry a small bag; inside is a face mask and small bottle of hand sanitizer along with a portable speaker for my music. With the pandemic upon us—with many holed up indoors, absorbing the news on the uptick of positive Covid-19 cases, one must get outdoors, to engage with the environment—to breathe. I walk by a few consignment stores—a specialty store offering varieties of tea, a Laundromat frequented by many in the Latino community, and clusters of mobile homes. I pass by streets with names such as Rutledge and Brooklyn. Brooklyn, a borough of a city and I too am a city dweller—born and bred—but now dwelling in the green landscape of a small town, and the greenness is dwelling in me after residing in the area just under a year. Other things dwell in me—voices: Spanish, Chinese, Tagalog; and African-American voices—their tones, highs and lows—their poetry and songs move inside me. These things are part of my inheritance—like my skin.

I am a fan of oldies—the sounds, the words blend in the greenness all around me. The branches on trees seem to move with the sounds of those old songs—songs I grew up with in the city, songs that I cannot forget, songs that have followed me to a small town. I listen to a song, "Natural High," as I pass through the landscape—stunning views of Japanese maples and other foliage—and the lyrics

Take me in your arms
Thrill me with all of your charms
And I'll take to the sky on a natural high
Loving you more 'til the day I die

Then it's the music of War—"All Day Music" then "Slippin' into Darkness." And I slip into greenness; ahead are streets, passing cars; beyond me, the mountains that appear to cradle all in their presence. It is a peaceful walk. But I am keenly aware of my skin. I know that a walk can turn into tragedy. A walk, a run—such as in the case of Ahmaud Arbery, a young black man jogging in his neighborhood in Georgia—can end your life. People of color understand this: that we can be shot for the act of walking, jogging; that another's perception of us can become our reality—is our reality. The perception formed by what Toni Morrision referred to as the white gaze—in the case of Arbery, a gaze accompanied by a rifle, a handgun and a camera that caught it all—can turn a seemingly inconsequential moment into tragedy. We walk into the virus of racism, of white supremacy, and with it we know that our reality can change—a walk, a jog, requesting that a dog walker leash her dog—can turn into an unleashing that can result in our last breath.

I continue walking. It is quiet, peaceful. I pass houses, windows with curtains. Curtains have eyes. I have eyes too, always aware. I approach the end of the road towards the main highway. It is moist. I come upon a puddle at the edge of the road. From behind, I hear the sound of an engine, wheels approaching. I wait for the car to pass so I can circumvent the puddle. I look to my left. It is a truck. A voice calls out.

"Where you go?"

It is a brown man, brown like me. His face is moist with sweat.

"Walking," I answer. "Exercise."

He looks at me. There is a kinship in his eyes, his skin. I've never seen him before but he sees a familiarity in me and me in him.

"Where you from?"

"Filipino," I answer.

Where am I from? I have been asked this many times. The question often insinuates that I somehow do not belong. I know where I am from: a city in California. I know what he means when he asks, what he really means.

"Come te llamas?" I ask, in the little Spanish I know.

"Saul," he says

"Yo soy Tony," I say.

He nods at me, begins to pull away on the road.

"Gracias, hermano," I say. He pulls away, waves.

I walk towards the intersection. I think about the connection with Saul. Perhaps he saw something in me, on a road, alone, heading towards something. I walk and come upon a butterfly hovering near a bush. It is yellow, a bright burning yellow with black spots and streaks. It floats free. I walk and think of those who have died for the act of walking, jogging, breathing into someone's distorted perception of what it means to be human. Gracias, Saul. I walk on in hope's direction.

Tony Robles was born in San Francisco and is the nephew of Manilatown and I-Hotel Poet Al Robles. He is the author of *Cool Don't Live Here No More—A Letter to San Francisco* and *Fingerprints of a Hunger Strike.* He was short-listed for Poet Laureate of San Francisco in 2018 and was named Carl Sandburg Writer in Residence at the Carl Sandburg Historic Home in Flat Rock, North Carolina in 2020. He is currently an MFA candidate in creative writing at Vermont College of Fine Arts where he is working on his first novel.

Growing Up in San Francisco
Gerard Clark

I came to San Francisco with my family when I was 12, now more than half a century ago. San Francisco looked nothing like it does now. My family moved here from Albany, New York. I immediately went through a very positive culture shock. Albany was monochromatic, reminding me of the movie "Pleasantville." Culture and the arts were not a part of our life there, but with the cross-country move, that was about to change.

The most dazzling thing to me about San Francisco was its diversity. We lived in the Mission District, which was said to have been predominantly Irish at one time, but then—and now as well—was populated by the Latin community. The music, cuisine and art made it a place of wonder for me. The people were warm and kind and patient with a white kid who was ignorant of their culture but very eager to learn all he could. I soon found that there were multiple cultures just waiting for me to discover. I was always a bit shy and a bit agoraphobic, so I discovered San Francisco by foot and it was a delightful way to learn "The City," as everyone called it back then; I don't hear that designation much any more, but times change.

I walked out to Ocean Beach from our apartment in the Mission, on 16th and Albion. I discovered the Russian Jewish community in the Richmond District. There were not as many Asians making their homes there then but the faces of most of the districts have changed radically, as all cities and neighborhoods do over the course of time. I love this city like no other. I cannot stay away from it for long. When I was young she was a gorgeous, young and wild town, in the midst of the Hippie era. The Haight was a communal Wild West show with drugs, sex and Rock 'n' Roll, a wild ride for a young man coming of age. I was really still a child, but it opened my mind to a universe of possibilities.

I remember my first experience of stumbling through Chinatown on a Sunday morning and picking up a huge bag of dim sum for a couple of bucks. Then I wandered over to Cafe Trieste for a latte and walked over to Washington Square Park to sit on a bench and watch the City wake up. Later I would wander down to Fishermans' Wharf and watch the boats sail off for a day's catch and return filled with every amazing creature of the sea for that night's dining. Yes, back then there really were fishermen at Fishermans' Wharf and the restaurants were owned by the names on the signs that hung above the doors. It seemed to be a city built by families from around the world, and from my point of view they represented the best of those rare and beautiful places. I could explore the world without a passport or anyone having to approve my travel.

I have lived in Florida, Southern California, upstate New York again, and five wonderful years in Sicily. I enjoyed my time in those places, but the lights, laughter and warmth of San Francisco always drew me back. I realized that I was in love with this town and all her flavors, scents and sounds. Those sojourns were enjoyable and broadening, but none of them could ever be home for me. MY city is like a beautiful lover who does not care if I venture out because she knows her smile, scent and form will always bring me back, happy to come home.

At Marina Junior High School, I was one of a handful of non-Asian students. Many were "Fresh Off the Boat." They relayed tales of Hong Kong and mainland China. They would share their beliefs with me, and we would talk of dreams and goals, family, duty, likes and dislikes. That was one of the places I learned we all were not so different. I was also introduced to so many things, including the films of Bruce Lee, the martial arts, and Chinese calligraphy and watercolor art. I would go to Chinatown and see exhibits and demonstrations of these art forms. An old man held a bamboo brush and made it dance and exposed the depths of its magic before my eyes. This was so meaningful to me as I had always loved to draw and delighted in art in all its forms.

I discovered that all of the museums were free to minors (not so now—a mistake in my opinion). I would play hooky and spend the entire day going to museums: the DeYoung, the Academy of Sciences, the Japanese Tea Garden. These were my classrooms and what a magical education they provided. I always took my sketch pad and drew whatever I could. I would also hang out at the San Francisco Zoo, which was also free, and draw all the animals, the people and scenery. I would lunch on the zoo's pink popcorn bars, hot dogs and coke...Whatta life!

San Francisco was a beautiful, patient and loving friend who seemed to provide everything for immigrants like me as well as all the foreign born who came to her shores looking for freedom from oppression, freedom of expression, freedom to worship without fear of harassment or ridicule. As in all democracies we, the artists, writers and those who climbed up on soapboxes would test the patience of the more conservative, and less imaginative, among us. But often those people, exercising their First Amendment rights in one form or another, open our collective eyes to beauty, justice and knowledge.

Often real learning is a poke in the eye because it challenges us to examine our beliefs and see if they stand up to the light of truth. The year 2020 has tested our patience. None of us have gotten through the year without a black eye. The coronavirus pandemic, the damage to our economy, the wildfires making it so hard to breathe—all these things have created new challenges for San Francisco and beyond. I believe that it can still be the City of my youth, where diverse cultures live in harmony and learn from one another. Immigrants built this country and made San Francisco the unique place that it is. Americans have died in this country's wars to fulfill the promise of freedom and liberty for all. The last year will live vividly in our minds and hearts for as long as we live. It has presented an extreme challenge to the San Francisco life I had as a young man. The challenges before us may seem insurmountable, but we can, and we must, work together to overcome them.

Gerard Clark was born in St. Louis, Missouri, in 1954, lived in Albany, New York until he was 12, then moved to San Francisco. He studied at the Academy of Art College. Gerard's unique perspective developed while working at many occupations, including restaurant cook, hotel and hospital security guard, massage therapist, bookstore manager, artist, illustrator, cartoonist. Now retired, he is working on a graphic novel.

Webster Street Moon
Nellie Wong

Music of the lute and erhu wafts down Webster Street. The chair caner walks by, a pine chair hoisted on his back, unconcerned with the clacking of mahjong tiles, a woman's voice cascading out the window singing of separation from her love. Above the Silver Dragon café, night's tendrils snare a young girl's ears, her Baba drinking V.O. and playing pai gow—a respite from his day of buying beansprouts, breast of lamb, ground beef, salt, flour and granulated sugar; paying the cooks union dues, adding, subtracting and dividing on his abacus. The Great China operated six days a week, even on New Year's. Cow's ear cookies and custard pies no longer fill the window of New Home Bakery. The girl anticipates the aroma of cinnamon, Chinese apple pies wafting from ovens at 8 o'clock in the morning. Live chickens no longer squawk, no more duck feathers flying from the poultry monger's hands. The herbalist, barber, bookseller, noodle maker, and women buying winter melon, star anise, fresh pork and oranges disappear into their homes. Night-world moon lights up the girl's curiosity: Who is that woman in the cheongsam of sequined phoenix and peonies on the arms of an elegant man wearing a three-piece suit of gabardine, his fedora framing his handsome features? The girl watches him, another time, with another woman, older, his wife, walking into the insurance office that he manages. At the kitchen table the girl breaks down the sentence: subject predicate verb object nominative declarative interrogative imperative. No dangling participles, her teacher admonishes, when she writes her composition. Sipping scorched-rice soup, the girl thinks of diphthongs, saving for a new pair of Spalding saddle shoes, and how she'll sing of what she doesn't yet know.

Nellie Wong has published four books of poetry. *Breakfast Lunch Dinner* was released in 2012. Her other titles are *Dreams in Harrison Railroad Park, The Death of Long Steam Lady,* and *Stolen Moments.* Work, poetry, and socialist feminist activism are central to her long life.

White Woman Tries to Pass
Jeanne Choy Tate

"White Woman Passes for Black." A little over a year ago, this headline burst across front-page news. Rachel Dolezal, who was white, so longed to be black that she lied, not just to others, but to herself so she could access power in the African American community's fight for racial justice.

Rachel's story disturbs my morning coffee and roils the placid waters of my own oh-so-carefully constructed bicultural identity. Like Rachel, I feel passionate about racial justice. Like Rachel, in my longing to participate fully in the fight for civil rights, I too have tried to leave my white heritage behind. Borrowing another culture's story was easier than claiming painful contradictions in white culture's deep divides.

With Rachel's exposure, the burden of whiteness I have tried so hard to leave behind returns to haunt me. So, while I don't condone the lie, I identify with her desire for a passport to a different racial heritage.

A Navy child, perpetual outsider, with each new school—thirteen in all—I peered through the diamonds on a chain-link playground fence, separated from the promised land of peer acceptance. Tired of constant arguments with my father over civil rights, I dropped out of my southern women's college and crossed the continent in my cousin's top-down, red TR. The year was 1964, one year after Kennedy's assassination and Martin Luther King's "I have a Dream" speech. Bob Dylan had just released his "The Times They are A-Changin'." I was nineteen. Wanting to live as far away as I could get from my family and still be in the U.S., I came to live and work as a church volunteer in San Francisco's Chinatown.

Its own small town within the larger city, Chinatown then—as in its earlier history—was still largely a bounded enclave of Cantonese-speaking immigrants with a burgeoning population of second-generation youth. It was just starting to spill into the streets of North Beach, crossing over Broadway—that previously rigid dividing line where, not many years before, Italian and Chinese youth lined on either side to hurl taunts across the thoroughfare.

Ironically, while teen-age rebellion against parental heritage was an accepted Western rite of passage, my Chinese American peers were proudly laying claim to their ethnic identity. Like many white liberals, I orphaned myself from my inheritance. I defined myself, not by who I was, but by what I was against. A continent away from my East Coast home, I slammed the phone on differences I could not bridge, joining instead with Chinese friends making fun of people of color who tried to pass for, or act as, white. Oreo, coconut, banana, we called them—our jokes filled with prohibitions on unacceptable behavior.

There was no name for whites who tried to pass for black. There was no need—no one wished to cross in that direction. Back then, I tried to raise my street cred by laughing at myself as Egg—white woman trying to pass for Chinese, white woman with an Asian soul. In my early twenties, it all seemed funny. Today, in my seventies, I wonder that I did not perceive my fragile shell.

I so envy people of color, their racial pride, their certainty of cultural identity. I, on the other hand, am divided within, a hybrid mix of ethnicities and clashing versions of history. In my mushy mix of European cultures—Danish, Irish, Scotch, Jamestown settler—like many white Americans, I don't know which heritage to claim while liberal and conservative versions of white America's heritage lock battle with each other.

If I cling too closely to the Chinese American community it is because, oddly enough, this is where I most feel a sense of belonging. Here in Chinatown, where everyone was connected or in some way related, I found the community I longed for. I was a *faan gwaai*–white devil or ghost. Finally this barbarian had a place and an accepted identity.

I begin to understand why Rachel's story jars me so. Recently I mentioned, proudly, my *faan gwaai* status to a non-Asian friend. I held the term out lovingly, a sign of my belonging, till I saw reflected in her eyes that what to me meant belonging to her said 'racist.' For here, in Chinatown, in the only community I have ever known, I stand on shifting ground knowing I can never fully belong. I will always be a guest and outsider, on the receiving end of hospitality.

In Chinatown, I am Caucasian, forever the foreigner. In broader San Francisco and in my East Coast homeland, I am white. My outward appearance both defines and confines me. The color of my skin speaks volumes. It shouts of privilege, dominance, oppression. In reality, I am a cultural hybrid, a mestizo mix: biracial marriage, parent of a biracial-bicultural adult child, white person in the Chinese American community, Chinese-identified in the world of whites. White outside, inside I am some ever shifting mix of East and West, foreign and familiar, rootedness and ever-emerging being.

In 1975, when my Chinese American husband and I married, miscegenation laws against interracial marriage were still on the books in my home state. Fortunately, we were in our thirties and both sets of parents were simply happy we were finally getting married.

But in Chinatown then, to marry outside your race was a betrayal of community. Racial ethnic ideology said: "Marry within your race or you will abandon your race.... You will sell out to the white oppressor.... You will lose your roots.... You will become the feared 'Other.'" While our church community joined with us in celebration, Chinatown activists were not so accepting. Some friendships disappeared forever.

And so, I worried that marrying me might draw my husband away from his Chinese culture. No one worried that I might somehow change to become the forbidden Chinese 'Other.' For white remains the dominant American culture. Its tentacles are pervasive. This view however ignores the strength of Chinese culture. The Chinese self knows its clear identity, as a race and as a culture. I am married to that clarity. In my marriage, I daily engage a strong ethnic identity lived with conviction. If anyone has given up their culture, I am that person.

In marriage—particularly interracial marriage—differences are up front and in your face. Yet, over time, the Other moves inside to clash and blend, to challenge and enrich. Though each of us retains our own unique integrity, we now are married, irretrievably, within. What was once 'them' and 'Other' has long ago turned into 'me,' no longer enemy, but friend. I have become my own diversity.

In truth, I am a hybrid of identities alive with contradictions. To live on the border between two cultures is, like architect Maya Lin, to live on "the place where opposites meet." I crackle with the tension of opposing sides. "Do I contradict myself?" Walt Whitman writes, "Very well then I contradict myself, (I am large, I contain multitudes.)" Where charted waters fall off the edge of the page, I map new worlds and weave a story fresh with meaning. I am a builder of bridges, creator of the in-between. Who I am I know as fluid, always shifting, part of an emerging culture that even now is coming into being.

Jeanne Choy Tate. At age 19, in 1964 Jeanne Choy Tate crossed the American continent to "find her identity" as a live-in volunteer at Cameron House in San Francisco's Chinatown. Building on her experiences as a bilingual/bicultural early childhood educator in Chinatown, a Presbyterian lay pastor, partner in a biracial marriage, and parent of a bicultural child, Jeanne writes of life lived on the borders, in the tension between individual and community. Her experiences inspired an M.A. in Values and a Ph.D. at the Graduate Theological Union. Her book, *Something Greater: Culture, Family and Community as Living Story*, contrasts the intergenerational relationships valued in Chinese communities with the individualism of American child rearing.

Broken Hourglass
Kelechi Ubozoh

One

She still haunts me. In another timeline, my future stepdaughter....She has her father's sea green eyes and long blond curly hair. To call her doll-like would be offensive to her strength and grit. She's not the delicate type, but my god she's gorgeous. More importantly, baby girl is smart. She hears the unsaid words of adults and is always listening. She can charm her way out of trouble, and is unfamiliar with the word no.

She holds my hand as we walk into the toy store. I tell her to pick out any toy she wants, my treat. Her eyes widen and she runs to survey the store. I feel the tiniest bit of panic for my bank account. She returns with a brown baby doll. "I want this one, she's beautiful and she looks like you," she says. She thrusts the brown baby doll into my arms and starts to look for accessories.

Such a simple statement, so casual. I'm winded, thrown, and melted. I hold onto the precious moment, it will be our last.

Two

He is a *good* white man, he reads "White Fragility." Shows up to all of the Black Live Matters protests and brings baby girl. He works in social justice and I am in awe of his "allyship" and his political astuteness.

We're the perfect interracial family. Holding hands with loving gazes, we confront all types of racism. In San Francisco, it is praise. White strangers telling me how happy they were that we were together, so they could feel comfortable in their discomfort? When his southern rooted father decides to never speak to him for proposing to a black woman, my love swiftly disowns him. I am loved truly.

He does and says all the right things. Except...he decides to move to Sonoma County and assumes I'll move there too...when we are married. There is no conversation, no discussion. He just moves. He doesn't quite understand consent, though he swears he is a feminist.

I tell him about the Confederate flag I catch sight of entering county lines on my drive up from Oakland. He brushes off my fear...but, I thought he was an ally? Wait, how does one become an ally? Is it an identity that you achieve? Do you have to take recertification classes? Is there a board of woke-ness that approves your progress? And who is on this board? It can't be your one black friend from high school/college/work/church. What if you were an ally on

Monday, but on Wednesday when your fiancée told you that she was scared because she saw a Confederate flag you decided to take PTO, does your allyship still count? Later I'll learn that allyship is not an identity but a verb, it is not a destination, it is action.

Three

Today is calm.

I hold baby girl's hand and we walk toward the playground. I'm surprised to see several Muslim families playing. Boys and girls immaculately dressed in white and running everywhere.

My guard lowers.

Baby girl looks at the other Brown faces and slowly stops playing. She runs to us.

"What's wrong honey?" Her face framed by blond curly Q's says, "There are too many Brown people on this playground."

Punched in the gut and fury rising to my cheeks. Heat. I take a deep breath.

"Are you afraid?" I ask.

Her eyes widen and she gives me a knowing look.

"Yes," she says. Almost with a sigh.

Crushed, collapsed, broken.

Who taught her this hate? She was just buying brown baby dolls. I need to walk and I need someone to blame. He blames me for getting upset, and I blame him for bringing her here, for breaking her innocence, making her a copy of his father. But...is it this place? Have I given it too much power? The real question trembling underneath the surface that I fear the most. Is it him? She cries and holds on to my leg. How can she cling to me for protection from people who look like me?

"I want to go with you!" she starts to wail.

I gently shake her off. It hurts when she touches me.

"You can't. You can't ever come with me."

She leaves me in broken doll parts. Shocked and undone. Angry, twisted, and confused.

***

This is not forgiveness, this is release. It is time to release my anger at a frozen 6-year-old. I don't live there anymore, and I am not this story. It is a tiny patch of fabric on a complex quilt that is my life. I will take these lessons as gifts, pain as truth, and rage as power. I have my own reflection to attend to. I must say, it is beautiful chaos out here.

From Vampires to Zombies: 2020 in Review
Hussain Yusuf Abdulhaqq and Wei Ming Dariotis

Hussain Yusuf Abdulhaqq: *Facing down a policeman is like facing down a vampire at your door*

You gotta know the rules

I've never studied law, I just remember the things that police tell me when they have me. So many times I've sat kneeling in the dirt by the side of the road with my hands chained behind my back while a man holding a gun pacing circles around me with his zipper at my face telling me that he's doing this for my safety. To ensure my safety? What is the alternative? Do I want to know? I'd rather just be safe. I don't even ask why or who called him out on me.

Why do they always have to have a hand on their gun if we're just talking?

Wei Ming Dariotis: I've learned from living with a Black man, being married to a Black man, walking down the street with a Black man: You never invite the cops in.

It was a beautiful late summer night. We were visiting my aunt and uncle on their farm in rural Washington state, in the verdant Skagit Valley—famous for its annual Tulip Festival, and visiting snow geese. My Uncle Chris is my father's brother; mostly Greek and Swedish, with some Scottish, English, German and Pennsylvania Dutch (yes, that's another kind of German) thrown in. My Aunt Margy and he met on the over-55 international weight-lifting circuit; they're both world masters. Aunt Margy is also white.

I'm Chinese, Greek, Swedish, etc.; raised by my Chinese immigrant mother and my Chinese American stepfather in San Francisco, on the edge of Chinatown. My husband, Hussain, is Black, and Lenape and Irish, raised in Atlantic City, NJ.

Hussain was taking an evening stroll on the road that led to only their house and one other house further down. I felt safe in my aunt's warm kitchen. Suddenly,

---

Previous page: Kelechi Ubozoh is a Nigerian-American writer and mental health advocate. She is the first undergraduate ever published in *The New York Times*. Her story is featured in *O, The Oprah Magazine*, *CBS This Morning with Gayle King*, and *The S Word* documentary. Her work is published in *Endangered Species, Enduring Values*. Her first book with L.D. Green, *We've Been Too Patient*, was released in 2019.

Hussain came running in, shouting, "Don't invite him in!" Warning: "If you let him in, he can grab me!"

HYA *There doesn't need to be a reason.*

No crime, no infraction. He's never seen you here before. That's enough.

He can take years of your life just by touching you. If he grabs you then you become his legal property until he dismisses you.

He can mark you or your home for others to come or he can drain you of life sustaining blood on the spot.

Do not invite—

Not by vocalization or gesticulation

He will suggest that he is already inside

Or that he has the right to be

He will suggest he came here simply to speak with your companion

He is lying

Do not invite him in

Ever

When invited in, he is free of many rules and you are free of many rights.

WMD: Aunt Margy and I were still trying to process. I was still shouting after Hussain, "What?" when the local sheriff came to the door and asked to be let in. His hand rested on his gun.

Despite our assurances that Hussain was our family and that we were safe, it took far too long to convince this stranger, this man with a gun, to leave.

HYA: *The vampire, at least, is restricted in the moment; he cannot break his own rules.*

Vampires fear the light of day. They know that they're evil, embodied. A policeman will lie to protect himself from consequence—even lie to himself.

WMD: The neighbor down the road had seen Hussain standing under the street light in front of my family's home and had begun chasing him with his truck, despite Hussain's attempts to appear friendly and unthreatening. Hussain was on foot. The neighbor chased him back and forth, without speaking to him, then called the cops. Hussain held up his hands to show he was unarmed, to a man in a 10,000 pound truck, pointing it at him like a weapon.

Which one of them should have felt threatened? Which one of them was justified in their fear?

HYA: *Know when a policeman is going to be willing to break his own rules. There's only so far he can rough you up before he needs to explain why.*

I told Aunt Margy if they weren't a white family I wouldn't have come back to the house. I would have ghosted that cop and come back at midnight. White witnesses with more money than a cop's family: that's the only real barrier.

I don't think he would have respected the residency rules if the people he was pushing past were Black or even Asian.

Gotta know when a cop is going to be willing to break their rules to come after you. If he breaks the rules but gets a hold of you, he doesn't have to answer for it; but if he breaks the rules and you evade him, he gets mistreated by cops who want to man up on him.

You can't call in a collar and then not bring in a bond.

And if a cop is alone, he doesn't have to follow any law. He is law. I don't play that.

WMD: Aunt Margy was also slow to react to the danger. She lives in her community and perceives the cops there as helpful to herself and other similar law-abiding members of society—why shouldn't she? She and my uncle are white property owners.

HYA: *I have had a cop try to sneak up behind me and cuff me while I was walking down the street because he thought I fit a description. Never trust them.*

They don't have to follow the rules that a soldier does but they will take on the training of a soldier. Many policemen feel as if they are going to war every day. Some actually are. These white knights are on a crusade of purity.

They are rarely in danger but are taught to act as if they always are.

He does not protect me, my family, or my community. In his eyes, he protects his community from me and my family. My children, my aunties and uncles, cousins, and brothers are—to him—a threat to his way of life. A threat to his hold on power. My life is a threat to his freedom.

WMD: My Greek-Swedish etc. father once asked me, "Why do groups of Black men have to look so scary?" The question was apropos of nothing. I didn't know how to parse it. "Do you mean, why do they feel compelled to act scary?" I asked. If that was the question, the answer was simple, because groups of white men wanted to attack them and kill them just for being Black, just for reminding them of slavery, the original sin of American wealth and power (right after that other original sin, the theft and colonization of Indigenous land).

Or, "Do you mean, why do Black men look scary to you?" That's the media, I told my father, reminding him that most of the Black men I knew personally, like my childhood friend Malik (now a law professor), or my grad school friend Darryl (now an English professor), or a myriad of other Black men I have known, were nerds who wore glasses and liked to talk about Star Trek.

Of course, most of them are not 6'7", like Hussain, who has had other Black men remark to him, "They must just want to take you down as soon as they see you." Yet, Hussain is a Black nerd, too. He likes to talk about Star Trek, cries openly, draws flowers, plants vegetables, and studies dinosaurs.

HYA: *He is allowed to point a loaded gun at me. Safety off, ready to slip free a round. If he feels I could threaten him, this is his right: to hold my life at his sweaty index finger.*

The hard and fast of it is that he doesn't have to feel threatened, he only has to claim he does. A white lie becomes law and the rule of death is his.

WMD: Why did the Black Lives Matter movement catch fire and not let go? Because white people finally started to see what Black people have been saying for years was true.

Saw it with their own eyes. Not just one Rodney King in 1991; in 2020 the visual evidence was overwhelming. And the pile of Black bodies—people murdered by police—keeps growing.

Black people in our family and community—even my Black colleagues with their PhDs and respectability—all know it could happen to any one of them. And to any one of their Black children.

How did any Black people or the people who love them work this year?

HYA: *You died because you were shot. You were shot because he said he felt you were a threat to him. It was his right. It was your blood. None of this was his fault as far as he's concerned and when he returns from a short but paid vacation for his troubles, he will be treated like he was the one harmed by his violence.*

They will care for him and praise him after he stood there watching you bleed to death in handcuffs. Medically trained in emergency services, he will not act to save you. You put a victim of an accidental shooting in handcuffs to watch him die.

No report for the public how many are killed.

Shoot from fear. Shoot to kill. No emergency medical care. No lawsuits. This is his job. This is his training.

He is a professional.

WMD: Whenever Hussain goes out for a walk at night I get nervous. I asked him to quit the job he had because he came home after midnight. Our neighborhood in San Francisco is under-policed in a way that translates into the use of extra force, extra violence.

Once, when a patrol car came up our block, I lost my cool and started yelling at the cops. I told them I was watching them and that I would know who they were if they ever touched my husband, who was a good man. "He's an artist who cares for the earth and teaches children to garden!" Gently, from our door, he told me to stop wasting my breath. "They'll remember my face," he told me, "but they won't remember your words—only that they know me from somewhere, which must mean I am wanted."

What can I do to protect him?

Since we moved to the Bayview neighborhood in 2014, I've gotten to know every police captain assigned to our district (of 100,000 people, but often has fewer than 10 active officers). Actually, I stopped getting to know the police captains after the fifth one rotated through in as many years.

The liquor store on the corner has been the location of at least one shooting a year since we moved here, with the last one involving six wounded and one young person killed.

Our block had an entrenched crack dealer for forty years who brought prostitution and threats of physical violence. Our community worked together

196

with the DA to successfully end this activity using a stay-away order. No Black men were put in jail. The dealer moved to a new location, his business broken. Did all of the misery end? No, but our children can play in the street.

None of this is easy. Hussain wouldn't go to the meetings at the police station because he legitimately fears not being able to leave. I use my privilege as a mixed Asian American who can pass for white or Latina to protect him when and where I can.

Which is ridiculous. I live a sedentary life as a college professor who likes to eat potato chips while lying down and watching British murder mysteries.

What can I do?

HYA: *While visiting or vacationing, I take extra care walking through darkness down tree-lined roads. I love walking alone at night, breathing the air, looking up at the stars and the creatures and plants that come out at night that are different than those that come out at daytime.I always put between myself and any pair of headlights, a telephone pole or a tree trunk. A sharp ditch will do. Anything that would stop a runaway pickup truck.*

Breaks can fail suddenly out here on these lonely nights.

When those haunting blue and red lights and that eerie wail calls from out in the darkness, I follow the teachings of my elders:

Grab my phone

Check for cell service

(A cell tower is the church steeple cross, these days)

Connection to protection—or at least an honest witness

I set myself in order

Text my wife my position. Set my phone to her number.

Turn on my live video stream and tremble slightly as I wait for the specter to pass me over

Pray he doesn't stop for me

Pray for the soul he's come to take

Prey for the hunter

Men out hunting innocent men. Armed men who stalk civilians.

WMD: In late 2019, Hussain and I became fost-adopt parents to a six-and-a-half-year-old Black girl.

The urgency with which we address these social issues is now intertwined with learning how to soothe a child's nightmares ("there are no monsters..."). We found a way to be family with a traumatized child who, in March—just four months after we first met—was suddenly at home with us all the time, physically cut off from everyone else she's ever known.

We learned the new rules of COVID-19, and our daughter learned interesting vocabulary for a now seven-year-old: quarantine, disinfect, pandemic, Zoom.

For her, more than ourselves, we've become healthily paranoid. Most of all, we avoid the maskless.

San Francisco is filled with them—generally affluent people who seem to think they are too special to get sick. We dodge these zombies every time we try to leave our home to take a walk or just to get sunlight.

We dream of taking a walk in a forest, or by the ocean, without seeing other people, especially people with their maskless dogs running around off-leash. Dogs can get COVID, too.

Barking zombies.

It seems like everyone in San Francisco is dreaming of moving to the country, or at least to Marin County. We want some space to move around in some fantasy place where houses don't touch other houses, and people don't touch other people.

Hussain tells me he no longer has anxieties because all his childhood fears have come true.

Donald Trump became president.

Zombies took over the world.

And yet, also, something he never imagined would happen, did. People started to say Black lives matter, and seemed to finally believe it. White men and women put their lives on the line to say it loudly enough for the world to listen: Black Lives Matter!

We believe we can change the world for our Black daughter. We must.

Her life *does* matter.

Hussain Yusuf Abdulhaqq: Gardener and homemaker in San Francisco's Bayview. Nurturer, student, teacher, guardian.

Wei Ming Dariotis, PhD: Dr. Dariotis is Faculty Director of the Center for Equity and Excellence in Teaching and Learning and Professor of Asian American Studies at SFSU. Dariotis co-founded the Critical Mixed Race Studies Conference and co-defined the field. Her publications include *War Baby/Love Child: Mixed Race Asian American Art* (UW Press, 2013) and *Fight the Tower: Asian American Women Scholars' Resistance and Renewal in the Academy* (Rutgers, 2019).

"Black Lives Matter," Oakland street mural. Photo by Edsel Rivera.

Instructions
Kimi Sugioka

Render
tooth, jaw, femur, lung
Resist nothing
embrace everything
the shelter
the storm
the paroxysm of despair
the wedge of hope
the padding coyote
smug crow
wisp of fox

Arrangements
cannot be made
Plans
are not required
Sleep is
imperative and
impossible

Vows are paper wishes
belong wherever
 you are
make peace
with the demons
and the angels

remember only
the ancestors and
the first peoples

they are the only ones
who can help us
to resurrect
the innocence
we abandoned
so long ago

Kimi Sugioka, is an educator and poet. She earned an MFA at Naropa University and has published two books of poetry; the newest of which is *Wile & Wing* on Manic D Press. As the newly inaugurated Poet Laureate of Alameda, she will try to engage the community in a multi-cultural and intergenerational exploration of poetry and literature. Her work appears in anthologies such as: *Civil Liberties United, Endangered Species, Enduring Values, Standing Strong! Fillmore & Japantown, Colossus,* and *Colossus:Home.*

knowledge

Artist Karen Seneferu with her piece "Call Yo Momma"
at *The Black Woman is God: Divine Revelation* exhibition at the
SOMArts Cultural Center in 2017.

From one teacher to another
christl rikka perkins

Dear Rona,
I'm going to teach exponential relationships this week
You are the prime example
Of how the curve goes upward, neatly tabled evidence ample
We graph the cases doubling and the number of deaths per day troubling
As we make tables and model the flattening that we seek
The peak, the elusive peak

But then again it's hard to preach the importance of algebra 2
When a mom calls at 2:32 am saturday of week 2
Sorry to be rude
Yes we got the laptop and the hotspot too
But what we need is food

Dear Rona,
I'm going to teach about supply and demand curves
Widgets and guns versus butter this week
You are the prime example
The supply of hospital beds, ventilators, protective gear
The demand of the people for life, work, to get back to the pursuit of
happiness
We'll play the stock market game

But then again it's a luxury to lecture economic theory
When a student texts from a neighbor's cell phone
Teacher, I can't talk unless you call me
'cause our phone is cut off
we just moved and then my mom and dad were laid off

Dear Rona,
I'm going to teach about the food chain
The biology textbooks say that humans are on top
But you are teaching me otherwise

homeschoolin
adrienne danyelle oliver

Baby, we are quarantined
Quarantina as in forty
Baby, we are being cleaned
Here we go, as in lawdy lawdy

Forty come from four
as in corners on a page
when we know we so much more
than words in a cage

Trapped in the white space
Instead of the black keys
single instead of double space
on our prayer hands and knees

Instead we in here like stars in space
floating around in the black of a shelter in place
We got our living room in here. All the paintings. In place
this the kitchen table that's gone be your learning space

Wishing suddenly we had more natural light
So dark in here makes Mama miss the sunray's flight
through windows, big and bad, with nature's view in sight
instead, we got one back room letting in sun with all its might

We gone call this our Vitamin D room
We gone call this our sippin' tea room
We gone call this our room of we room
We gone call this our room of peace room

West Oakland light shine in and let us see clear
We be quarantined like Black skin with dogs chasing near
outsmarting the wolf again and pretending we can't hear
knocking on our brick house from white knuckles too near

While the wolf roams around us
We light the fire without a fuss
We keepin your lesson robust
This ain't the last stop on this bus

We pushing ahead of them pushing us around again
hanging on by the hairs of our chinny chin chin
withstanding the growls and howls to get in
we let the wolf stand outside while we safe within

We might be quarantined like sardines
getting salty like a sack of saltines
for your art project running out of magazines
and making do with anything we got on the scene

But that's alright, baby, we okay
We gone be the one that got up, up and away
We ain't got nothing but time to play this spade
What you think about all that? What you got to say?

Mama, why the schools closed down?
Why can't I go outside?
Why are you wearing that mask around?
I miss going down the slide.

Where is my teacher? I miss Ms. Lila Honey.
Can I go outside? Can I have my lunch money?
Mama, I'm tired. Mama, I'm hungry.
Mama, why you laughing? I'm not being funny?

Mama?
Mama?
Are you still there, Mama?
When will it go back to normal, Mama?

Mama, I'm bored. I don't want to sit down.
Can I have a snack, Mommie? Pull the cookies down.
Mama, I already know how to write contractions.
Mama, that's not the way Ms. Honey does fractions.

Mama, what happens to a dream quarantined?
Does it ooze out the window like a syrupy treat?
Or does it grow so numb, it forgets to weep?
Or does it explode into this new you and new me?

What does all this / computer light do
to my eyes / Mama?

I know I said ask me anything
But, whew chile, that's a lot
Let's see what the day bring
We gone work with what we got

We might run out of snacks
and ease up on the fractions
we might be behind the racks
on addition and subtraction

We ain't got no slide or swings that I can count
But we got the Vitamin D room
And a bed...I guess I'll let you bounce
When you jump in the bed don't jump past the moon

We want the mattress firm
Mama, need a place to gloom.

---

adrienne danyelle oliver is a poet-professor, hip-hop scholar from Little Rock, AR currently based in the SF Bay Area. Her previous work has appeared in *Storytelling, Self & Society* (Wayne State University Press 2018) and The Museum of African American Diaspora's poet corner. Some of Adrienne's favorite authors include Maya Angelou, Gloria Naylor, and Tyembia Jess. When she is not writing, Adrienne is reading or watching documentaries. She also leads a monthly healing writing circle for Black women.

Photo by TaSin Sabir.

lesson plan
adrienne danyelle oliver

0.

H - Her legacy is my inspiration
A - Abolition state of mind
R - Returning not an option
R - Responsibility to educate
I - I take up my mantle
E - Everybody loves the sunshine but nobody like the run
T - Tell the truth in love though I feel lost

1.

Pre-pandemic.
after school program.
third, fourth and fifth graders.
nine-year-olds
can't sit still long.
Pre-pandemic college.
19-year-olds sit still
like zombies in desks.
in both places Black writers
get distracted easily
can't cursive
between lines
of notebook paper.
can't sit still at desks.
class is a sentence.
second language learners
are doing better.
it's the Black kids
having the hardest time.
all the training.
degrees ain't working.
separation of self.

2.

I ask the after school
program coordinator
what's wrong with Samej?
She says his mother was on drugs, she
　　　　suspects that he was one of those
　　　　　　　　'crack babies'
So sad
　　　　me and the other teachers agree
　　　　　　　　　　　　　　　　we understand now
A week later I'm reading
　　　　　　　　　　Killing the Black Body
　　　and realizing　　　　　　　　　　　　that answer
　　　　　　　　　　　　is too convenient

I witness bureaucracy
　　　　　　　　　　　　the failing of education
too much home unschooling days
　　　　　　　　　　　　　　to count
present
　　　　　　absent
present
　　　　　　absent
　　　　　　　　absent
absent　　　　　　　　　absent
　　　　　present
absentabsentabsentabsentabsent
　　　　　　　　　　　present
A classroom of 35 with a waitlist on the first day
　　　dwindles
　　　　　　　to
　　　20
　　　　　　　18
12
　　　　　　7
　　　　　　　　　　　　　　"I am an essential worker"
"I have to take care of my kids"
　　　　　　　"I slept in my car last night"

207

"My mother died"
                        and the unsaid
"I'm addicted"
                              "I'm depressed"
            "I'm barely living"
                                          "I'm suicidal"

3.
With all of the remote instruction
I think about the nine-year-olds
like Samej
who can't sit still
who become 19
who become numb
who cannot take another
shot of screen time
without overdosing
who can't find
his self
in the light of
his headline
his hashtag
his riot
his vigil
his classroom sentence
digital divide is more than a trending concept
the Sade song, 'a bulletproof soul' is on repeat
at my knees

4.
They say Wal-Mart taking over public education
somewhere in great America charter schools like
privatization be in a police state of mind
nationally guarded Little Rock Nine
I'm the Black little girl walking solo down the line
housewives growling with picket signs
I'm grown up now
It's hard to remember the details

                              we still dreaming

About Making the Grade
Margot Dashiell

In September 1950, we lined up in front of Mrs. Benjamin's 3rd grade bungalow. Standing in front of us she said, "Children, you have been promoted to 4th grade. You will go into Mrs. Mather's room upstairs and show her what well behaved children you are."

The main building on San Pablo Avenue and Virginia Street in west Berkeley looked like an old wooden ship beaten dull grey by the wind and rain blown off the bay. At its entrance the sign read "Ocean View School built in 1856." Before it became Berkeley, the Ocean View community built it. The school's name now was Franklin and it was the oldest school in Berkeley.

A tortoiseshell pin held her light brown hair on top of her head. Mrs. Mather was an older teacher, probably about 50. I thought she was different in a good way. She said that we would sing from popular tunes on the radio or the TV. I liked that. Mrs. Mather preached the goodness of brown bread and against things like CocaCola, just like my father did. She told us she would bring in reeds and teach us to make baskets like the one she carried her lunch in.

Mrs. Mather was white like all the teachers except for Mrs. Bruce who looked white. My mother put her forefinger to her mouth to let me know not to tell anyone. Negro teachers were not hired in schools outside of south Berkeley. Mrs. Bruce made us proud and we kept her race a secret. My parents said the NAACP was going to get more Negro teachers hired.

I was eight and the youngest in class, but I was tall and was proud I could reach the top of the fancy old metal coat hooks in the cloak room. We were big children now and we would dip long black pen holders into inkwells to write our papers.

Mrs. Mather said "Face forward children" when she took the long wooden pointer with a rubber tip to the blackboard. In 3rd grade Mrs. Benjamin gave me gold stars for reading. I wanted to show Mrs. Mather that I could read the sentences that she pointed to, but she usually didn't call on me. Claudette was the only other Negro girl in the class. She hardly ever called on her either.

For social studies we learned about Mexico, our neighbor to the South.

Mrs. Mather asked us to draw the map of Mexico with crayons. I drew the map in a pretty orange color. It came out long and skinny. Mrs. Mather gathered the drawings at her desk, stood up, removed her glasses that hung from her neck with a cord, and held up some of the maps. She said, "Look class, Margot's map looks like a tooth." Some children laughed. I smiled.

I had a hard time waking up in the morning. Every morning my father or mother came to my room and said, "Margot, you will be late for school. You have to get up." Slowly, I dragged myself to the bathroom to wash up. My father told me it would help me wake up if I splashed my face with cold water. The rains came down that winter for many days at a time and in my galoshes I slowly sloshed my way to school, kicking the waters moving along the gutters.

I didn't tell my parents about the map and that I wasn't doing well at school.

But they saw my report card which had a lot of checks in the "improvement needed" column. My parents said, "Margot, please try harder. We know you are able to do it." I didn't feel smart.

The Crawford family lived next door. They were the only other Negro family on our block. Mr. Crawford was a "race man." He belonged to the Negro National Council. A man named Willie Magee in Mississippi was on death row for something about a white woman. The Negro National Council was taking Mrs. Magee around the United States to ask people to help save her husband's life. Mrs. Magee was staying at the Crawford home and my father was a foot doctor. He went over to treat her feet. My father said they were blistered from walking so much. My father told my sister and me to pray that Willie Magee would not be killed. He had little children like us.

That week Mrs. Mather stood in front of the class and said that "People were in town saying 'a Negro man was not guilty' but he had assaulted a white woman. Children, that is a serious crime." I told my parents. My father looked down and shook his head from side to side.

June came and I looked forward to being out of the classroom. Then Mrs. Mather sent a note home that she would not promote me to 5th grade unless I could turn in a writing assignment I didn't finish. The semester was over and the book could not leave the classroom. My father found the text book at a publishing house in San Francisco. There were two pages of questions I responded to in one afternoon. It wasn't hard. My mother delivered them to the principal. I was free to try again to see if I could be a good student in the next grade.

* * *

In the Sheltering-in-Place time of 2020 the images of Breonna Taylor and George Floyd and Ahmaud Arbery and a distressing trail of others stretched back to my nine-year-old self when I first feared for a Black man who could not be saved from death row in Mississippi. Since then, locked in my inner sight line, I have absorbed seven decades of racial killings, and personal experiences that reveal how little Black Lives Matter.

But the spasms of the 2020 decade, with the pain of pandemic deaths and police killings, have also brought inspiring signs. Maybe the "Black Lives Matter" slogan will fade as others have, but I find hope in the hundreds of thousands of people of all colors and ages and classes who packed the streets across the United States in protest against wanton police violence. I am encouraged by the signs that demonstrators, news commentators and even some elected officials have shown an understanding that Black people are deeply undervalued and that systems—criminal justice systems, educational systems, health care systems, economic systems, financial systems—are responsible for maintaining the massive disparities in the wealth and welfare of Black people. For the first time, I hear a new crop of political leaders acknowledging the need for "systemic change." There will be opposition, of course, and I expect progress to be slow.

In the meantime, through my childhood memory, I see again how much families, neighbors and communities have laid it on the line to save individual futures like mine. This Sheltering Year, I've come to the conclusion that communities must build an advocacy industry which prepares citizens to advocate for themselves and others—in police corridors, in hospital halls, in principal's offices and school boards. There's always been informal advocacy in African American communities. It has to be expanded and coalesce with other communities until there is enough people power to assure that US institutions can finally make the grade.

Margot Dashiell. I retired from wonderful work teaching sociology and African American Studies at the Peralta Colleges in 2004. Today, while Sheltering-in-Place in 2020, on ZOOM I continue wide-ranging advocacy work in support of families helping members living with serious mental illness. Currently I'm editing a memoir of years traveling to Ghana where I added a second son to my family.

For All The Girls Like You
Janae Newsom

You're having a baby.

You're twenty years old. The law says you're grown, but still not old enough to walk into the liquor store down the street and buy alcohol. It's not like you drink it anyway. Still, you are having a baby. You try to go to college, I mean really try everything you can to succeed. You show up to office hours, and you actually study the text, even though you wish they taught a course on how to study. Your favorite class is the creative writing one, that you take on a fluke as an elective. The teacher is white, and so are most of the students in your class, in fact you are the only black person. This class is still your favorite, but that doesn't mean much. The spark doesn't ignite in you. Besides, you still have to pass that remedial math class. This time you would be done, done for good if you failed again. The seventh time.

It's like the movies. You're sitting in your car holding your grown belly and crying reading the letter. San Jose State university has to disqualify you, your "failure to complete the remediation courses within the allotted time has resulted in..."

The car is your silver 2001 Lexus, with the black leather seats, it is a hot September day and the windows are rolled up as you have your tearful meltdown. What would you do now? What kind of mama could you be to the baby who you learned is a daughter? You are having a girl. This is a task for you. Was she the karma that your mama always talked about, would she be worse than you? Despite all of your efforts would she end up hating you? Or running away, or getting into fights in school, and smoking weed at thirteen? Would she be pregnant before her twenty first birthday?

You had the baby. She takes over all of your life, when you look at her you see stars, and flowers. Your actual heart becomes liquid flowing around the inside of your chest. Her soft coos as her little mouth moves make your cheeks hurt from smiling. She does nothing but be the cutest thing you have ever seen. Your breasts produce milk for her and she drinks it. For weeks you are on a cloud, you give baths for the first time, you change her first diapers, you know which cry is which, she is yours. You are a mother. You had gone down to the social services agency at Eastmont mall and got on Medi-cal, and Calworks. The cash assistance and the Medi-cal and the WIC help you to continue to smile, and enjoy not working, so that you can keep staring into the face of your daughter every day. You live in your great-grandmother's house, she passed away in 2006 and her funeral was on your fourteenth birthday. But her house is home. Your grandmother, her daughter, got you a crib for the baby and a futon. You didn't have a babyshower but you have all that you need.

Some months later you get a job. You fill up vending machines and although you don't always know it, it is one of the best jobs you will ever have. You wake up at 3 or 4 am. You get your daughter dressed and somehow have a bag ready for her in all of the unorganized chaos that is your new apartment. You buckle her into her carseat with the darkness of early morning hitting your back. And you drive from your apartment in San Leandro to 89th, and park in the middle of the street leaving your daughter in the warm car as you call for her father to wake up. He eventually wakes up, and you hand her off and make your way to work cruising through back alleys all the way there. You park on the long street and walk up to the gate and wait there as it opens. You say "what's up" to the guys coming out of the warehouse, or loading up their trucks. You go into the building and clock in, hoping you'd get either a route by yourself or with your favorite co worker Rian. You know if you ride by yourself you can run your route how you want, and take breaks to do homework. If you rode with Rian you knew you could sleep on the ride and discover new food places along the route, and talk about your problems while walking down the long building corridors, pulling your dolly behind you. Most days the warm sun would begin to peek through as you unloaded the truck on your first stop. But some days it rained, then you'd slosh around in the wet pulling those loads of bottles, cans, and food items. You get off work at 1pm and rush to school for 1:45pm. You miss your daughter, thirteen hours a day.

You graduate with your Associate's Degree. When the back doors open to the paramount theatre, and the line begins to move you look around at all the black women in the line with you. Some with stories the same as yours, some different. You see the smiles stretching across their faces, the nervous excitement buzzing through their bodies.

When you get closer to the entrance and step foot inside, you see your cousin standing on the side of the ropes. On the inside of the theatre you hear the music coming from the auditorium, the cheers, and laughter. Your cousin is holding your daughter, her small two-year-old body cupped between loving arms. Your daughter smacks her small hands into each other and smiles at you. You get into the auditorium and sit in your seat. When it is your row's turn you all stand, and follow each other to the stairs, the closer you get to the top you think you might throw up. Finally, you get there and they call your name. This name belongs to you and now it carries a title of mother, although you still feel fourteen on the inside. As you leave the stage you feel a spark, one that you thought your daughter had given to you. You learn that her existence forced you to see what was already there. You hoped that if you could teach her this lesson, then she would not have to wait until she is a mother to learn it. That despite all the ways that she ignited the spark in you, you hoped that maybe her spark would be ignited by her, and her alone.

My name is Janae Newsom, I am a writer and mother of two from Oakland. I work as a college counselor, and I am in my final year of the MFA in prose program at Mills College. I am currently writing my first novel. My goal is to tell an authentic story woven from the fabric of my community, and for black girls who can relate.

Joan Osato, "Tanya Orellana, Scenic Designer," f
rom the photographic portrait series *unseen labor,* 2020

Don't Tell Me How to Say My Name
Ariella Pinedo

With a bounce in my step and a smile from ear to ear
My feet made their way into white stone walls
"Maybe you should say your name
like this,"
he says to me.
"Clients get confused when you say your name
          your way.
They don't get it."

He swivels in his chair,
his chest puffed,
his words masked as wisdom.
Anger flowed up and down my spine.

Brown bare feet and hands, covered in sand,
running across the street and back,
running around, avoiding cars and lighting up fireworks,
Warm nights, spent listening to my grandfather's stories
next to a tree I climbed early that day.

Millions of immigrants crossing to safety,
holding on to each other
for that and the sweat on their backs is all they brought.
          It's the calloused hands that grip the shovel to move mountains
          to stride onto new land.
          You know, safe land.

Don't tell me how to say my name.

The way I say my name is not a trend.
The way I say my name is not a commodity
to be used, or changed just because you "don't get it."

Sitting in the back of my dad's truck
barely old enough to formulate proper sentences,
desperately trying to memorize where I'm from although
I've lived there my entire life.
How does a child convince the man in firm green
we are the same?

I'm not yours to mold,
So don't tell me how to say my name.
The way I say my name stands on the shoulders of those who rose before,
of those who dance like the world is on fire and there is no tomorrow.

Do you want to know my name?
My name is three words,
And no, I will not change how I say it.
My name is Ariella Pinedo Vanegas.

Sin Comunicar
Ariella Pinedo

I recollect blurry visions of tattered yellow books and cassette tapes
a gift of a migrant parent and a son of migrants
   They wanted me to own el idioma inglés

Time lapses to fourth-grade lectures and Missions of
San Diego de Alcala
   Built out of paper and popsicle sticks but mostly I recall
Getting in trouble for finding the peeling ceiling and fluorescent lights
Far more interesting

Among the scattering of rules for conformity
   and petty elementary school crimes
Came a teacher's assistant to take me away
   from a classroom of 25 to a class of 5
To take a test after test after test that only bilingües
took
No matter how fast I finished and how many I passed they continued
And so did I
Poseyendo el idioma que tanto querían negar mío

Ariella Pinedo is a Mexican-American poet born and raised in Southern California, whose passion for writing was spurred by her studies of multiple languages. She has an enthusiasm for empowering others and finds value in showcasing the true you in all aspects of your life. Since moving to the Bay Area, she has been a regular contributor at poetry readings and open-mics.

Starboy
Juan Hernesto Gómez

"THERE. IS. NO. 'THERE.' THERE."

And of course you would say that, sitting on Parisian cushion with your entourage of giants while I'm forced to telescope your traces of stardust left behind on withered pages of books from my repressed memories of high school; everyone knows *Gatsby* is assigned reading and, well, what can I say, I sympathized and shared the need to flicker my way into the verdant nebulae of preppy Ivy scholars. Columbia College for me—Manhattan, not Chicago (I felt the need to say).

For four years I sought to recreate between semesters the utopic, ideologizing walks of his *Moveable Feast*, who knew Certeau pre-Certeau, but who, like you and your pre-digital crew, could not help but proclaim your beloved *Paris* the Big Bang of all Wastelands to come; I'd make a more sophisticated allusion, but I must profess, I never made it past two for fear of murder by death of water— that is, the icy cold waters of boredom.

"But wait!" Professor Emeritus of Ladida would be quick to say. "He is not even in the same *period* as the expatriates!"

Let's be clear: any debate predicated on clearly defined demarcations of periodizations is doomed to give way to the hollow scholarly tantrums tantamount to the incessant *honk! honk! honk!* of the Canadian geese gliding pacifically the tip of the iceberg on this fine wintry night—at least, that is my theory, borne out of the plethora of readings and lectures which could not provide for me the answer I did not know to find outside all aesthetic-literary modalities.

Welcome to the age of silicon. Traverse with me, wave by cyberkinetic wave, the teleinformatic membrane of our new world order 'til we've MC Hammered it with intellectual funk into vibranium crystal, resemanticizing Oak-Town 'til Wakanda-Forevered.

I Make Promises Before I Dream
Tongo Eisen-Martin

No unclaimed, cremated mothers this year

Nor collateral white skin

No mothers folding clothes to a corporate park preamble
No sons singing under the bright lights of a lumber yard

Quantum reaganomics and the tap steps of turning on a friend

New York trophy parts among
       the limbs of decent people
             Being an enraged artist is like
             entering a room and not knowing what to get high off of

             My formative symbols/My upbringing flying to an agent's ears
                         I might as well be an activist

                    Called my girlfriend and described
             All the bottles segregationists had thrown at me that day

             Described recent blues sites and soothing prosecutions
                         I feared for my poetry

You have to make art every once in a while
       While in the company of sell-outs
       Accountant books in deified bulk
       Or while waiting for a girl under a modern chandelier

                       Or in your last lobby as a wanderer

                       The prison foot races the museum

                       My instrument ends

          I mean, what is a calendar to the slave?
             Also, what is a crystal prism?

                    "He bought this bullet,
                       bought its flight,
                   then bought two more"

legacies

Malik Seneferu, "Aesthetic Ascension," 30 x 15 inches, 2005.

Artist statement: This piece was inspired by the fists raised at the 1968 Olympics by Tommy Smith and John Carlos. I decided to add an extra for balance which represents the pride that was emoted throughout the world.

Karen Seneferu
Artist Statement

At the center of my work is beauty. Despite what I create I want beauty to be resistance to annihilation. Oftentimes public and private domains are structures of trauma for the Black body that distort how the individual views the self. I want to challenge the dehumanizing depictions by rooting beauty in the African esthetics. I use iconic patterns, forms and colors associated to the cultural value of Africa form and in some cases, integrate those components with technology to speak to the contemporary concerns. This allows for me to dialogue with traditional African art while attempting to advance the medium of the work.

Reoccurring patterns and shapes emerge in my forms. One is the cross, that for me symbolizes peace. The shape represents the crossroad figure who becomes the place of struggles for Africans in America because the binary construct demands one give up one's cultural identity for the possibility of belonging. However, within Yoruba spiritual practice, the cross is God. The Kalunga line establishes a threshold or boundary between the world of the living and the dead associated through bodies of water, like the Atlantic Ocean. Triangles are also embedded in my work. These three sides or three corresponding faces create multiple possibilities of existence through a prism, which gives me glimpses into sacred geometry, where I attempt to unify something broken, something lost. The metaphysics of my experience is exemplified by the art piece "Grandson, Mureed, the Seeker" an ode to my grandson, who is the third generation with the same first name. He represents tri- or trinity, or completion. His life experiences have already indicated a shift in reality.

This leads to a very important component in the process of my work. I like to invite family, community into my space, to create something unifying. In each exhibit, I have a piece or work either my family member created or had some hand in the making of that work. This inclusion is important, for the exhibition space is designed to separate the community apart from the individual whereas I try to gather parts of myself, my family, and my community into the work to not only celebrate the beauty I produced but how that production could not have existed without them. The implementation emerges as various assemblage pieces that show the constant battle of claiming the self. However, it doesn't always turn into, but can sometimes become, a beautiful struggle.

Karen Senferu, "The Heir Done Been Pulled."

Karen Seneferu is a mixed media artist whose work challenges the idea that beauty exist outside of one's cultural reality. Her work has been exhibited at the Oakland Museum, the California African American Museum, Yerba Buena Center, Skirball Museum, Tuft's University Museum, and the Museum of the African Diaspora. For the last seven years, Seneferu has been developing and co-curating an exhibit entitled *The Black Woman Is God*, which has changed the artistic and cultural landscape of Black women's art. Many of the artists in this book have participated in *The Black Woman Is God* exhibitions.

Karen Seneferu, "Techno Kisi."

Techno-Kisi developed from an ancient form designed as a container for spirit forces in the Kongo Basin. A traditional Nkisi has nails all over a wooden sculpture, a few charms around the body, and a sealed box attached to the belly. The lid of the box is a mirror that reflects those that stand before it, to keep watch over the viewers' intentions.

I adapted the tradition to create a memorial for healing the cultural obliteration that happens when the Black Woman's body is dehumanized. I replaced the traditional Nkisi nails with fabric-covered charms made of clay balls wrapped around hidden properties.

Shizue Seigel, "Imperatrix Mundi," acrylic on canvas, 52 x 28 inches.

In an homage to Japanese American grandmothers, I replaced the emperor's head in the Ingres portrait "Napoleon I on His Imperial Throne" with the smiling face of a Japanese immigrant baachan. She wields a broom and a staff topped by a bright red daruma, traditional symbol of resilient spirtiuality. Centered on her chain of office is the Buddhist Wheel of Dharma. Napolean reigned for only ten years, but Baachan is still glows in her grandchildren's memories fifty years after her death. She was the beloved Empress of a large extended family that she led with humility and compassion.

Wanda Sabir, self portrait in MAAFA SF Bay Area Mask.

Wanda Sabir covers Black arts and culture in print, radio and the web on *Wanda's Picks* (https://wandaspicks.com) and a column in the *San Francisco Bay View* newspaper. She is a Depth Psychologist, with deep roots in the bayous of Louisiana where she was born. Her interests and expertise are trauma and trauma healing—Maafa, specifically ancestral memories, dream tending and the use of art and guided Appreciative Inquiry (AI) to stimulate those forgotten conversations, especially among Diaspora descendants. She holds a master's degree in writing from the University of San Francisco, and teaches at College of Alameda.

Mythology Attached to Blackness
Wanda Sabir

The references to burial sites is lost perhaps to those with shovels, but for those persons whose ancestors wanted dead not alive once stock options expired could not miss the six feet apart references

Six feet under
Six feet…

I walk among the dead. I am a ghost, a ghost with
possibility extinguished at birth

6 feet under I see kin swimming nowhere, anchors attached to nooses
attached to preexisting conditions like covenants…
and expired insurance policies

There's a mythology attached to blackness…like we don't swim
We just drown
Perhaps the tears we tend to wallow in create sinkholes
Jaws open
Swallowed
We swim inside a belly
Dark…we search for light and find more darkness

The mythology attached to a narrative of supremacy
One where black people are not people
You know…we die but not with dignity afforded even beasts,
domesticated pets

This mythology attached to blackness leaves my people
Alone
Isolated
Looked upon with contempt
Systems supported by cheap labor spin on wheels oiled by
dispensable humanity

Black mythology
People step off curbs
Yell expletives
It would be funny except
For Baba Emmett it was too late

The JOKE
White people have no humor
Six feet under
Emmett's body chained to narratives that say: black boys don't get to grow up
Black people as surplus
Emmett linked to a genetic circuit passed through inheritance
Auction blocks and stocks marketed differently now with the same result
Covid19
Corona
Crown

Beheaded

Black people stumble into graves
Six feet under
Six feet below sea level
We reach for sky and find more dirt
Gravel
Broken ladders and distilled promises
Even with pink super moon…its largess was only an illusion
The moon is still 238,855 miles from the earth and even further from the sun,
93,000,000 miles away.
Even though it looks close…like broken legislative amendments
to an anemic constitution…
Justice sitting with her sister Liberty, both marooned on an island
off the coast of a Big Apple

Apples laced with poisonous promises
Black mythology

It's a question of resilience
If only…
But we don't
Black people don't bounce…we jump, remember? We run, remember?
Chased…we cannot slow down, except through death
Running is what people do who are alive
Walking is for the dead
 Balls bounce like *boomerangs*—Sankofa symbols in pyramids
We do return…
Blackness indivisible
Permanent like dark matter that births life
But this is a philosophical wonder that has limited practicality

as one is running from police or stopped at a red light
or unmasked in the face of Covid-19
Top soil
Pressure cookers
Steam kettles
Tip over historic landmarks
Six feet under

Applied racism
Like applied math is practical
Resilience looks like:
Hypertension
Prostate Cancer
Liver disease
Sugar diabetes
Kidney stones
Tumors
Glaucoma
Gout
Renal failure
Asthma
Persistent trauma

Inside Greedy Monster's belly
We take small breaths
Disappear or at least try to with passwords etches in DNA

Swallow stinging nettle to stop itching
Racism covers epidermis
Solitary confinement
Shelter in place…anxiety

We are magic. I think I remember a poem about magic…oh yes, Joy Holland
spoke about magic and voodoo and blackness in one sentence

I count steps…just as I time hand washing rituals
"Out spot…" the Queen said. However, when she looked her hands were still
covered in blood.

This nation is covered in blood—cleanliness is a myth too like blackness.

Wanda Sabir, "Man in Ancestor Masque," Lip Festival, Senegal,
digital photograph, 2010.

Wanda Sabir, "Eleke Couldn't Save We," Rufisque, Senegal, West Africa, digital photograph, 2010.

Ancestors
Lorraine Bonner

The sisters love the ancestors
call their names and pour out water and rum
they love Dia de Los Muertos
because they love to build ofrendas

I don't build ofrendas
I don't want the ancestors to come
nature, nurture, the ancestors
of the ancestors
of my father and mother,
how could I trust any of them?

People say they gave you life
you should honor them for that
They don't know in a life spent longing
for death, how the days I wanted to live
are like tiny islands in the sea

It's true I feel unanchored, drifting
as if dropped without a backstory
into a movie I have never seen
the camera rolls on
takes me down a wet path
through ancient trees

I see a figure crouched in shadow
at the riverbank lifting deep brown mud
squeezing out the water, caressing the clay
the camera shifts, I am in her hands
I feel her shaping me

the camera shifts again, I am the shaper
I press a neck into your form
shift again and I am in your hands I was whole
now head and body
I know myself

I kiss your face your eyes and mouth emerge
you kiss my face I see your eyes

you are made of night and stars
you are made of earth and water

I touch your heart
I feel pain and the secret of healing
rush down my arms to my hands
which I have shaped just to hold these gifts

 I create your womb, plant two seeds
you create my womb I am carrying twins
This one I name Esperanza
This one I name Cassandra
Hope and the prophet of doom

I form your legs, they are of the river
my legs are of the river, I can't be still
I climb down from your hands and run
I release you from my hands
you are running away
I am running toward
my feet form the path as I run

I watch you disappear into the dark forest
already you have forgotten

but see
these
wet footprints

Lorraine Bonner Artist Statement

I was born a scientist.
As an undergraduate, I studied metamorphosis in insects, the way caterpillars grow, shed their skins, and transform into butterfies.
I began practicing art in response to personal trauma, and the art quickly metamorphosed into the larger skin of politics.
The political morphed into the spiritual and the scientist in me began asking questions too large for molecular answers.
I use clay, earth-flesh birthed as magma in the sea, raised to the mountaintops, and washed down to riverbeds, to create tactile and visual witness to the metamorphosis of our species.
www.lorrainebonner.com

Incantation for Black Lives to Remain in Focus After the Outrage Fades
Yeva Johnson
With gratitude to Community of Writers
and the BIPOC Writing Community's Carrie Mar

O, Wise One, we call on your essence.
We cleave to justice, but find only feather

pillows after the owl's flight, a shifting enemy.
We seek, O Mother, a path to prevent

more deaths, more suffering.
Let not our hearts' desires

immolate on scattered alliances fanned
by misbegotten echoes of promises

already broken. This time, let the sword strike
at the root to end this senseless cycle.

Yeva Johnson, a Pushcart Prize-nominated poet/musician/physician whose work appears or is forthcoming in the *Bellingham Review, Genre: Urban Arts' House Anthology No. 2, Sinister Wisdom*, and elsewhere, is a past Show Us Your Spines Artist-in-Residence (RADAR Productions/SF Public Library), winner of the Mostly Water Art & Poetry Splash Contest, Marin Poetry Center Board Member, and poet in QTPOC4SHO, a San Francisco Bay Area artists' collective.

Ajuan Mance, "Eve and Her Daughters," ink and digital collage.

"Eve and Her Daughters" depicts women from five of the oldest tribes on the planet, arranged in the style of a medieval tryptich. The central figure, a member of the San tribe symbolizes mitochondrial Eve, the common ancestor of us all. The halo-like sun is a collage element made from a remixed photo of the Ngorongoro crater, site of the earliest known human ancestors.

Ajuan Mance is a Professor of English at Mills College in Oakland, California and a lifelong artist and writer. In both her scholarly writing and her visual art, Ajuan explores the complexities of race, gender, and identity, Ajuan has shown her work at exhibitions and festivals from the Bay Area to Brooklyn. You can see more of her work at AjuanMance.com

joan tarika lewis, "Dancing on Water," 48 x 24 inches, 2018.

joan tarika lewis is a visual artist, musician, author, and political activist. At 16, she became the first woman to join the Black Panther Party, and helped create space for women to be seen as radical defenders of community and culture as Panther Lieutenant and graphic designer for the Black Panther newspaper. After leaving the party in 1969, she became a graphic artist and jazz violinist. She toured internationally with saxophonist John Handy and taught visual arts and jazz to inner city youth. She founded of the Oakland Black String Ensemble and works with women at the Healthy Babies Project.

Identity Poem
Xiomara Larkin

They ask me to write down my race
And I think and think very seriously
And consider writing down the truth
And have my answer read.

I am the sister of eleven with the mother who has no food
But spiritually I have plenty
Even with no shoes to spare I am free
I run through the wilderness and drink the spring water
I eat the mango off a tree
But I am not greedy I share with others
I have freedom
Inside this body.

I am a child raised by a child
I am the son of a father who went to war
With God on his side he survived
I am as strong as an ox
But as swift as a gazelle
My love for my brother is forever more
And I have love worth fighting for
Inside this body.

I have the faint whispers in my ear
The sound of Spanish music dancing in the air
I feel the love of my life whose heart beats
And the little girl who sees me
I smell the scent of arroz con leche
And chicharron de pollo
I have my country
Inside this body.

I have the punch of one thousand waves
And the kick of a kangaroo
But I have the flow of a streaming river
And the peace of nature

I have the fighting spirit planted into me
I have the determination to succeed in life
And the perseverance to accomplish anything
Inside this body.

I have the Spanish culture run through my bones
And African in my blood
My ancestors' conscience runs through my head
With all of the world stopping instead
I have the unfailing love in my heart
So that we will never be apart
My destiny runs
Inside this body.
But I stop and simply write down

Black

Xiomara Larkin lives in South San Francisco and is a senior at Sacred Heart Cathedral Preparatory. She has written poetry since she was twelve years old. She enjoys karate, swimming and dancing.

X
flight

on grief
Melissa Chen

My mom calls me one night when I'm in my brother's car. I don't pick up. I let it ring because my mom always calls, frantic, when there isn't an emergency. She calls my brother, and I hear her through the speakerphone. She cries and cries. Please take me to the hospital, I've been burned, it hurts, it hurts. My brother drives home. Our ceiling is singed and I hear my mother cry like I never have before, wailing like a yearning infant. It hurts, she says.

We take her to the hospital. She lies on the bed and cries. It hurts, she says. Can't you do anything for her? I ask the doctors. She tells me it hurts so much. They give her morphine, and she grows still for a while.

What feels like an eternity but is mere hours later, she asks to go home. What are they even going to do for me? She asks, lying on her side with her burns exposed, flesh raw. I don't understand how these can be classified as third-degree burns, these marks of fire and molten plastic that had ripped through my mother's flesh. I won't wait here forever, she mutters.

I do as she says, like a good daughter, and ask the doctors to send her home.

When she goes to meet her friends—even now—she tries to cover up those brown plumes of smoke billowing from her skin with long, flowing dresses and a wide smile.

/////////////////////////////////////

I'm 25 when my mom calls me, frantic.

I'm across the country, grabbing lunch on a workday. Sometimes I think I leave home so that I can screen her calls. I don't want to pick up. She calls again. Frantic, I can hear the panic, the tears. Your dad has cancer, we thought it was a stroke, but it's not. Your dad has cancer, I don't know if he has long. Please come home and see him.

I leave work in haste. I don't know why I'm sad. I never had a good relationship with my father, but something wells in my heart.

I fly home. He's in a hospital gown when I see him. Tattered. Puts his hands on my face gently. His hands don't smell like anything. It's weird. He used to hit me with those hands that always smelled of history burning.

My father
a giant I always feared
now small and frail.
///
I wrote a poem once about my father beating my mom.

My professor reads it, and tells me to consider carefully before sharing it. I hear in his voice that he would rather I not. It's...too personal, he says. I think I know what he means, but then again I don't. I nod.

In my dorm that night, I look at my ceiling, and wonder which parts of me are too raw to expose.
///
My father doesn't smell like cigarettes. It's strange. His hands are soft, sweaty when he reaches for my face. I left money for you, okay? He tells me with a thick voice. For you to buy a house. I nod, and sit in a chair that makes me stiff for hours.

I'm restless.

I go home that night, lying on a hard bed.

Go to sleep, my mom says.
///
Don't tell your parents how long he has, my cousin tells me. It will just upset them. I roll my eyes.

Terminal. Stage 4. How many people have Stage 4 cancer?

Does my father become 1 in a long string of numbers to fall into memory? What does it mean to grieve someone you never really understood?

A white man asks me about my dad and his cancer. I say matter-of-factly that my father had smoked for all his life. The man stops me. We don't judge here, he says. The insides of me snap, like twigs turning to cinder. This stranger knew nothing of how I often looked at my father with fearful eyes, watching plumes of smoke rising to our yellow ceilings.

He doesn't know of how I dig through my memories every now and then, remember when I'd asked my father to stop smoking as a child. You're so smart, he'd dismissed me. I will.

When I see *The Farewell* for the first time, tears well up in my eyes and I cry in the dark of the movie theater. What is fact or fiction but narratives spun and woven differently?

I let all the grief I hold in my heart spin out onto the screen staring back at me. Lulu Wang sees me, and I feel real.

//

A child of Chinese immigrants. How far back does my origin story begin?

I'm a child of knots, of convoluted memories and staggering contradictions. I'm a balloon filled with things I don't say. I like to think that my parents loved me with what they had, but not what I needed.

I'm stiff. My muscles strain, trying their best to wring out all meaning from me.

What does it mean that I can feel trauma from generations beyond my memory? What does it mean to ache for people I never even knew?

I always carry grief in my pocket. I can feel the ache of it in every cavity of my body.

Where do I begin? What does it mean that my mother married a man to go to America in the 1980s, traversing across uncertainty, through a Hong Kong muddled by fear for the Handover to come, to arrive in America, mei gok—land of gold and beauty, so that the children she bore could live a better life than she had?

So that I could live this life away from her?

Everything I do, I do for you, she tells me over the phone, sullen. Why raise children when all they do is leave you the first chance they get?

I don't have any of the answers. All I ever do

All I can ever try to do is try to be brave and think for myself and to wedge myself open

to fly

for my forebearers who couldn't.

Melissa Chen is a second generation Chinese American hailing from New York City. She graduated with an M.A. in Asia Pacific Studies from the University of San Francisco, and continues to reside in the city.

240

untitled
Shayna Gee

Ma and I have never seen snow.

she says the color

white is for funerals only.

                    & that

the only way to attend a funeral is
if your face is whiter than the dead one.

                    She never buys anything in white

only
sumac stained
gold doused
colors that shout—   *I'm alive!*

                    She kept us away from white:

shoelaces
hair ties

                    among other dead things with no
                    names

ahma,

                    whose cheek

I imagine

                    halved,

crunchy
pyrus pears

                    pillowing in a crate

six

                    feet apart—

I mean,

                    below.

During ma's graveyard shift

she pats layers of
                              concealer
using a sponge   & ring finger
until it is
                    the only thing
on her face.

                                        When ma devours

I imagine   it

        congee   salt   pork

scallions   gelatinous century
egg   perfuming her nose
the concealer   melting
in the steam   bowl.

I imagine
                                gesso on fresh canvas

        bone   white   snow

what the thing would look like,
spotting
                                red gold
                                vermillion
                                to name a few.

Shayna Gee (she/they) is a first-generation non-binary Chinese poet living on stolen Ramaytush Ohlone land also known as San Francisco, California. They have a degree in sociology from Mills College and will be forthcoming in *West Trestle Review* and twice in the zine space *All Female Menu* in 2021. They are a tiger in the Chinese zodiac and a middle child of two sisters.

gulper eels drink agua fresca when they're daydreaming
Lina Begonia

in a past life i was gulper eel
deep sea depths / wandering in the dark / always

hungry / for books? / for money? / for love?
i don't know / insatiable urge / it's always been

normal / every shot / every blunt / every
puff of nicotine / spliff / clouds of blue dream

spent my youth daydreaming in sweatpants / hot cheeto fingers
fluorescent dust wedged under acrylic nails / fire hydrant

red was my favorite / i was never allowed color / church didn't
want us dreaming / mama hid the polish / my fresh set stained

white choir togas / grubby red fingers / cracked hands couldn't
cleanse the red / baking soda made it brown / pale yellow / never

white / i've seen it before / your childhood best friend losing their home
all consuming / bloated parasites / an empire of silicon / glittering

gold pavements only for the imported / skilled / upper middle class
white / the city never cared for us / liccardo doesn't give a shit

we only had each other / my best friend & i / greedy
starving / cherished morsels of nacho fries at la vics

swimming in orange sauce / we tucked our bodies in art museums
searching for a new story / playground / an adventure hidden in

plain sight / we used the hilton for free restrooms / ran fingers against marble
walls / sat on steps to listen to the jazz concert gated by fences / they could
never

stop us / music cannot be restrained / we are gulper eels / accustomed to
deep sea pressure / the notes float on pollen / filling stuffy noses with

peppermint / skin glistening & browned by the heat wave we drank
fresa / piña / agua fresca till our bodies felt sick with sugar

guess i'm thanking you, mother bird
Lina Begonia

for all the overripe permissions / purple orchids / dusty bundles of
kale washed carefully by hands that serve garden cats / your kindest captors
you are my green thumb / patis / sweet & sour sauce / bean sprout lumpia

no pork / the way papa likes it
the voice in my head telling me to make my bed
wipe down counters / scrub the grime / don't become your father
if i scrub hard enough / do i become an altar?
cleanliness is next to godliness / or clamp

shut? / like mother like child / i was never your daughter
searching for you everywhere
succulents / ginger / ceylon tea
scarlet red tomatoes that'll never be as sweet as
the ones you grew & broke soil / backs / blistering skin
 all those summers searching for

you in people / ravenous mouthfuls of skin, tissue, & fragments of
a lover / all bones
mouthfuls of affirmations / lungs of smoke
all the blueberries in the world in lieu of
a love i would never receive / how would you know?
you were never given the chance

to taste honey / figs / gulay / seafood pasta / opposed to
thorny mouthfuls / applicant rejections
greedy fingers / foul mouthed daughters
worms in my teeth / disjointed sentences / death by a stubborn god

what was the last thing you said to your mother before
you never saw her again?

i never asked / we fought too much
gnawing at my tongue / cheek / drawing pools of
blood / there are cops at the door / when did i learn to be afraid?
Did he ever touch you anywhere? / mother's averting eyes tell all
like mother, like child
she swallows her tongue in shame
the weight rests upon buckling knees & weary shoulders

the pacific has cleansed me of all the muck & grime
Am I holy enough for you now that I've drenched myself in salt water?

that whiskey in belly / curry steams on top of a bed of rice / morning
throwup / dirty teeth / burning of my fingertips when i get too close to the
flame

i smoke through every phone call / the blunt is next / the white noise is
paralyzing / mama's disappointed chatter in my brain passed down

like a mother bird tryna feed her baby
but they choke instead

Lina Begonia was originally born in the heart of Downtown San Jose and now
lives in the Sunset District, SF. Lina looks for inspiration within Filipinx myths,
nature, and the upturning of family secrets. Currently, they're a student at CCSF
studying for their certificate in Youth Work after completing a degree in Asian
American Studies (BA) and Race & Resistance Studies (Minor) at SF State.

Shizue Seigel; detail from "Luko Loco," mixed media photograph.

The Tongue Remembers
Romina Saha

In Malabon where I grew up
the market vendors
sold vegetables in shapes and colors
and textures and tastes
considered strange in Silicon Valley.
They sold whole fish for frying
with heads on till the eyes bulged
and the scales were crunchy
and the tails crispy.
We ate chicken feet and intestines
impaled in bamboo sticks
and barbecued on the sidewalk
sour fruits dipped
in salty fermented tiny shrimp
crushed chilis in vinegar or fish
sauce.
We braised beef tripe and innards
ox tongue and pig knuckles
for hours till tender
Boiled pork blood in vinegar
And chicken blood with green
papaya
Roasted whole pigs on a spit
And fried chicken with crispy skin.
We ate rice flavored with *pandan*
And sticky rice wrapped in banana
leaves.
We drank green mango juice
And calamansi nectar.
We ate avocado with milk and sugar
and caramelized wax gourd.

In Silicon Valley where I live
I eat skinned chicken
And steaks trimmed of fat
Beheaded fish
Descaled, too
Oranges and apples
And giant bananas
Crusty bread dipped
In balsamic vinegar and olive oil
Pink salt from Trader Joe's
Rice vinegar and brewed soy sauce
From Whole Foods.
Here no market is wet
No haggling is allowed
No shouting is permitted

Sometimes in San Jose
When I swallow
there's a lump in my throat
and an ache in my stomach.
Memories of that home
conflict with memories of this home.
I think I will go to the Asian store
and buy my remembrances.
I will cook *kare-kare* or *adobo*
or perhaps *sinigang*.

pandan – an aromatic plant popularly used in Southeast Asian cooking
kare-kare – a Philippine stew often cooked with beef and vegetables in a
peanut-based sauce
adobo – a dish typically made with chicken or pork braised in soy sauce,
vinegar, and garlic
sinigang – a Philippine soup dish that can be made with beef, pork, fish, or
shrimp cooked with vegetables in a sour tamarind-based broth

Twelve Grapes
Jesus Francisco Sierra

At the end of a year I'd rather forget, I've thought a lot about this ritual of ours. The last New Year's Eve I spent in Havana was at the end of 1968 when I was eleven years old. There are two things I remember about that night: the panic I felt at the sound of gunshots and the comfort I sensed eating twelve grapes for good luck—fear and hope wrapped in that singular infinite stroke of midnight, lasting a moment, lasting a lifetime.

When I asked, I was told that those were gunshots into the air to celebrate the arrival of the New Year. It scared me to think about where the bullets might fall. "Don't worry about it," my Mom said. "We're safe here." But then I thought about how the bullets went up in one year and landed in the next, fear crossing the threshold of time.

My brother and I sat in the living room and watched Mom fret over the ritual that had been a part of our lives since we were born. Her voice echoed from the other room, imploring us to never forget the grapes at midnight, because that would always bring us hope.

My older sister reached into the fridge and retrieved five small bowls, each with twelve grapes. She placed them on the table. There were only four of us, but my Mom insisted on putting out five bowls, the fifth in memory of my father who'd died three years before.

"And the bucket?" she asked

"I'll get it," my sister answered.

"Make sure it has plenty of water in it. Fill it to the top," my mother added.

At midnight, Mom emptied the bucket of water into the street ridding us of the evil spirits that might have entered our house in the previous year.

Hearing the pop of gunshots, I looked up to the flat concrete roof above us and wondered if it was strong enough to stop a bullet. We'd survived worse. After my father died, Mom protected us. She'd always been the roof over our heads. I ate my grapes and hoped the new year would bring us our visas, because it was what she wanted.

Nine months later, we emigrated to the United States.

* * *

In December of 2019, when I'd been living in San Francisco for fifty years, a pandemic rose on the other side of the world and lifted stealthily. Unlike the strident sound of rising bullets, it dropped with a loud thud the next year, spreading unimpeded throughout the globe and devastating those who were caught without a roof to protect them. I'm one of the lucky ones. After building a business over the last twenty years, so accustomed am I to good fortune that I don't recall if I ate any grapes December 31, 2019, but I must have, because that's what we do, and because good fortune can be fleeting.

Forced to shelter for the greater good as the virus spreads. I find optimism in my seclusion. Like most Cubans, I'm used to not having. I'm used to doing with less. I'm used to understanding that it's not what comes, but how I receive it that counts. Isolation, at first a curious challenge, inspires innovation. The time alone for a while is a welcome respite from my rushed and frantic work life. Being trapped at home, I am left with only my imagination to get me through. I record videos of my girlfriend and me dancing in the kitchen. I set up a home office, work in my pajamas, read books I've put off reading for years, binge on TV shows, and I begin that novel I've always wanted to write. I find ways to keep busy and pass the time, and like everyone else I suspect that it won't last, that normalcy is a matter of weeks away because our intelligence and intellectual superiority will overcome it all. I figure it'll be a fun experiment, that I'll laugh about it with friends a month or two later.

Then people begin to die, and I am engulfed by a sense of darkness. My life flattens into a world where human contact is reduced to the two-dimensional plane of virtual meetings on computer screens leading to what feels like a collective depression, where hope seems elusive. I watch in disbelief as people in their desperation align themselves with a despot that stands for everything that's wrong with this country, as if hatred and divisiveness will somehow lead them out of despair.

Too much of my life and my routines are disrupted. The end of the pandemic has faded and has disappeared into an uncertain future. Fear once again crossing the threshold of time. And now, as human contact wanes, it leaves behind a chill that reinforces my need of touch. I miss the feel of a handshake, the warmth of an embrace, the sound of a shared laughter, a slap on the back, a kiss on the cheek. I miss being around my community, my friends, my family. Yet, I've rediscovered something I've lost by living a life that often feels like the only goal is to get ahead, a mad dash to get my own. It's as if the universe has hit the pause button and forced onto me the time to recalibrate and evaluate what's really important, to consider change. It is then that I remember a day, back in Cuba, when we were celebrating my sister's sixteenth birthday. A group of her friends came over. I was only a kid then, but I remember them dancing to the music from a tiny record player when the electricity went out. The collective moan that followed soon rose into a song, and even in the dark, everyone joined the chorus and continued to dance.

With vaccines on the way the end of the pandemic is by now at least a notion, even though the virus is mutating ahead of the vaccinations, trying to escape our attempt to regain normalcy. In light of all that the year has taught me about how much we ought to value each other, I wonder if others feel the same. They must, because in our absence we've never been more aware of each other. But I also question whether normalcy will instead serve to devolve our collective appreciation for each other and hurl us back into public isolation.

December 31, 2020, the family gathers at my sister's home. She walks in from the garage with a bucket filled with water and places it near the entrance to the house. She opens the door, and we count down to midnight. When the clock strikes twelve, she opens the door and launches the water out onto the sidewalk and with it all the bad that has transpired in the previous year. We all reach for our grapes. My brother, my sister, and I look over at the two bowls in front of empty chairs. I remember where we come from and I think, despite how far we've come, even when it's dark, we still dance. I decide then that hope can indeed exist alone, without the fear, and be wrapped up in that singular infinite stroke of midnight, lasting a moment, lasting a lifetime.

Jesus Francisco Sierra emigrated from Cuba in 1969 to San Francisco's Mission District. His work has appeared in *Zyzzyva, Solstice Literary Magazine, The Acentos Review, Gulf Stream Literary Journal, The Bare Life Review,* and *Lunch Ticket* among others. He is a member of The Writers Grotto, a VONA Voices Alum, holds an MFA from Antioch University Los Angeles and is a structural engineer.

Code Switch
Lorraine Bonner

Scars are bilingual
they speak fluent pain
vocabularies of terror and sorrow
stories of a single moment of inattention
or a lifetime of powerlessness

Scars' second language
an algebra of engineering
a bridge that not only joins
but draws together the land
on either side
creates a smooth seam
out of a raw gash

scars translate pain into healing
into empathy or hunger for revenge
comradeship born of shared struggle
or retreat into bitter solitude

some forsake their mother tongue
to pass for unscarred among the unwounded
others code switch with ease
dance along the waves of rupture and redemption
letting light shine out
through poems written in their skin

Lorraine Bonner, "Mending Takes You to Another Dimension."

Lorraine Bonner turned to art to deal with personal trauma. Her work has moved from personal/political betrayal, in the *Perpetrator* series, to a vision of humanity beyond socially defined "color" in the *Multi-Hued Humanity* series. She calls her current series *Mending*, creating new beauty from our scars and broken places.

Thirty
David Renteria

I'll tell you about a peculiar evening. We were just Johnny and me taking hits on his balcony. The hour was pleasant enough for the Bay. The sun went down easy. There was the ever-present Oakland chill, like a whisper crawling up the back of your shirt. We got to talking about English, the silliness of it. Trough versus through and so on. I asked Johnny when they let him stop taking ESL classes. Dude, he said. I was born here. I never took an ESL class.

It didn't occur to me that most people I know didn't learn English. They know it as a birthright, the way I knew Spanish. Johnny told me about his parents, who came from Laos before he was born. They only let him watch, read, and speak American: Sesame Street, Harry Potter, Power Rangers. His mom herself knew only a little English, so the house was mostly quiet while his dad was at work. He started learning Lao when he was 12, after his grandmother said she would stop visiting unless they showed their heritage some respect. I didn't get to tell her anything worth telling, Johnny said, because she died of breast cancer a year after that. Do they regret teaching you so late, I asked him. He said probably him more than them.

I said, Johnny, I didn't know you had a grandma. I didn't even know you had parents, that's how little about you I know. Johnny didn't take offense. He's more private than most—not aggressively private, but he knows that's how it comes off sometimes. He just turned his head and exhaled, the smoke stacking in the air above his shoulder. Eye for an eye, he said.

I thought for a bit. Okay, I said. Here's a good one: I was six years old when we got to the U.S. My mom told me not to tell anyone we were from Mexico. She said, if anybody asks, we're from California. Don't tell. My expatriate aunts warned her of neighbors tattling on neighbors. They said there would be a knock on the door, stocky men in green jumpsuits, and then—blam!—back to Mexico, quick as you like. Don't tell, she said. And it was true: neighbors really tattled on neighbors. La Migra really did pull into driveways. Some of us really were deported.

A few months after we got here, mom dropped me off at Edward Kemble Elementary School for my first day of second grade. During recess, Giovanna Trujillo told me about her brother. She said, did you know my brother has three snakes? I asked her how big. She said, two of them are babies, but the other one—she stretched her arms out wide—is this big. I said, well did you know my family's from Mexico? She said, mine too. No, I said. Like I was born there. Ohhhh. She got it, the gravity of it. I was pleased. I told her, but if anyone asks, tell them I'm from California.

Johnny asked me if I had liked Giovanna Trujillo. I told him I had. She'd had red glasses and a long braid and soft cheeks and a kind face. I didn't know English, so when I needed to use the bathroom she'd ask Ms. Rochelle for me. I would stand next to her while she got the ok. Then Ms. Rochelle would look at me and nod. I might as well have been sucking my thumb.

He asked if I still talked to her. I didn't. I moved the summer before fourth grade, then three times after that. The depth of my friendships ran pretty well shallow, I told him.

He said, I can't imagine that. Living somewhere they don't speak my language. I said I couldn't either.

We let that sit for a while, the thought dissipating in the dark currents of concrete airs and bellowing freight trains. I did the zipper on my coat.

Johnny took another hit. It's out, he said, and spilled the ash onto the bannister. He asked me if I was staying over. I told him I wasn't. He let me know to lock the door before I left. Then he went inside.

I remembered one day about ten years ago. I was doing homework in my room, in the house where my parents still live. I heard the heavy duty rumble of dad's truck pull into the driveway, which put me on edge because the sun was still out. Dad usually got home well past 8 in the evening, unless he forgot something. If that happened, he pulled in, opened the garage, grabbed whatever he forgot to load up that morning, and went right back to work. That day he came in through the front door. I heard him walk to the kitchen, to his room, to mine. Ey Beto, he said. Y su mama? I told him she was watering the plants in the backyard. Okay, he said, and left.

One beat. Two beats; shouts. That was mom. Dad doesn't shout. I heard mom go into her room. I sat at my desk until I heard the truck start, then recede. She wiped her eyes when I walked in. I asked her what happened. She sat on her bed and very calmly told me dad wasn't getting paid for his last job, at a house he'd been working for almost two weeks. I asked her why. Porque no quieren, she said. Pero no se preocupe. She promised we'd be okay. Ya dios sabra. She told me to go do my homework.

I know why the thought came up that night at Johnny's. I hope to tell him about it someday, if we get close enough. That most days I understand why they brought us here. But sometimes I think of my dad's truck pulling in, and my mom sitting on her bed. And I wonder why anyone would want to live in this country.

David Renteria is 26. He's lived in Sacramento, Berkeley, and Oakland. He's been undocumented since he was 6.

mestiza
Lina Begonia

mestiza (n.): of latin american origin, also used in the philippines to denote a woman of mixed race. commonly refers, in the context of the philippines, to a mixed filipina woman.

Anytime a white woman looks at me,
she does not paint me mestiza, she cat
- egorizes me as ambiguity, the bridg
- ing of two cultures, two lands, two
people who never committed in the
first place.

She allows me to take her purse, not
without removing her wallet, laugh
- ing as she says,
     - "Just in case!"

She does not see me as mestiza, or
grant me the keys of whiteness.

She leads me to the gate and slams the door in my face.

*Asian invasion"
"Beware the Yellow Peril"
Enjoy your chow mein

—Max Leung

ars poetica II
vanessa diaz cabrera

I want my words to dance in your heart
skin unpeel and let the words set the rhythm

I want words of resonance
humming, thrumming across a page near you

the words of my dreams
negligently cared for but always loved
fixtures of my life:
el salvador, ghosts, lakes, birds,
all the women and none of them at all

the way I look at you, with love
amassed words I could never tell you

these words I dedicate to you, all of you.

Seigel, Comparsa, Oaxaca, Mexico, 2013.

Bruja Halfbreed
Deborah K. Tash

I have never tried to pass for white
Submerged in the confusion of assimilation
As my mother impugned
"Don't tell people you are Mexican!"
Her pride that people joked about me as a child
"Where'd you steal the big Swede from?"
Her black black hair in contrast
To my blonde blonde curls

Bruja Halfbreed

When Swedes and Norwegians spoke to me
Their language incomprehensible
I always explained my heritage
Claiming my otherness
Not like my mother who told people
She was Italian rather than Mexican
While demanding I learn Spanish
Because Abuela refused to speak English

Bruja Halfbreed

I never tried to pass for white
Though others assumed me to be
I coped by thinking myself incognito
But always spoke up to claim my heritage
Bearing the legacy of my mother's self-hatred
In never feeling good enough
Not just because of polio and sexual abuse
But also because I always felt an outsider

Bruja Halfbreed

I searched for a way to answer my blood
The reverberations of the land calling
Echoing in the ways of the natives of the plains
And once again assumed to be a white woman
When I went to powwow and gatherings
Still I claimed myself Mestiza
Determined to claim all of my heritage
Regardless of blue eyes, fair skin, blonde hair

Bruja Halfbreed

Such a disappointment to my mother
Schooled in internalized racism
Purify the race by marrying a white man
While I longed to understand my blood
Dancing beneath the moon in a staghorn circle
Teasing her because my brother looked like Cochise
Refusing to fully assimilate and pass for white
Though others assumed I was

Bruja Halfbreed

Now I write at 2:30 in the dark of night
Unable to sleep because once again
I am accused of passing for white
And my soul demands I take note
To set the record straight
That I am a Bruja Halfbreed
And my blood roars in protest
To claim all that I am

Deborah K. Tash: Born in 1949 in Oakland and raised in Alameda, I was shaped by a dual heritage. A Mestiza, I have explored the Mexican half of my heritage from my mother's line, recently discovering that both of my maternal grandparents may have been Yaqui. I am also exploring in my poetry and art my father's English/Irish/Scottish line which includes strong Celtic influences.

Left: Deborah K. Tash, "In the Shadow of Childhood."

What It Is (No. 2)
Irmin Arcibal

This is a grasshopper
with exoskeletal issues
still trying to shed sticky, discarded narcissus scar tissue.
Can't shake it, or flake it away.
This is a thank you, a blank stare
written into thin air, bluffing.
Nothing up my sleeve, this is a trick.
This is walking the line
between catharsis and carsick.
This is vomiting butterflies on the carpet.
This is alarm clock karma marmalade,
formulaic, but non-habit forming.
This is a foray into euphoria,
an unforced error, unmistakably inescapable.
This is the most honest thing I've ever said.
This is pure sediment— inevitable. Eventually
this is all numerical, empirically.
This is filling sidewalk cracks with confessions.
This is sessions spent scrawling similes on freeway signs.
This is signing my name on nothing that means anything.
This is an arbitrary word count placed upon the value of a picture,
the exchange rate between pixel and syllable.
How ephemeral.
This is the fine line between sublime and subliminal.
This is our glass, no halfs,
filled with nothing,
filled with everything.
This is an hourglass.
This is hourglass sand
flipping, flipping, flipping.
This is an hourglass sandbox.
This is hourglass sandcastles crumbling into the vortex,
mixing into fresh mortar for more hourglass sandcastles.
This is our glass box.
This is a fine lattice.
This is tracing old light with my fingertip.
This is slippery.
This is a rainy day picnic in the park.
This is the lifeline impressed upon the flesh of my palm.

This is oxygen rusting my tongue.
This is a must-see trust fall with the earth's crust.
This is mustard cutting.
This is the fireworks show that comes from fairy dust combusting.
This is the cusp of sunrise in the east.
This is gastric bypass in the belly of the beast.
This is bees stinging.
This is bees being stingy with their stingers
because they see the ghosts of bees past.
This is where the bees go.
This is what beats.
This is a blessing.
This is throat clearing.
This is chest weight lessening.
This is uncomfortable.
This is comforting.

Irman Arcibal. Vallejo-born & raised, San Francisco artist/poet/educator Irman Arcibal immerses himself in the concepts of interaction and synchronicity. His visual art involves drawing & related processes; his poems incorporate rhythmic rambling, musical wordplay & crafted chronicle of sensory experience. Irman earned his Art Studio MFA from UC Davis, after a Bachelor's in Biological Sciences at Cal Poly SLO. He also studied art & poetry at Solano College.

Victor Navarette, untitled, mixed media. Photo by Martin Revolo. Bio: p. 258

A Prayer for Extinction
Vickie Ya-Rong Chang

The water pours obediently from the hard metallic neck like a domesticated grey wolf. On, off gushing, dripping, moving at the flick of my hand, as if I am Shiva himself. I mechanically lean on the plastic lever and the alchemy of fat and water stamps my yellow palm. The hands meet, as they do, again and again through the day, cleaning.

A spark of fear—COVID-19—washed away.

I gaze numbly out the glass as if I am a translucent film projected on a screen, a frozen piece of what man calls art. Day 3 of interminable torture caused by hundreds thousands millions of moments of disrespect of violent ripping from our beloved powerful mother.

Smoke

Poison

Lungs

Air

The eye follows the bright green hollow stems—竹子 (zhú zi, bamboo)

up

up

up

and a miracle.

Perched at the tip, swaying slightly in the wind, is 蜻蜓 (qīng tíng, dragonfly).

The eyes close and open rapidly, in shock. I had literally forgotten they existed. The lips creep up. I breathe in delight as the spongy twin lobes, the magical lungs, expand.

A message. She lives. I live. We are connected. There is hope.

Weeks pass, then the heat rises and I feel the dryness in my thick raven locks, immune to coconut oil, as the wind caresses my cheeks like a lover and I feel the curl of dread in the belly.

Fire.

On an innocent sunny afternoon as the moon ripens to fullness, time pauses and again the air is filled with the screams of wise elders (wood), of tiny creatures, the pitter patter of their limbs indistinguishable to my gross ears so I watch them in the yard. Busy moving secure in their purpose. Destiny not a question.

Their bodies burn burn burn.

I go to the sea, my mother. I watch her ripple beckon dance. She is always changing, she is alive, like I long to be. With no mind colonized by the white man by immigration by Chinese patriarchy and the violence of capitalism, always hungry for more more more and becoming ever more empty inside.

I watch my mother, the sea, I feel her in my belly, and I see the Ohlone. In boats, swimming, striding across the land with the wind at their backs. Man and animal. Unlike any man I know in this domesticated, unceded land. Where the wind the moon the stars as they pound the heart and move the blood guide each movement, every dance, the very shape of their days. Picking blackberries at the height of ripeness, loved to juiciness by the sun, the salt in the air moistening them just so. Where blackberry like acorn is a friend a sister a mother, not a commodity to be raped to extinction, to be bought and sold, rushed to bloom with poison created by men, always men, in white coats, glass tubes, in wooden boxes so far from the sun the moon the wind that they have literally forgotten their own names. The vowels of 妈妈 (māmā, mother), 亲人 (qī rén, loved ones) confusing the tongue.

The sea laps gently against the strong jagged rocks that hold my weary heart, grief rage pain heavy in my limbs.

She is timeless
she has seen it all
she gives everything
and we only take.

The heavy head bows in sorrow and then the thought lifts the eyes in wonder—

Should I pray for human extinction?

Is that how we protect our mother—the winged ones floating on her wide body, dotting the sky, falling dead in the hundreds thousands in the southwest as these fingers curl around a piece of plastic and the heart writes and the tears fall.

Some cultures see suicide as an act of honor or perhaps a thinly veiled remnant of hyper masculinity wrapped in the unappetizing figure of patriarchy. For the choice of death when given the ultimate gift of life is the worst form of cowardice.

No, no, I decide.

And clarity straightens the spine and clears the throat, fills the dull head pounding from inhaling death, from the pain of living beneath wood rather than the open blue sky.

The 飛龍 (fēi lóng, dragonfly) comes alive inside as I pledge myself to her once again.

The vow like a holy seed planted long long ago in rich soil.

Time unravels backwards across generations, lifetimes, dynasties, continents, worlds.

We were hers from the beginning.
We are her.
There is no separation.
We are always together.

The second daughter of Chinese immigrants, Vickie Ya-Rong Chang was born and raised in the Bay Area. In her work as a psychologist and writer, she is dedicated to personal = collective liberation. She is shaped by her relationship with the land/culture/people of the Divine Buddha Temple (Taiwan), Arunachala (India), Sangre de Cristo Mountains (New Mexico), and Chinese ancestral practices.

Victor Navarette grew up near Santiago, Cuba, and studied art in Havana. He left the country in 1980 in search of artistic freedom. After working for the Spanish-language press in the Mission, he bought Radio Habana Social Club 20 years ago. His Valencia Street café is filled with powerful surrealist sculptures created in his studio at the Hunters Point Shipyard. Often created from cast-offs, his work celebrates the redemptive power of art in face of oppression.

When I Am Spent
Leslie Yee-Murata

life as we know it has ended
systems come crashing down
all motives come under scrutiny
fear and doubt loom large
into my seventh decade of life
will i be forgotten?
did my life really matter?
did i make a difference?
did i tell everyone i love them?
did i squander my time
in the shadows in
the same damned stories?
why keep wallowing in the dark side
aren't i sick and tired of the bullshit
can i forgive myself and forge new thoughts?
can i swallow the bitterness of regrets
pushing myself uphill to new vistas
thinly disguised attempts to keep connected
finding us both just flapping our lips
there is a sense of urgency to tie up loose ends
black becomes white
white becomes black
colors lose their luster
all collapse into a dull gray
how i long for real, not fake, news
when did i become obsolete?
feeling I'm being swallowed down an hourglass funnel
into the dark endless pit inside of me
crumbling into grains of sand
melting into molten glass by icy flames
cooling and then shattering into shards
with all its jagged edges i cling to those shards
my fingers bleed as i frantically try
to glue the shards back together
those fragments of self lost forever
should i let go and free fall
to freedom from pain and despair
or will it just be more of the same
what happened to my JOY for life?

in my room first light
illuminates motes of dust... ash... skin cells
suspended in artificially charged air

and yet my crystals emit glorious rainbow sparks
to dance
distracting my mind with spiritual drumming
delving into uncharted vistas of molecules
far away galaxies and internal dimensions
while being held hostage by a minuscule virus
yet my heart silently screams "choose life!"
new reflections new directions
do i have the courage to escape the prison of my mind
to be reborn with renewed resilience?

Leslie Yee-Murata is a native San Franciscan, fourth generation of Chinese Immigrants. She attended City College of San Francisco, San Francisco State University, and San Francisco Art Institute in graphic art and art education, and became a graphic artist, art teacher and jewelry designer. Currently devoted to writing and the healing arts, her writing appears in the anthologies *From Both Shores* and *Window*.

Some Sort of Samsara
Kimi Sugioka

The finches are the boss of the bird feeder; they scare the chickadees and
juncos away
People with covid are overflowing the hospitals

A curfew of curlews and a contradiction of dowitchers excavate their dinner
at low tide
The undocumented and poor cannot work; cannot provide food for their
families

A committee of terns dives for minnows
They cannot pay their rent and are being evicted

Murders of crows are learning to find food in the tidal zone
The red and black and brown people are dying the fastest

A colony of gulls is dejected about the lack of McDonald's scraps
The factory and farmworkers live and work in close proximity, in large
unprotected groups

A paddling of buffleheads settles on the estuary
The Hopi and Navajo have set up roadblocks

The pelicans have left for the winter
There are no hospitals on the reservations

The egrets dance the Egyptian as they fish for their dinners
The wealthier people work from home; comfortable and safe

The snowy plover forage in a loud and busy ponderance
The rich are getting richer off the impoverishment of the people

A water dance of grebes dive in serpentine synchronization
The people are lonely and desperate and may not gather in gaggles, flocks or
murmurations

but we watch the birds as though our lives depend upon their wings

Time Does Not Pardon
Nicole Henares

Trauma is a time traveler and time is a goon that does not pardon. Time is also as pendular as it is circular. The past, present and future are always swirling around us. Yet, when there is violence, if it is something that we don't guard ourselves against from a place of love, we can never find a better future.

The conditions that many of us have been feeling since 2016 are laughable to what we are facing now—A global pandemic, cultural unrest, political unrest, systematic racism that has gone backwards to 1965, and reporting for Title 9 horribly effecting the ways students are supported if and when they come forward about sexual assault and intimate partner violence.

My school is no exception to these problems. As I face another semester of distance learning and realize I will be teaching a staggered synchronous and asynchronous schedule of six 35-minute classes a day, I have never felt clearer about who I am and what I bring to the classroom.

Compassion means to suffer with, and to celebrate. I celebrate that teachers are encouraged to move towards project-based assessment and meaning in our curriculum rather than tests and quizzes.

I see this moment in education as pivotal, requiring us to bring out our best selves, rooted in compassion—this moment of a global pandemic where some students are working 40 hours to support their families, or are living out of a garage. And yet I must not confuse my compassion for pity, superiority, or condescension. Compassion is a way to say, I have been there too. But I realize my high school experiences were nothing like what my students are experiencing now.

Though I was not teaching over the summer, to say things were challenging would be an understatement. Between Herr leader firing rubber bullets and tear gas on peaceful protestors, an unarmed SF youth killed by Vallejo police, mass protests, some with masks, some without, COVID-19, my father's ailing health, and ghosts, my school has erupted with students past and present coming forward with detailed allegations of sexual assault. I still am facing memories of what happened to me as a teenager, and what happened to my peers, both males and females, and the feelings of powerlessness because I did not know how to say what had been happening, much less where to go or who to ask for help.

In 1989, when I was in the 10th grade my friends and I were being groomed by a 30-year-old man who worked at the skating rink and was part of the same roller skating community we belonged to. He said he enjoyed being around us because we made him feel young. His niece skated at the rink too and we all thought of him like an uncle. At this time I was a very shy 14-year-old being raised by a single mother. I was estranged from my father, and grateful to have the attention of someone whom I regarded like a father figure. I was also a survivor of early childhood sexual abuse by an adult older cousin—something that I also never told. My grandparents were immigrants who had worked in the canneries and the fields. My father, the Executive Director of Big Brothers and Big Sisters for Monterey County, was trying to start programs to give more support to Latino youth. I was well aware of the privileges I had that my father and my grandparents did not have. I did not want to bring any shame to my family by discussing what was happening to me.

I never wanted to believe what was happening until one of my friends called the man out for shamelessly putting his hands over BOTH of our chests in a photo as a "joke." That photo says a thousand words—my friend's face is frozen in horror to see what he was doing to me because he was doing the same thing to her, and both of us have our hands up pushing his hands away. We were 14 years old. He was 30. A few months later he bought alcohol for my best friend and took advantage of her when she was very intoxicated. It was just a few days before her 16th birthday. Her parents filed a police report when he brought her home drunk. A male officer came out to her house to investigate, but he shamed her for underage drinking and she never told any adult what else had happened, and neither did I.

The spring of 1989, I was in a Health Class at Carmel High taught by a male teacher who had notoriously married one of his former students when she was an adult, though granted, it was after she was his student. The subject and this teacher made me feel overwhelmed and uncomfortable, so I pretended to sleep during sex ed. I should have held the teacher accountable for how uncomfortable he made me feel, but I didn't have the agency. I should have ditched, but I was terrified of my mother, so I pretended to sleep. The teacher threw erasers at me and never considered my perspective or his subject matter. He never even thought to go to my mother or my counselor about how and why I would be sleeping during sex ed. What particularly baffles me is that this teacher was also the teacher in charge of Peer Counseling. I got a D- in the class. He's dead now, but if he were alive, I would confront him. I'd like to think he'd understand. I'd like to think if my Health teacher had been more aware and gone to my counselor that maybe I would have told and my best friend would have gotten help—my best friend would have stopped blaming herself for what happened. She was never the same after what happened to her, and to this day still blames herself.

I have blocked out so many things about my teenage years for decades, and yet I realize I have always striven to be the kind of friend and adult who empowered those around me instead of exploiting them. I found resilience from teachers with whom I felt safe—in the spring of 10th grade, my band teacher had me play the Vivaldi Violin concerto for the Spring Band Concert, and when I was signing up for courses in the fall, my English teacher encouraged me to enroll in her Honors class. Looking back at all that I had been experiencing, I realize how much those things helped me find resilience that empowered me in high school and beyond into my adult life. Sometimes young people do not have safe adults in their lives who can listen, much less adults they feel safe talking to. This makes the harm of predators so much more poisonous and isolating. That's exactly how predators work, they look for those who are vulnerable.

Listening to the youth who are sharing their stories is the most powerful thing adults can do to support and empower them.

Sometimes young people cannot share their stories. They still deserve being seen and empowered instead of exploited. Those who work with youth in any way have a responsibility beyond just being a mandated reporter—they also have a responsibility to model and consistently keep mindful of what being a safe adult means. I should not have experienced what I did. I should have had more education and support to be able to report what was happening to me. While the effects of these harms have been lasting, in finally facing them they have informed me in how I can use my voice to ensure no youth experiences what I did.

Shawn Ginwright's *Hope And Healing In Urban Education* argues for the essential belief that we as educators must respond to the crisis of hopelessness among youth of color and advance the following three ideas:[1]

- Structural oppression harms hope
- Healing is a critical component in building hope
- Building hope is important political activity

The school I teach at is an academic magnet school where students are stressed about grades, test scores, college apps. Those are not bad things to be stressed about—if they can manage whatever pain they are carrying. Our school has higher expectations than most, and the students have to test to get in. And yet, we have huge issues surrounding equity that do not account for the effects of systematic violence. Exposures to violence have a direct correlation upon achievement test scores. Ginwright says, "We have to view structural issues such as poverty, unemployment, underfunded schools, incarceration, lack of access to quality health care, and poor quality housing as the root causes of violence and causes of trauma. Violence, and its root causes, are not simply experienced as individual phenomenon, but rather they represent collective experience shared by young people and their families."[2]

This is not even touching upon sexual violence, or the effects of violence that happens in multiple languages, and, of course, the traumas caused by respectability politics.

Ginwright says, "The most significant impact of structural violence is how it erodes young people's sense of hope."[3]

This summer I have been forced to recall the memories within my body from what happened to me the summer of 1989. Reliving the somatic experiences have been difficult. For thirty years I have struggled with panic attacks, flashbacks, and bad dreams of having a bullet in my third eye. I am finally healing now that I understand more about the trauma it comes from, and how my story connects to the stories of others. I had the realization—every girl I was close with the summer of 1989 got pregnant as teenagers from boys they thought they were in love with. The first of my friends to get pregnant had her baby a month after her fifteenth birthday. That summer I was still 14. I took a geometry class with a troubled boy I knew from the rink who was good at tests and bad at grades. In August he was joining the Marines and he was taking the class only to get a better score on the ASVAB. It was before he started using and dealing drugs. He was the only person I told about flunking my Health Class. He is the only person who asked why and understood how. He told me he struggled with violent thoughts. I never wanted to believe him.

Upon reading my diary from 1989, I found myself thinking of Diotima and Plato's ideal forms. Empirical knowledge, the basis of Plato's ideal forms that comes from knowledge of the senses,[3] utterly fails to address what it means for the woman's body. There are memories in my body. In Plato's *The Symposium* Socrates quotes what he learned from Diotima. She taught him not to confuse the idea of love with the beloved, and used the metaphor of a ladder to explain the different stages of love—love for the body, love for all bodies, love for the soul, love for institutions, love for knowledge, love for love itself. I have never been powerless. None of us are. No matter what the world around us has said.

Even when I feel hopeless in my own life, I know that I want to bring hope with me into the classroom. I want to encourage my students to find light when there seems like there is no light to create from. Sometimes all I can do is to notice the power of whimsy—and keep my light shining as a way to help my students.

1. Ginwright, Shawn. Hope And Healing In Urban Education. Routledge; 1 edition (August 13, 2015)
2. Ibid, pg 3.
3. Ibid, pg 8.

Nicole Henares has taught high school in San Francisco since 2003, and is currently a PhD candidate in Women's Spirituality at California Institute of Integral Studies where she is researching the history of the women in her family who worked in the canneries of Monterey's Cannery Row.

The Company Of Strangers
Leslie Yee-Murata

My well intentioned parents
warned me of the dangers
Of befriending total strangers

But not the parent of my friend
He who would inflict
Wounds that never mend

Who do people believe—
Child or perpetrator
How could he deceive

Something's terribly amiss
The hidden danger
Of just a customary little kiss

To betray the trust
Of his own daughter
For his twisted lust

Forced smiles mask the lies
I know the reason
why her sister always cries

Who will take the blame
If truth be told
All will share the shame

Cowardly I flee
Today I lost my best friend
Pretending not to see

The company of strangers
can feel safer
when home is filled with danger

Sinking Teeth to Save a Life
Randy James

> "*I am not wrong: Wrong is not my name*
> *My name is my own my own my own*"
> —June Jordan

Every day I wake to a wrong world, and every day I try flight.
On good days my wings can
beat back any lingering
paper bags.
On lesser ones I am photonegative.

My body speaks the fired neurons
of the griot, the chattel, the maroon.

  Yes, I wear my crown. See,
                   I am   a big queen   because I am   quiet.
I travel
      sans entourage,
  wear no
        cape.
                My gait   clears sidewalks
                I convert   into runways.

      I am   cunt affixed   to daisy-lilies   & rose-orchids. See,

I   mimic   casual   felines.

    My skin rankles their Californian faces.
          They deepen my laugh lines, California.

I am   a queen   of a nation   of One.
  My king   he is   smitten.

          I am   a left-handed   punk   sinking
          teeth   to save a life—fuck a grill—
     my buttons button on the left side.
I am   a loud queen
because   I am
        quiet.

In a barber's throne, shears shape me into a vision even *real men* must admire.

Yes, the world is antiblack
"no homo" & legally loopholed.
Yes, my body is a racist cop or watcher away from death. But I do not fret.
>   I wash my face with charcoal,
>   kiss my body with coconut oil,
>   Tory Burch my collarbone, trim
>   my nostrils & pepper beard,
>   balm my lips with peppermint—
>   call it a day.

Randy James received an MFA in Writing from the University of San Francisco. He has also studied at UCLA. His work has been published in *Myriad*, *Westwind*, *Red Cedar Review*, *Palette* and *FEM Newsmagazine*. Randy has performed in venues across Los Angeles and the San Francisco Bay Area. His chapbook *Shifters* is available on Nomadic Press.

Seigel, vintage clothing window display, 2007.

My Name Is Gold
Mel (Prince)

I can feel myself shaking,

"It's just..."

How... do I say the words?

I inhale, trying to calm my erratic pulse.

there's something I need to tell you—" I'm ready to cry.

What if she rejects me? I was born Anderson saying my deadname *hurt.*

I could feel tears of frustration collect in the corners of my eyes,

It hurts, it hurts it *hurts*— "I'm trans..."

She kisses me. holds me so gently and carefully that her touch calms the rush in my brain but accelerates the flush on my skin.

"This," "is not new to me. You're still Gold. You've always been Gold. And you'll always *be* Gold."

"My Gold."

I'm crying, pulling her to me kissing her telling her how much I love her because I'm Gold, always have been Gold, will always be Gold.
Her Gold.

Mel (Prince) is a bigender writer who prefers sleeping in over running in the mornings. Born and raised in the Bay Area to Mexican parents, he tries to reflect personal relationships of family, love, and growth in her writings. An aspiring novelist, you can find him always listening to music on Spotify's friend activity tab or binge watching whatever she can find on streaming platforms.

My Hands Are Pretty Because Of You
Mel (Prince)

It's pretty. The way the tips curve into a soft point. The way the nail beds are shaped like pillows and the edge of them say "Look! Look!"

It's pretty. The small scar on my knuckle that serves as a reminder of an accident I don't remember. The shape of it hidden within the folds of skin. Like a secret. Like a private event between my mother and my younger self I am not privy to.

It's pretty. The length of my fingers, the height of them extending out out out as if stretching forward and *forward* to touch and reach and feel—

My knuckles say "Halt!" Halt! to rings, to jewelry daring to adorne the digits. They are indeed more stubborn than me. Stubborn and good. Only those worthy, only those more stubborn than even my knuckles are allowed to pass. But it's pretty.

It's pretty and my palms agree. Square and steady and strong. Supportive. Like my mother. Like my family. The shape of my palms is from my mother. My mother who holds my hand and runs her fingers along the back of them and says, "You've never worked a day in your life," "Why are your hands so pretty?" "They're long and thin and pretty—"

They're pretty because of you.

They're pretty because of what you gave me. Because of your words. Because of your touches. Because of your kisses.

My hands are pretty because you allowed them to be pretty. They're pretty when they hold your hand and when they support your back and when they find warmth in your embrace.

My hands are pretty because you let them be.

Next page: Mirah V. Lucas is a poet and actor. They identify as genderqueer and as a Filipinx American of indigenous origin. Their writing and photography have been published in national and international journals, and Mirah has received fellowships and grants through the James Irvine Foundation and the Djerassi Resident Artists Program. Mirah's poetry tends to focus on everyday moments that can easily be overlooked.

A Story About Dad
Mirah V. Lucas

When I look at my face in the mirror, my jawline and freckles line up with yours. Even though I haven't seen you in years, I've memorized these features—they've become like a photo of a monument, familiar and unchanging.

When I think of you, I think of San Francisco, of the damp fog and warm Irish coffees. Of Daly City—where you and mom ended up after immigrating in the '60s.

I can still hear your voice, asking if we want to go pasyal, on a daytrip to visit the pier, next time we see each other. To not "work too hard," to "enjoy life." The timbre of your voice weaves through my memories, real and imagined, every day ever since you died.

Where did you go?

I haven't spoken to you in five years. You had two strokes in that time—the last one leaving you stuck. Physically. We stopped getting your voicemails on our birthdays. No more written cards in your sloppy cursive. No more holiday Christmas songs sung onto a one-way recorder. We never returned your calls anyway. And now we can't.

I scrolled through my phone the other day to call the auto shop. "Dad" was right above "Danny's Auto and Body Repair." I thought about dialing your number just to see if you were really dead. It would be a really, really bad joke. And that wasn't your type of humor.

It was a Thursday morning when my sister called me to tell me about what had happened to you. That you passed the night before, that your body was "just tired."

That COVID took you.

I stopped breathing, my heart immediately felt tight and suspended as if God was clutching it so it wouldn't sink. My thoughts were trying to grasp what was real and what was imagined. But what was real was the fact that we weren't allowed to say goodbye.

Instead of calling the auto body shop, I tucked a persimmon into my pocket—your favorite fruit—and I decided to take a walk.

As I walked along familiar paths, I only hoped that you were dreaming of walking along the pier, drinking an Irish coffee when you left, nearly one month ago.

friends like us:
Dena Rod

we fit on the couch with ross, rachel, and chandler
slotted side by side for the cold open
and for once, chandler can talk about how
his dad is a transgender drag queen without shame
as he sips his coffee, longing for a cigarette he won't let himself have.

this time, there is no agony over inviting chandler's dad
to his and monica's wedding because
she won't be the only trans person there.
after all, we're invited too.

no one can hear the laugh track
this time because we remember
marsha and sylvia, but it's clear that if
we weren't there to listen to chandler,
the shame would creep back into his face
as t word slurs and laughs would fall out
of ross and rachel's mouths
and who knows what joey would say?

i saw the way he looked me up and down
when we first walked in through the coffee shop
doors and i immediately want to
throw a ring of salt around myself to keep
the *how you doing?* away from my person.

but it's too late. too late for those of us who are no longer here,
too late to blast this coffee shop open with the girls who were
on the corner before we marched in like ants for a morsel
of conquest, beans and all.

maybe if you saw us on your tv screen in central perk, friends like us
would also include the ones who are laugh tracked away from their humanity.

unsafe
Tommi Avicolli Mecca

born unsafe
born queer
gender non conforming
I couldn't hide
I tried
they always saw
through me
the incredible
walking x-ray
sometimes they
played along with
the pretense until I
came screaming out
of the closet
my Mardi Gras moment
every time I hear of
another beaten or
murdered queer or
trans person
I think

it could've been me
it was me that summer
night in State College
me outside that theater
in Westmont, NJ
me in Philly on a cold
subway platform
I started flying in my
dreams to escape
the replay
I don't have wings
only arms to flap
and they're tired
like the rest of me
tired of living where
I'm not wanted
tired of always watching
my back
tired of worrying that
someday they'll come
knocking on the door

---

muzzled
Tommi Avicolli Mecca

I'm muzzled
walked on a six-foot leash
at least a dog gets treats
forbidden from hugging
or kissing
I'm highly suspect
every sneeze or cough
sets off an alarm
I've been down this
road before
with another deadly virus
a condom won't help

this time
my sperm's been
cleared
my droplets are the
guilty party
they're quarantined now
I'm like Bella Donna
look, don't touch
I may be beautiful
but I'm deadly
again

menstruation as prayer
danny ryu

may I carve out
slough away –
to bleed as practice
to say no & mean it

may I shed
what prepared me
for futures
that never came

may I be
raw & unready,
a nest
not yet gathered

may I rest
my frayed fantasies—
let the current flowing from me
be my balm

may I bleed

danny ryu is a student of the human experience as a healer and their poetry echoes through themes of interconnectedness, memory, grief, and (dis) integration. They find home in liminality and the creative form that comes from being somewhere-in-between. danny is indebted to the legacy of queer trans/bipoc creatives who have challenged injustice through their art and they hope to write alongside poets seeking liberation.

a rift in reality
vanessa diaz cabrera

I was born split apart
from the middle
half truth, half lie

they say truth lives
at the back of the throat

I wish I had been told
I would be a witness
a confessional stand
visitors would clamor
to tell me
"this is who I am"

forgiveness evades me
I don't want her
I don't want to be free
in that way
I would only be opening the grave
to let you rest.

singular relief

Rebecca Samuelson

there will be pain in the night but
joy in the communal mourning
floodgates of forgotten emails
ignored texts flash incessantly
during those late-night scrolls
or on a clear Tuesday morning
or at the third yellow light
or when a scent drifts in on
wings of parking lot crows

the space following sun streaks
between clouds sprinkler rainbows
in the front yard during summer
plunge into pavement cracks blender
set to high beat concrete slabs
& coffee table disagreements
& choosing plastic portraits
& celebrating death anniversaries
the same frequency as birthday parties

dust settles quicker than it used to
blankets across reopening wounds
ignited by exposed noses above
saliva dripping out of gnashing teeth
purchase bandages with intention
before tweets cover up your moment
before ventilator beeps never end
before final words become encased
in heavy duty bubble wrap

Rebecca Samuelson is a poet from Hayward, CA. She writes from the intersection of caretaking and grief to add fresh perspective to the contemporary poetry landscape. Education is a top priority exemplified by receiving her MFA in Creative Writing Poetry from SMC and BA in English Creative Writing from SFSU. Her work has been featured in *Transfer Magazine* and *MARY: A Journal of New Writing*. She is Filipina-Mexican American.

XI
sustainable hope

Carla Caletti, "Stronger Together,"
acrylic, wax and paper on canvas, 2018.

I articulate the less rational and more mysterious realms of being human
through abstracted figures that bridge the seen and unseen.
I am drawn to practices of mending and repair; gathering
disparate parts and fragments and creating new forms and associations. The
process of adding and removing materials creates a sense of time
and speaks to the impermanence of the physical realm.

Carla Caletti is a self-taught artist, born and raised in the Bay Area and now
living in Northern New Mexico, She teaches classes and offers quarterly
Art Residencies at her Mining Time Studio and Gallery.

next

VOL. 3   NOV 2020

**THE ART OF MENDING
BROKEN THINGS**

**FUN THINGS TO DO
IN GEORGIA THIS
WINTER**

**CELEBRATING
NATIONAL &
INTERNATIONAL
SAVASANA MINUTE**

"WE ALL HAVE PTSD NOW"
AN OPEN LETTER
BY C.K.ITAMURA

365 SUSTAINABLE PLANT-
BASED MEALS TO MAKE
WITH RENEWABLE WIND-
GENERATED HYDRO-SOLAR
POWER

FREE

6 009800 461091

C. K. Itamura, "next," photography, written word, graphic design
November 7, 2020.

C. K. Itamura
Artist Statement for "next"

"next" is a visual mixed-media piece in the form of a fictitious magazine cover that is a composite of these components that are emblematic of 2020:

- Text: The text on this fictitious magazine cover are titles of articles that came to my mind on November 7, 2020— the day that the last of the States finished the presidential count and the New York Times announced Biden/Harris as the winners of the Election. Thus the "date" on this fictitious magazine cover is shown as "November 2020".

- Costume: My standard, everyday Covid pandemic "work from home" footwear: mismatched socks & zori.

- Set/Location: The photo was taken while standing on the cement outside a small women-owned local bakery in Sonoma County during the phase of the Covid pandemic when they could only serve socially distanced, masked customers through a small pass-through window. The worn "x" taped on the ground indicated the spot where customers were allowed to stand while waiting for their pastry and coffee.

- Color: the saturated hue of blue light is a subtle political statement (Democratic Party); blue is also the color of sky and water/fresh air and clean water.

NOTE: This is a visual mixed media piece only. No articles were written.

Wish List for the Other Side
Yeva Johnson

When we are all vaccinated or immune

I'm going to book a massage at the Kabuki because Osento is closed
I want to feel someone's hands touch my whole body before I soak

When we are all vaccinated or immune

I'm going to Alemany farmers' market for corn and dry farm early girl
tomatoes
I want to eat food that I picked out myself on the same day it was plucked

When we are all vaccinated or immune

I'm going to catch a flick at the Balboa or the Castro, or a play at The Marsh
I want communal shared disbelief, laughing or crying in the dark next to
strangers

When we are all vaccinated or immune

I'm going to visit my children in person at home in SF or in their dorm rooms
I want to hold them, hug them, kiss them and repeat and repeat and repeat

When we are all vaccinated or immune

I'm going to throw an immune-compromised person's post isolation party
I want to invite all the poets, writers, and friends who helped me survive

Cindy Shih, "Case for Hope," ink, pigment, and gouache on plaster.

As 2020 came to an end, I started to feel hope again while working with a few political groups getting out the Asian American vote for the general election. These two pieces came from that glimmer of hope, as a reminder that in the end, hope always prevails.

Protest
Kim Shuck

This is where the tattered banner hangs
Taken by the freeway weather
Like feet slipping between chill sheets
Like hope
Song
Of no dreams
Have you
Have you heard music
Music that didn't hand you a memory
Feathers in a left hand
Feathers and tremble
Moth against glass
Banner
Wound into the chain link
Wound in wild weaving
Like feet
Sliding over unfinished floorboards
An idea of floorboards
A slow polish
Step and step
Bringing up the grain
Tree life
Written in dark ridges
Dark ridges the night foot cannot read
Have you heard the music
Music that keeps your memory
Is your banner hanging there
Woven into the metal webbing
Over the freeway?

Cynthia Branvall, "The Threads That Bind A Divided Nation,"
vintage texiles, 36 X 58 inches, 2020.

A map of the United States was pieced together from stained and heavily worn vintage lace, trim, ruffles, and bindings by a black female identified queer artist and historian. The textiles are potent signifiers of labor, trade, industry, slavery, luxury, baptisms, weddings, funerals, gender, and history. It raises questions about race, territory, and gender that confront expectations of whiteness as something pure with a reality that is stained, fragmented, degraded, and yet enduring.

Cynthia Brannvall is an art historian, multi-media artist, and faculty member at Foothill Community College. A California native of African American and Swedish descent, she holds BAs in Art Practice and Art History from UC Berkeley and an MA from San Francisco State University

Cynthia's artwork explores identity formation envisioned in an imagined deep time terrain of memory, reclamation, and the geographies of forced and voluntary migrations. Her artwork has been exhibited in the Bay Area, San Luis Obispo, Los Angeles, New Orleans and Washington, DC.

To Breathe
Tehmina Khan

Thank you to the wind for bringing us fresh air
and taking our brother on his journey.
—Michelle and Ashley Monterrosa, at the remembrance protest
   for Sean Monterrosa, murdered by a Vallejo police officer as he was
   demonstrating for Black Lives, June 5, 2020

Wind
              Fresh air
                          To breathe

To take oxygen into lungs so it can travel through veins.
Like our ancestor the fish, who ambled onto land.

Air in lungs, our animal inheritance.

Where does my body begin?
                        Where does it end?

Molecules enter and leave me, dispersing into air.
I breathe you. You breathe me.

We stand six feet apart,
cover faces
               sanitize surfaces
stay home.

All to protect this right to breathe.

              Then what of George Floyd?

He survives his birth,
Black boyhood
Black adolescence
young Black manhood.

He even survives the virus
and keeps breathing
keeps breathing.

If we hold our breath long enough, we will go unconscious
and our bodies will begin to breathe again.

To calm the chaos inside, spiritual teachers tell us:
Focus on the breath,
this miracle of air
entering and leaving our lungs.
Watch it, hear it, feel it.

Offer gratitude to this air,
this friend that accompanies us
in and out of our bodies,
on this terrestrial journey.

George Floyd survives the virus.

We stay home so he can recover.

And yet.

Recovered lungs cannot help him
when a murderer in police uniform
crushes his throat.

Son of a mother who pushed him
from water to air
and wept at his first crying breath,

he cries for her after his last breath is spent.

Tell us:

Who's breath are we protecting now?

How will we heal ourselves from this deadlier virus
that takes away the air in our lungs?

Umbrellas As Poetry
Maggie Harrison

                                                         sister

a peace officer is justified in using   deadly force
… only   when the officer reasonably believes
… that deadly force is necessary
… to defend against an imminent threat of   death
                          or serious bodily injury.…
        —Section 835a of Assembly Bill 392, effective January 1, 2020
our voice a collective
we chant
and unfurl   yellow   umbrellas
      names painted in black letters
        thick with tar smell of ink and paint
                        SEAN MONTERROSA
thinker   learner   student   of Latinx feminisms
                        (he read Audre Lorde, y'all)
      pre-apprentice carpenter
        brother   son   grandson
        his community of friends
          teachers
          mentors
          family
     feel   his   loss
his umbrella stretches taut and clicks into place
        next to
        ALEX NIETO   MARIO WOODS
      eighteen more Vallejo victims
             of state-sponsored gun violence
                since 2010
MARIO ROMERO   WILLIE MCCOY
   RONELL FOSTER   JEFFREY BARBOA
      With yellow umbrellas   we march
        to the billboard of Sean
        across the street from
          Vallejo police
          headquarters
          three months
          after
          the detective
            shot

Sean Monterrosa
from the backseat
of an unmarked
police   truck
he was on his knees
his hands raised
the universal sign   of   surrender

ANGEL RAMOS
GUY JARREAU, JR. CHINEDU OKOBI MILES HALL   STEVEN TAYLOR
when the officer fires a weapon   he says   "I'm afraid"
OSCAR GRANT
MICHAEL BROWN
GEORGE FLOYD
unarmed
yet the fear the cops carry   transforms   anything
to a deadly weapon
a bat
a hammer
a paintbrush

a pen
we've painted
a hundred and nine
umbrellas
each umbrella, a life
with a trajectory

one survivor
one hundred and two lives robbed
by US police
six lives stolen
by vigilantes
JACOB BLAKE

AHMAUD ARBERY   ERIC REASON
This is only part of the picture.
* * *
The searing   truth   came out
the inner circle of Vallejo police
barbeques
when one of their crew
a human   kills   a human
the ritual in this police force   is to gather   drink beer   eat meat   pat backs
bend
the four o'clock point   on   the killer's   badge

291

they see kills as their duty

they honor those who accomplish the deed
    (someone   must know   how they squander their honor)
fathers

pass police union jobs

to sons
and the hundred officers employed in
the Vallejo police department shoot
the highest number of people, per capita,
in Northern California

the third highest in the state

* * *

In the days after the vigil beneath the bridge, I open umbrellas inside my
living room and office, taking stock of iambs and trochees. On the sleeves,
print names of deceased and ages at death. 22. 28. 26. 23. 20. 33. 45.   21.
34. 36. 23. 33. 22.   18.   46.
    Black and brown.   Mostly men.   29.   25.   38.
There are more lives lost than umbrellas
    so we paint more

* * *

One thing I regret about the night I spent in jail: I didn't yell his name after I
crossed the threshold of the unlocked cell door, as I walked down the stairs
of the pod so
his elder sister Michelle

alone in a locked cell

could hear
My excuse: I was blurry and sleepless, giddy and shocked. I was leaving. They
had unlocked the cell door and I hadn't yet peed. I would be waiting
in god knows how many holding cells   to get my clothes   and
belongings
    and   discharge   I should pee   I couldn't figure out the
flush
    I was getting out   I was facing forward   I just awoke
I'm sorry

* * *

If they're going to shoot us when we surrender, then why don't we fight
back? Because we've got sisters.   Ashley   Michelle   a thousand more
with poetry on our umbrellas   we will find our voices   and use them
    no matter how grating   how distorted   we'll speak
until they hear us

SEAN MONTERROSA

I am a white, genderqueer woman, a parent of a 22-year-old son, who grieves the police murder of another 22-year-old from our neighborhood, Sean Monterrosa, and aims to challenge the white supremacist culture that enables state-sponsored violence against Black and brown community members by supporting the demands for accountability and change made by Sean's sisters, Ashley and Michelle Monterrosa. My Open Letter to Governor Newsom was published in *El Tecolote* and *San Francisco Bay View* newspapers.

Maggie Harrison has worked as a teacher of writing in the Bay Area for the last 28 years, now chairing the Women's and Gender Studies department at City College of San Francisco. Their creative work has been published in *Prism Review, Ignatian Review, Santa Fe Writers Project Quarterly, Entropy, Green Hills Literary Lantern, New Letters, Blithe House Quarterly, Harrington Lesbian Literary Quarterly,* and *Sinister Wisdom.*

Sean Monterrosa, a 22-year-old activist of Argentinian heritage, was shot and killed in Vallejo on June 2, 2020, a week after the death of George Floyd. On September 27, 2020, Monterrosa's family gathered with friends, supporters and activists in front of a billboard bearing his likeness. Located a block from the Vallejo Police Station, the sign serves as a daily reminder of Vallejo's long history of police violence. With 18 deaths since 2010, the city has the highest per capita rate of police killings in Northern California. Photo by Thomas Gase/*Times-Herald.*

Never Again is NOW
Tsuru for Solidarity

TSURU means "crane" in Japanese, and symbolizes peace, compassion, hope, and healing. In the traditional Japanese folk art of paper folding (origami), it is a popular, easy-to-learn figure that children and adults of all abilities can create. The cranes we fold today are expressions of SOLIDARITY with children, families, and communities that are under attack.

Tsuru for Solidarity is a project of Japanese American social justice advocates working to end detention sites and support front-line immigrant and refugee communities that are being targeted by racist, inhumane immigration policies. We stand on the moral authority of Japanese Americans who suffered the atrocities and legacy of U.S. concentration camps during WWII, and we say, "Never again! Stop Repeating History!"

Tsuru for Solidarity arose from a 2019 pilgrimage organized by Bay Area Japanese American leaders to the site of the Department of Justice Internment Camp in Crystal City, Texas, where over 2,300 families of Japanese ancestry had been imprisoned during and after World War II. We also protested at the South

Photo above: Members of the New York Day of Remembrance Committee and Tsuru for Solidarity joined in direct action outside of Elmhurst Hospital in Queens, New York. Photo: Michelle Chen.

Texas Family Residential Center, where 1,000 Central American women and children were currently detained. We grew into a national, intergenerational movement of Japanese Americans as we began planning a June 2020 gathering in Washington, DC, to protest the detention system operated by Immigration and Customs Enforcement (ICE). It annually imprisons over 500,000 immigrants in more than 200 prisons.

Our mission is to:

- educate, advocate, and protest to close all U.S. concentration camps;

- build solidarity with other communities of color that have experienced forced removal, detention, deportation, separation of families, and other forms of racial and state violence;

- coordinate intergenerational, cross-community healing circles addressing the trauma of our shared histories.

Tsuru's strength lies within our community and our commitment to healing and justice. We share some of our highlights in the challenging year of 2020.

In January 2020, we joined with Japanese Americans for Justice and 24 other social justice, community, labor, and faith groups to organize the Oshogatsu Protest to Close the Camps at Yuba County Jail in California, to end their contract with ICE, and to call attention to the inhumane conditions there. In February, as part of an incredible month of Day of Remembrance events, we partnered with La Resistencia, Densho, and the JACL, Seattle Chapter to organize a direct action at the Northwest Detention Center outside of Seattle in Washington State. Event co-organizer Stanley Shikuma noted it was "the largest Asian American protest action in decades."

The Covid-19 pandemic forced us to cancel our in-person National Pilgrimage to Close the Camps in Washington, DC, in June. Instead we launched the Contagion in the Camps project as a way to support Detention Watch Network's #FreeThemAll campaign, drawing parallels between our own experiences with epidemics and illness in the WWII concentration camps with what is happening today.

We never gave up on our vision for a national, intergenerational protest to close the camps, and we worked hard to transform it into an online experience. In June, we hosted Tsuru Rising!, our virtual protest to close the camps, and Kimochi Night, a space for cultural celebration and healing. For two days, we brought together 1,000 registered attendees, 30,000 viewers, and 22 healing circles for change. We connected dozens of artists, organizations, and activists in a cross-community gathering demanding a closure of U.S. concentration camps, and a national reckoning and accountability around anti-Blackness and police brutality. We gathered as a community moving toward transformative solidarity against all forms of state violence—a more expansive vision than we originally conceived. Additional information at *tsuruforsolidarity.org* includes links to all our recorded events.

In the summer, we started Community Conversations, a four-part series of community dialogues around identity and intergenerational trauma, anti-Black racism in our own community, and solidarity with other historically targeted communities. We had over 1,000 registered attendees, 25 healing circles, 12 affinity groups, and 13 amazing speakers. Community Conversations will continue in 2021!

Over the July 4th weekend, we participated in XMAP: In Plain Sight —a stunning effort to make visible the injustices of the largest immigration detention system in the world. In Los Angeles, led by Karen Ishizuka of Nikkei Progressives, the words "No More Camps" were sky-written over the Santa Anita racetrack which once held thousands of Japanese Americans during WWII. Up north in Washington State, kites were flown outside the Northwest Detention Center. Attendees heard stories from detainees and their families, learned about ongoing efforts to end immigration detention/ deportations, to work towards decolonization, and to reform Immigration and Customs Enforcement (ICE) and Customs and Border Patrol (CBP) as part of #DefundPolice. This innovative project is on-going with events and art installations that have continued throughout the year.

In July and August, we protested at Berks Family Detention Center in Pennsylvania in solidarity with the Black and Brown families enduring these inhumane, devastating conditions in the midst of the pandemic. We brought healing and solidarity to these actions, and we will continue to fight tirelessly to #FreeTheFamilies.

Our ongoing work includes supporting Detention Watch Network's national "Communities Not Cages" campaign to free people from prisons, jail, and detention during the COVID pandemic, supporting immigrants and asylum-seekers who are in sanctuary, and working in national coalitions and roundtables to develop a strategy for ending family detention in the next presidential administration.

In 2021 we will continue to:

- Demand the end to all U.S. concentration camps;

- Deepen our commitment to community building and healing in the Japanese American community;

- Collectively envision new ways to keep our communities safe;

- Listen to, learn from, and stand in solidarity with Black, LatinX, Indigenous, and other AAPI communities—and recognize that there have always been Japanese Americans who hold these identities.

In 2020, we learned how much we can accomplish when we move forward together! We thank our incredible Steering Committee of activists, educators, and visionaries for their hard work, leadership, and commitment.

With our deepest gratitude,
Tsuru for Solidarity Co-chairs:
> Satsuki Ina, Mike Ishii, Bruce Embrey, Lisa Doi, Joy Shigaki, Stan Shikuma, Carl Takei, Duncan Williams and Tsuya Yee

Tsuru for Solidarity is a nonviolent, direct action project of Japanese American social justice advocates working to end detention sites and support front-line immigrant and refugee communities that are being targeted by racist, inhumane immigration policies. We stand on the moral authority of 120,000 Japanese Americans who suffered the atrocities and legacy of U.S. concentration camps during WWII and we say, "Stop Repeating History!"

Co-founder Satsuki Ina is a licensed psychotherapist specializing in community trauma. Her award-winning documentaries *Children of the Camps* and *From a Silk Cocoon* explored the lingering multigenerational impact of forced incarceration and family separation because of race. She has worked with others to facilitate, coach, counsel, and organize groups, individuals, families, organizations, and communities victimized by various forms of human-perpetrated trauma. She supports victims of oppression to find their voice and claim the power to transform themselves and the systems that have oppressed them. www.satsukiina.com

It Take a ComeUnity to Heal from Covid
Tiny Gray-Garcia

How do You Shelter in Place if you have No Place? On May 25th, 2020, my birthday, something happened at our beautiful liberation village called Homefulness in Oakland. A guy in our own community, who worked on the land, and who also refused to wear a mask, came down with Covid. The next day my Sun Tiburcio literally collapsed, saying he was too weak to stand up. The following day, I almost fainted and another member of our Homefulness family also fell ill. We closed down everything we were doing, sent everyone home and got tested. Lo and behold, four of us formerly houseless residents of Homefulness had contracted Covid-19.

Now to be clear on the logistics behind this, I lived in the "school/office/ recording studio/Mac Lab building." I, as someone who literally was on the street houseless with my mama for all of my childhood, was happy and blessed to even have a roof, a home and safety. But in some ways at this moment we weren't as safe, because our private areas were public and we had no way to control that, so we weren't able to really prevent contact, especially if someone in our community wasn't acting carefully and consciously.

Most of the 830 families we support weekly at Sliding Scale Cafe/ Mercadito de Cambio at Homefulness live in communal housing and are unable to successfully "quarantine" if any of them gets sick.

ComeUnity saves us—it takes a ComeUnity to boost an immune system. While you could say that being embedded so deeply in community caused our collective virus to spread, it also was responsible for our survival, thrival and eventual health. First we went into an arsenal to bump up our collective immune systems, determined to not end up in the increasingly filled-up ICU. And we knew that Wite Science did not hold our collective cure.

Michelle Steinberg, the nutritionist and herbalist at Street Level Health Project, created a tincture blend of baikal skullcap, red root, boneset, elecampane, usnea, and licorice for each of us that we took religiously for 4 weeks—90 drops of horrible-tasting wonderfulness in water. Michele Kim, and her fierce mama, members of our POOR Magazine solidarity fam, created some beautifully amazing Korean healing soup. That was all me and Tiburcio and the other family members here could seem to eat.

Covid ain't got nothing on the trauma in our heads. Minutes leaked into hours, hours into days and days into weeks. Time passed in that molasses way that time passes for traumatized people who can't stop thinking, worrying, activating, working because the minute we slow down, even a little, everything that we are working so hard to forget fills our heads. We start obsessing and depressing and getting lost in the silent terror of our trauma. The past can lurk there in the shadows and drive us to seek the man's poison, dangerous killer substances, and our own death just to quiet the pain. We held each other—not actually, but spiritually and metaphorically—held each other's stories and

shared survival tips—tips for navigating thru the violence of our own dangerous minds, tips that have kept us alive this far even when we thought we couldn't go on any further.

Although we were eventually "healed" from COVID-19, I never felt exactly the same. None of us would qualify as "long-haulers" but I never got back my sense of taste or smell. Even after testing negative, for at least three weeks longer, I teetered on what felt like the knife's edge of getting sick again and amped up the garlic, ginger, mushroom, cilantro, mint, caldo de pollo (chicken soup), more doses of vitamin C, and on and on and on.

Wealth-hoarding kills—radical redistribution heals. Now let's get real about something, these tinctures and vitamins and organic food and produce aren't cheap. Health in amerikkklan is tied to access and resources. It is one of the many reasons we work so-o-o-o hard to get organic, homemade healthy food out to our Sliding Scale Cafe each week and why we collaborate with multiple bakeries to get fresh produce harvested and distributed out to all the hundreds of very low- to no-income families and elders we support weekly at Mercaditor de Cambio and across the Bay with houseless folks in RoofLESS radio.

What I can say is this colonial virus called Covid should be fought on every front. The answer is through the medicine, vitamins, sleep, and care that Mama Earth provides and has always provided. In addition, please overstand and understand that the other viruses called Poverty, PoLice Terror, Incarceration, Racism, Classism, and Isolation in this stolen land are also extremely dangerous and our lives as humans aren't meant to live in this hater, hoarding, I-got-mines bubble called krapitalism. And for all of you that know this poverty skola, people's souldjah is here, working my hardest, as I have always done, to resist, protest, manifest, implement, listen, pray, dream and walk with you into decolonization, degentriFUKation and liberation so we can all heal together from all of these deadly pandemics before they kill us all.

Tiny (aka Lisa) Gray-Garcia is a formerly unhoused, incarcerated poverty scholar, poet, visionary, teacher and co-founder of POOR Magazine/Prensa POBRE Homefulness Project and Deecolonize Academy, PeopleSKool and the Bank of ComeUnity Reparations. She is the author of *Criminal of Poverty: Growing Up Homeless in America,* and *When Mama and Me Lived Outside,* and a visionary force behind the books *Poverty ScholarShip-Poor People Theory, Decolonizers Guide to a Humble Revolution, Born and Raised in Frisco,* and *How to NOT call the poLice Ever* and the theatre productions *welfareQUEENs, Poverty Skolaz* and *Hotel Voices.*

The Sacralization Of The Earth, Of Life
Rafael Jesús González

In May 2016, I attended a Nonviolent Strategy Summit with the Albert Einstein Institution focused on Climate Change. There was so much of value (much of it ineffable) that we shared and explored, but in trying to determine a "Grand Strategy" the one thing that I found of utmost importance was articulating and arriving at a consensus of the "Grand Vision," of a whole (entire, healthy, integral) Earth capable of supporting all life.

This is our Grand Vision and our hope, though the Earth is already much compromised by our myopic vision and toxic values. Our utter disregard for our "inanimate" relations (the waters, the soil, the minerals) except as "resources" for our consumption has already caused the extinction of many of our animal brother and sister species, and many of our plant relations. And many of our human brothers and sisters throughout the Earth are suffering greatly from injustice, war, and the effects of "climate change" (droughts, hurricanes, floods); and there is much more suffering to come.

So we must hold two simultaneous visions, one "Grand" vision of our hopes and dreams for which we must strive, and a clear vision of the suffering we face now. Hence our "Grand Strategy" must be three-fold:

Image above: "Healer's badge," a button adaptation of the Earth-Justice-Peace Flag, an image to unify the work for Earth-Justice-Peace.

1) to struggle for justice and peace,

2) to mitigate "climate change" and heal the Earth, and

3) to prepare ourselves to deal with the disasters that we now face and are yet to come. I state the obvious, but perhaps the obvious must be said for us to truly own it, such as putting a "Grand Vision" into words.

What unified us all, upon which our "Grand Vision" itself is rooted, was love—love of life above all else.

Because our task is huge beyond imagining, we must be very clear about what motivates and empowers us to undertake it. The task is to foment and realize a world-wide revolution, a revolution of consciousness, of the mind and of the heart that transcends nation, race, ethnicity, gender, language itself.

And the Grand Vision for the Earth must include the demands for Climate Justice and for Justice in every aspect (racial, ethnic, gender, etc.) without which there can be no peace. All aspects in a strategy of nonviolent struggle are to be engaged simultaneously to put forth our point of view and cause—to win hearts and minds.

I cannot imagine a more irrefutable base on which to build such a world-wide revolution than love of life. Not life as an abstraction, but the concrete experience of the Earth in all its exquisite (as well as terrifying) forms. Is this not the very root of divinity we humans imagine? This is what the indigenous cultures can teach us. Our task is nothing less than the sacralization of the Earth, of Life. That is the revolution that we must propagate.

To change, convert the dominant culture on a huge scale, we must recruit and engage the most powerful agents of cultural change, the artists: the poets, the musicians, the dancers, the painters, the sculptors, all. Nothing is worth propagating if it is not rooted in love, informed by beauty and joy. If life is devoid of beauty and joy, what is there in it to love?

To propagate a belief and a cause we need symbols and signs, flags to identify and unite us. Obvious in western history are the Star of David, the Cross (*in hoc signo vinces*), the Nazi swastika, and the Stars & Stripes (not to mention the myriad logos on which corporations spend millions to sell their "goods"). Several folk at the summit said that our various organizations confronting "climate change" need a common symbol or symbols to unify, identify us in our common cause of Justice and Peace for all.

I put forward then and do so now the "Universal Earth-Justice-Peace flag" that adorned the podium at the summit as a fit symbol of all our struggles for Justice, for Peace, for the well-being of the Earth:

Here is its history: 1982 I took a leave of absence from teaching at Laney College in Oakland to work with the Livermore Action Group to organize the International Day of Nuclear Disarmament. Starhawk (author of many books, including her futuristic novel *The Fifth Sacred Thing*) and I advocated a universal world-wide holy day free of national, political, religious, partisan overtones, a holy day set by the Earth itself in her movement around the Sun. After long discussions (with the consensus process you may imagine how long it took), the date was set for the Summer Solstice, June 21, 1983.

A logo was needed that embraced the issues involved, and whose meaning went beyond language, nationality, political bias, etc. The organizers chose an image of the Earth, superimposed upon the Sun and spanned by the wings of Peace.

The day was a huge success in the number of actions and people involved throughout the world. At the Livermore National Nuclear Laboratory blockade alone, 1,000 of us were arrested for civil disobedience.

That was the first and last International Day of Nuclear Disarmament. We came out of jail and, exhausted from organizing demonstrations, the Livermore Action Group dwindled away. No one else took on the gigantic task of organizing a second day, and the logo of the action was forgotten.

Then on the Summer Solstice in 2011, the logo was resurrected during the Occupy Movement. Some veterans of the Livermore Action Group organized "Solstice in the Streets" to demonstrate throughout the financial district of San Francisco. The logo was superimposed upon the international rainbow flag for peace that was flown throughout Europe, Latin America, and the U.S. just before and during the last war on Iraq. We called it the "Universal Earth-Justice-Peace flag."

We wanted to have more flags made, but the expense was beyond what we could afford so we settled for having a button made, "healer's badge" we call it, extrapolated from the flag.

We have been giving the buttons to other activists for Justice, Peace, and the well-being of the Earth, and to healers, artists, folk of consciousness throughout the world. People invariably respond to its beauty and ask, "What does it mean?" We ask, "What does it mean to you?"

We have not met a single person who did not know how to interpret it, no matter what their culture or language, they identify the Sun, the Earth, the bird of peace, and the rainbow. We also ask that if they see someone else wearing the pin, ask how they came by it. Thus a connection is made, a net woven of folk sharing values: Earth-Justice-Peace.

There have been many stories related to the Earth-Justice-Peace healer's badge. Someone who was in Paris for the 2015 United Nations Climate Change Conference, COP 2 wrote:

"....this morning we got mega hassled on the bus en route to cop21. They kept trying to charge us for not paying and we tried to explain we were with the UN delegation and didn't understand the bus system. Finally I showed her the peace button and we explained in English and the crazy cop woman completely changed her energy, was begging us for forgiveness! I took off the button and gifted it to her. She kissed me and they let us go!!! The Earth, peace and justice button saved us!!!"

The power of symbols to transcend culture and language is enormous. We offer you this one to link and unite us in our movement to heal the Earth. The more widely that we use it, the greater the impact visually and psychologically. Imagine if it appeared in all our marches and demonstrations and direct actions, not only here, but throughout the world on flags, banners, posters, billboards, flyers, and T-shirts.

Our task of healing the Earth and bringing Justice and Peace to all is huge, daunting. But we must not lose hope. Let us undertake the task with heart, with joy, with beauty, and celebration. Let our struggle be a dance.

Adapted from an article on *Somos en escrito*: https://somosenescrito.weebly.com/poetry-poesiacutea/an-image-to-unify-the-work-for-earth-justice-peace

Rafael Jesús González, born in the bicultural/bilingual setting of El Paso, Texas/Juárez, Chihuahua, is an internationally known poet and peace activist who was named the first Poet Laureate of Berkeley in 2017. He founded the Mexican and Latin American Studies Department at Oakland's Laney College, where he was professor of Creative Writing and Literature. Four times nominated for a Pushcart Prize, he has been published in *Contact II*, *Midwest Review*, *Montserrat Review*, *Runes: A Review of Poetry*, *West Coast Review*, and elsewhere, His poetry books include *El Hacedor De Juegos/The Maker of Games* and *La Musa Lunática/The Lunatic Muse*, which was featured on Somos en escrito. His work may be read at http://rjgonzalez.blogspot.com/

Eth-Noh-Tec in Times of Change
Nancy Wang

In March 2020, much of the United States began to shelter in-place. What would this mean for Eth-Noh-Tec, the kinetic storytelling theater non-profit I co-direct with my husband Robert Kikuchi-Yngojo?

In 2019, we booked over 105 performances. Too busy! And, while performing, we also negotiated contracts for 2020—dates in Chicago and the Bay Area, including a concert-length mystery story set to premiere May 2020 at the SF International Arts Festival.

But theaters were closing and so were festivals, universities, museums and schools across the country. Emails and phone calls came in cancelling our shows.

All our work down the drain? Besides marketing, we must research, write, choreograph and rehearse in order to perform our ancient Asian folktales and myths and contemporary Asian American stories. As part of the global storytelling community, when we tour, we not only meet interesting people, but the storytelling festivals are like reunions, meeting again our compassionate and generous colleagues from across the nation.

So, when we ended up losing 27 gigs and tens of thousands of dollars in income, we also lost our community. And, like many artists that depend on live audiences, we were suspended in a no-man's land, dazed.

But, after our initial shock, we actually felt relieved. No more deadlines; no pressure to keep up the marketing, purchase airline tickets, organize a dog and plant sitter, rehearse-rehearse, memorize-memorize lines, rent a car, find the venue, troubleshoot the tech rehearsals. We could stay home to…declutter, read books, complete neglected tasks, watch online movies, and to stay in our pajamas all day if we so pleased! Yes, we felt free! A vacation at home!

Then a month passed, and we wondered if it was ok to feel free when every day, every hour brought another piece of bad news about politics or the pandemic. In a way, it felt unreal because we didn't know anyone getting sick or dying or having money troubles. But how could I feel relaxed when others were suffering? I began signing even more petitions, wrote get-out-the-vote postcards, made more non-deductible political donations, made masks for the homeless and health workers. But it still felt not enough. There were too many needs out there.

Then there was Eth-Noh-Tec's mission: to build cultural bridges, celebrate diversity and create compassionate communities through storytelling. How could we fulfill our mission with every gig cancelled and no prospects for more?

Robert and I decided to produce our story performances online. Little did we know how totally complicated this task would be: 1. We needed to build a recording studio—what did we know about that? 2. We needed to set up lighting suitable for Zoom or Live Streaming—with what? 3. we had to rig up a microphone just right—thank goodness Robert played with Tinker Toys, Lincoln Logs and Erector Sets as a child. 4. And finally for the recording studio, we needed to set up a nice but not distracting backdrop. What was that?

Then the technology! Which app was best for us? We are known for our stylized, highly choreographed movement. How do we fit our choreography in that small computer screen? How do we make a two-dimensional screen more like a three-dimensional live performance? We could only use one stationary camera because who has a cameraman hanging around? Besides, who would do the editing?! And, most importantly, how do we simulate the energy of live performance when performing to a cold-eyed camera? And, do we charge? Tickets? Donations? Or free? All the equipment was so expensive!!

Learning new technology and new performance practices has been exhausting. We started in May 2020 to broadcast our storytelling. By June, we left the city for the natural, tree-filled environment of a rural island that was

Covid-19 safer. And promptly ran into more problems. Not enough broadband? Our appearance online was all glitchy? OK…find someone who has more broadband than us…load the van with the camera, lights, microphone, monitor and computers and set it all up in a friend's backyard. But fall and winter brought shorter days and cold weather. So, we schlepped the equipment to the Orcas Center—back and forth for months.

It has been months and months, and it seems like all we do is work. Trapped in our own home, even with the trees, lakes, mountains, we are inside working working working. Of course, this is definitely of our own making. No one asked us to work on so many projects. No one makes us have so many zoom meetings. Probably, no one would miss us if we stopped, because everyone is doing online programming: numerous numbers of storytellers, scientists, theaters, musicians, yoga teachers, tap dancers, spiritual gurus! It is overwhelming! So much to choose from; it's just too much!

Yet, do I want to go back to live performances? Do I miss the audience energy coming back to us, the live feedback, the applause, and meeting our audiences—hugging, shaking hands, smiling and chatting? And then there's the gorgeous meals with colleagues!! Do I?

At first, we were glad not to have to travel. Now I would put up with the inconveniences to get out of my four walls! Waiting in the airport lobby is down time; sitting on the airplane is down time; driving to the hotel is down time; waiting for your turn to go on stage is down time while enjoying the performances of the other storytellers. But at home, there is no down time. It is work work work because it's there there there staring you in the face to get done done done!!

Those traveling days may be gone for some time. All the unknowns continue to baffle and overwhelm. Rules for what is open keep changing in every state and locality. How does one plan for a future? How do we keep relevant? Just keep creating…

So, for those monthly online shows, I chose stories from our 180+ repertoire that spoke to the horrors of our times. For example, we dedicated the 16th-century Chinese tale "Monkey King Saves 10,000 Caged Children" to all the children caged at our southern border. Mongolia's "The Khan Has No Head" was not just about the Khan, but our own heedless, headless ex-leader. We launched our "Red Altar" DVD about the racism my family faced and responded to in the 1850s onward as they started the fishing industry in Monterey Bay. It aligned with the Black Lives Matter movement and the rise in anti-Asian American violence. We felt we had to be a part of rewiring the way people of color are viewed in this country.

So, despite the exhaustion and uncertainty of our work, we were being purposeful. I have to remind myself daily how lucky I am to have the skills and platform to do this. And, taking a different perspective during this time helps. After all, we have electricity, shelter. We have heat. We have water, enough food. We have the internet. We can walk and drive without fear of arrest. We can talk on the phone or on Zoom to family and friends across the country.

I must take space for gratitude, acknowledge my resilience. And our country? I must have faith, that like our country, we are all a work in progress. We will overcome!

Nancy Wang and Robert Kikuchi-Yngojo are Eth-Noh-Tec's founding artistic directors. Since 1981, Nancy's dance, choreography and theater experience have synthesized with Robert's musical talents, in a unique and choreographed expression unlike any other Combining stylized gesture and movements with spoken word and music, Nancy and Robert perform age-old Asian folktales and contemporary Asian American stories around the world. They have recieved many grants and awards for their perfomans and workshops. http://www.ethnohtec.org

---

HUMAN EXISTENCE

OFTEN SO ROMANTICIZED

THE INSECT WALKS ON

Max Leung haiku

308

Erica "Nikki" Cooper with a detail from the Kate DeCeccio murals on the exterior of Two Jack's Nik's Place, a legacy business in the Lower Haight.

For the Long Haul: A Legacy of
Black-Owned Business and Cultural Pride
Erica Cooper

The first case of COVID-19 in the United States was reported in January 2020. Over the next two months, the insatiable, predatory nature of this novel virus was allowed to prey freely on the respiratory tracts of countless innocent Americans until it had reached community transmission. On March 16, London Breed—the first black woman to be elected mayor in San Francisco—instituted a shelter-in-place order, the first mayor to do so for an entire city in the United States.

It was a Monday, my last day off before having to return to work. I was at home with my two teens, whose schools had recently closed out of an abundance of caution, when my husband called me from work.

"I just heard London is shutting down the city because of the virus. I'm going to stop by Costco to pick up food for the house."

"What does that mean—shut down the city?" I asked.

"I think it means all businesses will have to shut down for at least the next two weeks and everyone will have to stay home."

My mind went into negotiation mode. Our restaurants, Two Jack's Nik's Place on Lower Haight, and Two Jack's in the Bayview have been cornerstones in San Francisco's black community for over 42 years. Shutting them down for two weeks was less than ideal, but manageable. And at this point, temporary closure was almost expected. During the previous week, the world watched in real time its own episode of "A Series of Unfortunate Events" as the NBA, MLB and Disneyland all shut down indefinitely due to the virus. I knew it was just a matter of time before we would have to consider doing the same thing.

I immediately called my parents, who own and operate our Bayview location, and told them the news. My mother's hesitancy about shutting down was noticeable, though I couldn't understand it at the time. After we ended our conversation, she called back within five minutes telling me that essential businesses, which included restaurants, would be allowed to serve take out and delivery—therefore, their location would remain open.

Fear and anger quickly consumed me as I imagined the destruction this virus would leave behind on my parents' 70-plus-year-old black bodies. I tried negotiating with them. I desperately wanted to avoid the front lines of this new war this country carelessly found itself in.

History has painfully revealed that our bodies are always offered up as front line sacrifices to meaningless wars. My parents empathized but remained resolute: Two Jack's would remain open.

Although I did not realize it at the time, it was that very moment I witnessed my own living legends live out what Nip meant when he said "ten toes down" and "the marathon continues." After fully feeling my fear and anger, I surrendered to their wisdom. The next day, I began putting chairs on top of the tables in the restaurant, converting the welcoming energy that I had worked so hard to reclaim from the pernicious influences of the crack epidemic, into our new business model: takeout only.

The following weeks and months revealed frightening aspects of the behemoth COVID-19, particularly within the black community. Everyday, news crawls recycled the number of increasing infections, deaths, and shuttering businesses across the country and globe. Coincidently, during this time, two black men and a black woman were violently murdered by white men, five of them being police officers.

However, it was also during this time that the faith my parents typified became palpable. It was as strong, as beautiful and as black as Aretha's voice singing "Mary Don't You Weep." It was solidified by surviving the first American pandemic of self-hatred that suffused the collective unconsciousness and manifested into police brutality, the pipeline to prison, and now, COVID-19.

For us, the new normal of social distancing is less new and more normal due to the mandatory shelter-in-place order that black people have had to live under in order to survive the brutality and systemic oppression that has been exacted on us with such deadly precision that it has been programmed into our psyche and allowed to expand over generations of black families since our arrival in 1619. The perpetuation of these physical and spiritual transgressions against black Americans—as well as the denial of the resulting generational trauma—is a form of self-hatred. In the words of our beloved Celie from *The Color Purple*: "Everything you done to me, you already done to yourself."

The longevity of my family's legacy is a direct result of social distancing from society's expectations of who we are supposed to be.

My parents instilled in me early on that being driven by the acceptance and elusive accolades of a system that is programmed to turn me against myself is insanity. Being driven by love for humanity holds real value. Having businesses within our own community pushes us to evolve in our authentic power and bring light to our hidden figures.

Two Jack's, like so many other black-owned restaurants, has been historically excluded from San Francisco's "foodie" culture. Restaurants that attempt to appropriate the soul in our food are mainstays on the "Best Restaurants" lists while 20- to 40-year-old restaurants remain quarantined from such praise, or no longer exist.

Yet, it's the darkness of isolation that allows the seeds of generational wisdom and strength to grow, blessing us with the opportunity to feed the unprotected, the neglected, and the ignored. So many of our dishes are seeped with the sacredness of African spirituals that our ancestors sang when preparing them. It is this generational spiritual renaissance that has allowed us to survive the intersectional oppression of two deadly pandemics that are—hopefully— shifting humanity to fully realize that no society can last forever unless it is built upon truth and justice for all.

Erica "Nikki" Cooper is the second-generation owner of San Francisco's first legacy business. Two Jack's Nik's Place has been a family-owned staple of the Lower Haight and the greater San Francisco black community since 1977. tBoth Two Jack's Nik's Place on Lower Haight and Two Jack's on Gilman are open for takeout. www.twojacksniksplace.com

Twin Walls Mural Company
Artist Statement' for "Our Ancestors' Wildest Dreams"

With a primary focus on healing and resistance, we aim to help heal society, ourselves and our loved ones. We have always been fascinated with methods of healing generational and current trauma through visual art, and this continues to be our goal with every project. This is also a personal piece for us because we aim to help heal one of the two of us. Twin one, Marina Perez-Wong had been battling stage four metastatic breast cancer for almost two years.

The central focus of our design consists of a Sakura Tree reflective of healthy lungs. Sakura trees are associated with the heart chakra, and its properties use feminine energy to bring healing and love. The idea of a tree also relates to a hidden chakra located underneath the heart chakra called the Hrit chakra (Wish Fulfilling Tree). It symbolizes the ability to manifest what one wishes to happen in the world)

The seven young women depicted in the mural are our future leaders, and their joy is the ultimate act of resistance. Four are from the Radical Monarchs and three are students from the Oakland School from the Arts. They are dancing on water over sunken colonizer ships, border walls, I.C.E and monuments that have been thrown into lakes and rivers that represent the dismantling of patriarchy and white supremacy. They are not just surviving but thriving, and they are their ancestors wildest dreams.

Behind the tree is circular vibrating energy painted in shades of green with stencil designs lining each vibration. We wanted to find a way to include women artists from our community (Cece Carpio, Nancy Pili, Priya Handa

and Lisa Max) that inspire us and who also create movement-related activist work. Each woman created a stencil with a symbol that represents their own personal healing medicine. Using those stencils we overlapped them to create texture and movement in the background. Women support one another in many different ways and we hope this collective feminine energy will activate healing in our community and in the people that experience the mural.

The tree's roots grow throughout the bottom of the wall creating balance and stability. Milagros are scattered on the tree. Milagros are traditionally left on shrines in Mexico when a prayer or calling has been answered. We are using them in the contemporary context of assisting in the healing of specific ailments or particular needs or desires. Cherry blossoms flow throughout the mural symbolizing our dreams and wishes coming to life. www.twinwallsmuralcompany.com

"Our Ancestors' Wildest Dreams" was commissioned by the San Francisco Museum of Modern Art in 2020. Assisted by Priya Handa and Lisa Max with contributions by Nancy Pili, Cece Carpio, and Suan Cervantes.

Elaine Chu and Marina Perez-Wong are the dynamic duo behind Twin Walls Mural Company. They believe in the power of visual narratives to capture and reflect a community's history, struggles, dreams and intentions.

They are motivated by the healing of trauma both current and generational, and the transformation of the viewer and themselves through visual language, color and collaboration. Their partnership reflects intricate visual stories of hope, balance, and community. Their work reflects growing up in the Bay Area, celebrating the women and individuals who inspire them, and changes they wish to manifest through bright colors and semi realism.

Index by Author

Praise for Write Now! SF Bay www.WriteNowSF.com
Workshops, events and anthologies supporting BIPOCs since 2015

Write Now! SF Bay's workshops are safe places where writers of color can grow and feel accepted for who they are. People feel safe enough to be vulnerable. I feel heard; I feel seen.

—Poet Norm Mattox, *Black Calculus*, Nomadic Press

Write Now! workshops provided me with a sense of cultural identity that I had yearned for. Sharing with a multi-cultural group is most comfortable—perhaps because I have not felt at ease in any mono cultural group. Shizue gives support and encouragement to all of us as we divine the passages and stanzas that come through us. Six years, and four anthologies later, I am very grateful to Shizue for helping us to safely incubate and birth our work within this fluid tribe of scribes of dream, wisdom, and survival.

—Kimi Sugioka, Poet Laureate of Alameda, *Wing & Wile*, Manic D Press

My very first publication—in Write Now SF Bay's *Endangered Species, Enduring Values*—launched me into a whirlwind of readings that introduced me to a vibrant and brilliant community I had no idea was under my nose in the Bay Area this entire time. Just three years later, my first poetry collection debuted.

—Dena Rod, *Scattered Arils*, Milk & Cake Press

Shizue Seigel is a writing evangelist who has convinced hundreds of people to write stories from their lives and to have their voices heard and read. Applause at readings is enthusiastic and sustained, and washes over the crowd like a warm shower of love and appreciation for writers from all walks of life and all hues.

—Francée Covington, San Francisco Fire Commissioner, former television producer, director and writer

Shizue's commitment to lifting up the voices of underrepresented and marginalized poets, essayists, artists, and spoken word performers is unmatched. She has a deep commitment to creating communities of truth telling, liberation, and connection.

—Sandra Bass, PhD
Interim Vice-Chancellor of Student Affairs
and Director of the Public Service Center, UC Berkeley